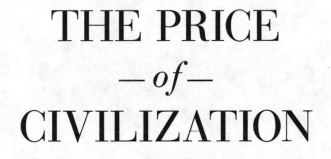

THE PRICE

—*of*—

CIVILIZATION

THE PRICE

—of—

CIVILIZATION

REAWAKENING AMERICAN
VIRTUE AND PROSPERITY

JEFFREY D. SACHS

Random House
New York

Published in the United States by Random House,
an imprint of The Random House Publishing Group,
a division of Random House, Inc., New York.

RANDOM HOUSE and colophon are registered trademarks of Random House, Inc.

Library of Congress Cataloging-in-Publication Data

Sachs, Jeffrey.
  The price of civilization / Jeffrey D. Sachs.
    p. cm.
  Includes bibliographical references and index.
  ISBN 978-1-4000-6841-8
  eBook ISBN 978-0-679-60502-7
  1. United States—Economic conditions—2009– 2. United States—Economic
  policy—2009– 3. Environmental responsibility—United States. 4. Social
  responsibility of business—United States. 5. United States—Politics and
  government—21st century. I. Title.

  HC106.84.S23   2011
  330.973—dc22   2011014631

Printed in the United States of America on acid-free paper

www.atrandom.com

9 8 7 6 5 4

Book design by James Sinclair

For my parents
Theodore and Joan Sachs
paragons of justice, compassion, and happiness

CONTENTS

PART I

The Great Crash

CHAPTER 1.

Diagnosing America's Economic Crisis

A Crisis of Values

At the root of America's economic crisis lies a moral crisis: the decline of civic virtue among America's political and economic elite. A society of markets, laws, and elections is not enough if the rich and powerful fail to behave with respect, honesty, and compassion toward the rest of society and toward the world. America has developed the world's most competitive market society but has squandered its civic virtue along the way. Without restoring an ethos of social responsibility, there can be no meaningful and sustained economic recovery.

I find myself deeply surprised and unnerved to have to write this book. During most of my forty years in economics I have assumed that America, with its great wealth, depth of learning, advanced technologies, and democratic institutions, would reliably find its way to social betterment. I decided early on in my career to devote my energies to the economic challenges abroad, where I felt the economic problems were more acute and in need of attention. Now I am worried about my own country. The economic crisis of recent years reflects a deep, threatening, and ongoing deterioration of our national politics and culture of power.

The crisis, I will argue, developed gradually over the course of several decades. We are not facing a short-term business cycle downturn, but the working out of long-term social, political, and economic trends. The crisis, in many ways, is the culmination of an era—the baby boomer era—rather than of particular policies or presidents. It is also a bipartisan affair: both Democrats and Republicans have played their part in deepening the crisis. On many days it seems that the only difference between the Republicans and Democrats is that Big Oil owns the Republicans while Wall Street owns the Democrats. By understanding the deep roots of the crisis, we can move beyond illusory solutions such as the "stimulus" spending of 2009–2010, the budget cuts of 2011, and the unaffordable tax cuts that are implemented year after year. These are gimmicks that distract us from the deeper reforms needed in our society.

The first two years of the Obama presidency show that our economic and political failings are deeper than that of a particular president. Like many Americans, I looked to Barack Obama as the hope for a breakthrough. Change was on the way, or so we hoped; yet there has been far more continuity than change. Obama has continued down the well-trodden path of open-ended war in Afghanistan, massive military budgets, kowtowing to lobbyists, stingy foreign aid, unaffordable tax cuts, unprecedented budget deficits, and a disquieting unwillingness to address the deeper causes of America's problems. The administration is packed with individuals passing through the revolving door that connects Wall Street and the White House. In order to find deep solutions to America's economic crisis, we'll need to understand why the American political system has proven to be so resistant to change.

The American economy increasingly serves only a narrow part of society, and America's national politics has failed to put the country back on track through honest, open, and transparent problem solving. Too many of America's elites—among the super-rich, the CEOs, and many of my colleagues in academia—have abandoned a commitment to social responsibility. They chase wealth and power, the rest of society be damned.

We need to reconceive the idea of a good society in the early twenty-first century and to find a creative path toward it. Most important, we need to be ready to pay the price of civilization through multiple acts of good citizenship: bearing our fair share of taxes, educating ourselves deeply about society's needs, acting as vigilant stewards for future generations, and remembering that compassion is the glue that holds society together. I would suggest that a majority of the public understands this challenge and accepts it. During my research for this book, I became reacquainted with my fellow Americans, not only through countless discussions but also through hundreds of opinion surveys on, and studies of, American values. I was delighted with what I found. Americans are very different from the ways the elites and the media pundits want us to see ourselves. The American people are generally broad-minded, moderate, and generous. These are not the images of Americans we see on television or the adjectives that come to mind when we think of America's rich and powerful elite. But America's political institutions have broken down, so that the broad public no longer holds these elites to account. And alas, the breakdown of politics also implicates the broad public. American society is too deeply distracted by our media-drenched consumerism to maintain the habits of effective citizenship.

Clinical Economics

I am a macroeconomist, meaning that I study the overall functioning of a national economy rather than the workings of one particular sector. My operating principle is that the economy is intimately interconnected with a much broader drama that includes politics, social psychology, and the natural environment. Economic issues can rarely be understood in isolation, though most economists fall into that trap. An effective macroeconomist must look at the big canvas, in which culture, domestic politics, geopolitics, public opinion, and environmental and natural resource constraints all play important roles in economic life.

My job as a macroeconomic adviser during the past quarter century has been to help national economies function properly by diagnosing economic crises and then correcting breakdowns in key sectors of the economy. To do that job well, I must strive to understand in detail how the different parts of the economy and society both fit together and interact with the world economy through trade, finance, and geopolitics. Beyond that, I must also strive to understand the public's beliefs, the country's social history, and the society's underlying values. All of this requires a broad and eclectic set of tools. Like other economists, I pore over charts and data. In addition, I read stacks of opinion surveys as well as cultural and political histories. I compare notes with political and business leaders and visit factories, financial firms, high-tech service centers, and local community organizations. Sound ideas about economic reform must pass a "truth test" at many levels, making sense at the community level as well as the national political level.

A macroeconomist faces the challenge of a clinical doctor who must help a patient with serious symptoms and an unknown underlying disease. An effective response involves making a correct diagnosis about the underlying problem and then designing a treatment regimen to correct it. In my book *The End of Poverty* I called this process "clinical economics." My inspiration has been my wife, Sonia, a gifted medical doctor who showed me the wonders of science-based clinical medicine.

I didn't train to be a clinical economist, though fortunately my theoretical training, combined with my wife's inspiration and some very good professional luck, enabled me to forge an unusual personal path to clinical economics. I was blessed with a first-rate education as an undergraduate and graduate student at Harvard, where I later joined the faculty in 1980. With life-changing good fortune, I became involved in practical economic problem solving in Bolivia in 1985, and from then on I have built a career at the intersection of theory and practice. I spent much of the 1980s working in debt-ridden Latin America to help support that region's return to democracy and macroeconomic stability after two decades of incompetent and violent military rule. In the late 1980s and early 1990s I was invited to help Eastern Europe and the former Soviet Union in their transitions from communism and dictatorship to democracy and market economy. That work, in turn, brought me invitations to the world's two great behemoths, China and India, where I could watch, debate, and share ideas about the world-changing market reforms of those two great societies. Since the mid-1990s, I have turned much of my attention to the poorest regions of the world, and especially to sub-Saharan Africa, to try to assist them in their ongoing fight against poverty, hunger, disease, and climate change.

Having worked in and diagnosed dozens of economies over my career, I've come to have a good feel for the interplay of politics, economics, and a society's values. Lasting economic solutions are found when all of these components of social life are brought into a proper balance.

In this book I will bring clinical economics to bear on America's economic crisis. By taking a holistic view of America's economic problems, I hope to diagnose some of the deeper maladies afflicting our society today and to correct the basic misdiagnosis that was made thirty years ago and that still sticks today. When the U.S. economy hit the skids in the 1970s, the political Right, represented by Ronald Reagan, claimed that government was to blame for its growing ills. This diagnosis, although incorrect, had a plausible ring to it to enough Americans to enable the Reagan coalition to begin a process of dismantling effective government programs and undermining the government's capacity to help steer the economy.

We are still living with the disastrous consequences of that failed diagnosis, and we continue to ignore the real challenges, involving globalization, technological change, and environmental threats.

America Is Ready for Reform

After a thorough diagnosis in the first half of the book, I'll get specific on what I think we should do. Those specific recommendations will raise several big issues. First, can we really afford more government activism in an era of huge budget deficits? I'll show that we both can and must. Second, can a program of thoroughgoing reform really be manageable? Here, too, the answer is yes, even by a government that currently exhibits chronic incompetence. Third, is a reform program politically achievable in an era when politics is as divisive as it is today? Successful reforms are almost always initially greeted with a broad chorus of skepticism. "That is politically impossible." "The public will never agree." "Consensus is beyond reach." These are the jeremiads we hear today whenever deep and real reforms are proposed. During my quarter century of work around the world, I've heard them time and again, only to find that deep reforms were not only possible but eventually came to be viewed as inevitable.

Much of this book is about the social responsibility of the rich, roughly the top 1 percent of American households, who have never had it so good. They sit at the top of the heap at the same time that around 100 million Americans live in poverty or in its shadow.[1]

I have no quarrel with wealth per se. Many wealthy individuals are highly creative, talented, generous, and philanthropic. My quarrel is with poverty. As long as there is both widespread poverty and booming wealth at the top, and many public investments (in education, child care, training, infrastructure, and other areas) that could reduce or end the poverty, then tax cuts for the rich are immoral and counterproductive.

This book is also about planning ahead. I'm a firm believer in the market economy, yet American prosperity in the twenty-first century also requires government planning, government investments, and clear long-term policy objectives that are based on the society's shared values. Government planning runs deeply against the grain in Washington today. My twenty-five years of work in Asia have convinced me of the value of long-term government planning—not, of course, the kind of dead-end central planning that was used in the defunct Soviet Union, but long-term planning of public investments for quality education, modern infrastructure, secure and low-carbon energy sources, and environmental sustainability.

The Mindful Society

"The unexamined life is not worth living," said Socrates.[2] We might equally say that the unexamined economy is not capable of securing our well-being. Our greatest national illusion is that a healthy society can be organized around the single-minded pursuit of wealth. The ferocity of the quest for wealth throughout society has left Americans exhausted and deprived of the benefits of social trust, honesty, and compassion. Our society has turned harsh, with the elites on Wall Street, in Big Oil, and in Washington among the most irresponsible and selfish of all. When we understand this reality, we can begin to refashion our economy.

Two of humanity's greatest sages, Buddha in the Eastern tradition and Aristotle in the Western tradition, counseled us wisely about humanity's innate tendency to chase transient illusions rather than to keep our minds and lives focused on deeper, longer-term sources of well-being. Both urged us to keep to a middle path, to cultivate moderation and virtue in our personal behavior and attitudes despite the allures of extremes. Both urged us to look after our personal needs without forgetting our compassion toward others in society. Both cautioned that the single-minded pursuit of wealth and consumption leads to addictions and compulsions rather than to happiness and the virtues of a life well lived. Throughout the ages, other great sages, from Confucius to Adam Smith to Mahatma Gandhi and the Dalai Lama, have joined the call for moderation and compassion as the pillars of a good society.

To resist the excesses of consumerism and the obsessive pursuit of wealth is hard work, a lifetime challenge. To do so in our media age, filled with noise, distraction, and temptation, is a special challenge. We can escape our current economic illusions by creating a *mindful society*, one that promotes the personal virtues of self-awareness and moderation, and the civic virtues of compassion for others and the ability to cooperate across the divides of class, race, religion, and geography. Through a return to personal and civic virtue, our lost prosperity can be regained.

CHAPTER 2.

Prosperity Lost

There can be no doubt that something has gone terribly wrong in the U.S. economy, politics, and society in general. Americans are on edge: wary, pessimistic, and cynical.

There is widespread frustration with the course of events in America. Two-thirds or more of Americans describe themselves as "dissatisfied with the way things are going in the United States," up from around one-third in the late 1990s.[1] A similar proportion of Americans describe the country as "off track."[2]

This is coupled with a pervasive cynicism about the nature and role of government. Americans are deeply estranged from Washington. A large majority, 71 percent to 15 percent, describes the federal government as "a special interest group that looks out primarily for its own interests," a startling commentary on the miserable state of American democracy. A similarly overwhelming majority, 70 percent to 12 percent, agrees that "government and big business typically work together in ways that hurt consumers and investors."[3] The U.S. government has lost the confidence of the American people in a way that has not previously occurred in modern American history or probably elsewhere in the high-income world. Americans harbor fundamental doubts about the motivations, ethics, and competency of their federal government.

This lack of confidence extends to most of America's major institutions. As we see in the data from a recent opinion survey (see Table 2.1), the public deeply distrusts banks, large corporations, news media, the entertainment industry, and unions, in addition to their distrust of the federal government and its agencies. Americans are especially skeptical of the overarching institutions at the national and global level—Congress, banks, the federal government, and big business—and more comfortable with the institutions closer to home, including small churches, colleges, and universities.

Table 2.1: The Public's Negative Views of Institutions Are Not Limited to Government

Effect on Way Things Are Going in the Country	Positive, %	Negative, %	Other, %
Banks and financial institutions	22	69	10
Congress	24	65	12
Federal government	25	65	9
Large corporations	25	64	12
National news media	31	57	12
Federal agencies and departments	31	54	16
Entertainment industry	33	51	16
Labor unions	32	49	18
Obama administration	45	45	10
Colleges and universities	61	26	13
Churches and religious organizations	63	22	15
Small businesses	71	19	10
Technology companies	68	18	14

Source: Pew Research Center for the People & the Press, April 2010.

Americans' loss of confidence in its institutions is matched by a loss of confidence in one another. Sociologists, led by Robert Putnam, have shown the decline of civic-mindedness in American society. Americans participate less in social affairs ("bowling alone" in Putnam's now-famous phrase) and have much less trust in one another. They have retreated from the public square to the home, spending their nonwork time in front of the computer, TV, or other electronic media. The loss of trust is especially high in ethnically diverse communities, where the population is "hunkering down," in Putnam's words.[4]

The two main political parties are not showing a way out of the crisis. Even when the fights between them are vicious—on taxes, spending, war and peace, and other issues—they actually hew to a fairly narrow range of policies, and not ones that are solving America's problems. We are paralyzed, but not mainly by disagreements between the two parties, as is commonly supposed. We are paralyzed, rather, by a shared lack of serious attention to our future. We increasingly drift between elections without serious resolution of a long list of deep problems, whether it's the gargantuan budget deficit, wars, health care, education, energy policy, immigration reform, campaign finance reform, and much more. Each election is an occasion to promise to reverse whatever small steps the preceding government has taken.

The general deterioration of conditions is taking its toll on life satisfaction in the country. Americans have long been a satisfied population. Why shouldn't they be, living in one of the world's richest, freest, and safest places? Yet we should listen more closely to the message over recent decades when Americans have been asked about their life satisfaction or happiness. As the economist Richard Easterlin discovered many years ago, America hit a kind of ceiling on self-reported happiness (sometimes called subjective well-being, or SWB) several decades back.[5] The trend line of happiness between 1972 and 2006 is flat, varying between 2.1 and 2.3 on a scale from 1 (not happy) to 3 (happy), even as per capita GDP doubled from $22,000 to $43,000, as we see in Figure 2.1.

Even as the GDP per person has risen, the happiness of Americans has not changed and perhaps has even declined among women, at least according to a recent careful study.[6] The citizens of many

Figure 2.1: U.S. GDP per Capita and Happiness Trend Line, 1972–2006

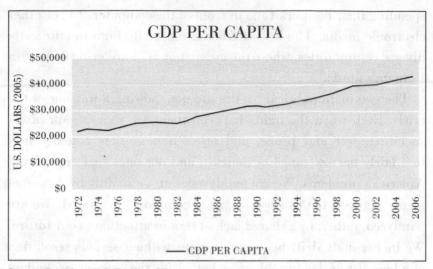

Source: Data from U.S. Bureau of Economic Analysis.

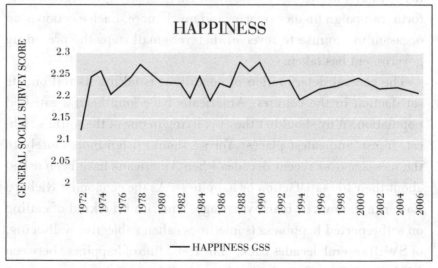

Source: Data from General Social Survey.

other countries now report a higher level of life satisfaction, putting the United States no higher than nineteenth in a recent international comparison by Gallup International.[7] Americans are running very hard to pursue happiness but are staying in the same place, a trap that psychologists have christened the Hedonic Treadmill.[8]

The Jobs and Savings Crisis

America's unemployment rate is nearly 9 percent of the labor force and has been stuck there for two years.[9] In all, 8.6 million jobs were shed from the peak employment in 2007 to the trough in 2009. Even before the current crisis, the 2000s had the lowest growth of jobs of any decade since World War II.[10]

The job-market pain is not felt evenly. The unemployment rate is by far the highest among lower-skilled workers, reaching 15 percent among workers with less than a high school education and 10 percent of those with a high school diploma or some college. Workers with at least a bachelor's degree have come through the crisis with more modest, though still very real, losses. Their unemployment rate hovered around 4 percent as of December 2010, up from around 2 percent in 2006.[11]

The widening gap in labor-market outcomes of those with and without at least a bachelor's degree is a theme to which we will return many times. In the figure below, we see the trajectory of earnings of workers according to their educational attainment, all relative to a high school diploma. In 1975, those with a bachelor's degree earned around 60 percent more than those with a high school diploma. By 2008, the gap was 100 percent.

Figure 2.2: Real Salary Growth Limited to Bachelor's and Advanced Degree Holders, 1975–2007

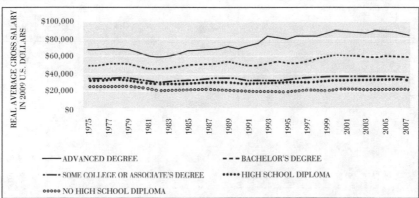

Source: Data from U.S. Census Bureau, Current Population Survey (2008).

The 2008 financial meltdown also deepened the financial distress of millions of Americans who kept their jobs but lost their homes and savings. The fall in housing prices beginning in 2006 spelled the end of a couple of decades in which middle-class households treated their homes as ATM machines, drawing on the ostensible value of the home through home equity loans. With the collapse of the housing bubble, millions of households found that their homes were now worth less than their mortgages, leading them to default on their mortgage payments.

This widespread financial distress is the end stage of a generation-long decline in Americans' propensity to save. The national savings rate, which measures how much of the nation's income is put aside for the future, tells a striking story. Saving for the future is the main kind of self-control needed for a household's sustained well-being. Yet starting in the 1980s, the personal savings rate out of disposable income began to fall sharply, as we see in Figure 2.3, and began a small recovery only after the calamitous 2008 financial crisis. In the three decades leading up to 2008, the nation as a whole, through countless individual decisions of households, lost the self-discipline to save for the future.

What occurred at the household level was echoed in Washington. Just as households were abandoning their personal financial pru-

Figure 2.3: Personal Savings Rate as Percentage of Disposable Income, 1952–2010

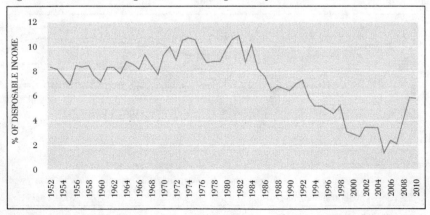

Source: Data from U.S. Bureau of Economic Analysis.

Figure 2.4: U.S. Deficit as Percentage of GDP, 1955–2011

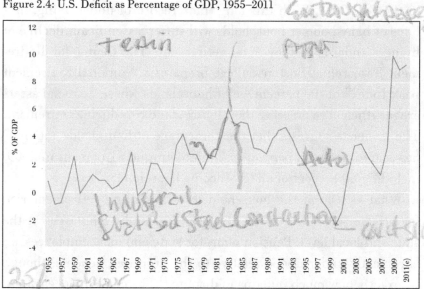

Source: Data from Office of Management and Budget Historical Budget Tables.[12]

dence, Congress and the White House lost the discipline of budget balance. The trajectory of the budget deficit is shown in Figure 2.4. For the period 1955 to 1974, the budget deficit was mostly below 2 percent of GDP. Then, from 1975 to 1994, it increased markedly, mostly above 3 percent of GDP. A squeeze on spending (both domestic and military) combined with higher tax collections during the years 1995 to 2002 temporarily brought the budget deficit back under control. Yet as soon as the surplus was achieved, the politicians were eager to spend it for political gain. In 2001, the new Bush administration cut taxes sharply while increasing military spending, thereby sending the federal budget back to deficit. The deficit soared in the wake of the 2008 financial crisis, which lowered tax collections, led to a financial bailout, and prompted Obama to push for a two-year stimulus package.

The chronic lack of saving by households and by government (especially state and local government) means an impending retirement crisis for baby boomers. The oldest of the baby boomers were born in 1946, meaning that they hit the retirement age of sixty-five in the year 2011. With this long track record of undersaving, millions of baby boomer households will suffer a significant decline of living standards as they enter retirement. The Center for Retirement Research at Boston College prepares a "National Retirement Risk Index" of the percentage of households whose financial assets are insufficient to preserve their living standards during retirement. The evidence suggests that the percentage of households "at risk" has soared, from 43 percent in 2004 to around 51 percent in 2009, including 60 percent of all low-income households.[13]

What is true at the household level regarding retirement risk for private-sector workers is also true for public employees at the state and local level. Pension plans for state and local employees are chronically underfunded relative to the promised benefits, though by exactly how much remains in dispute.[14] The consequences of underfunded pension plans will be some combination of a squeeze on public spending, a rise in state and local taxes, and a renegotiation of pension benefits.

The Investment Squeeze

The decline of net national saving has also meant a decline of funds available for domestic investment to build capital stock.

Whereas China, which saves around 54 percent of its national income, is building hundreds of miles of subway lines and tens of thousands of miles of fast intercity rail lines, America is building hardly any infrastructure at all.[15] In fact, our existing infrastructure is increasingly decrepit, a point of shock to foreign visitors when they arrive. The American Society of Civil Engineers (ASCE) has been our eyes and ears on the growing crisis, publishing every few years a report card detailing the estimated five-year investment needs to correct major deficiencies in key systems. The report card is sobering reading, with few passing grades. The roads are worn out; bridges and dams are vulnerable to collapse; and levee and river systems need major upgrades, as the tragedy in New Orleans shock-ingly exposed. The water supply is widely contaminated. The over-all grade is D, "poor," with an estimated five-year bill of $2.2 trillion to correct deficiencies in basic systems. At roughly $400 billion per year, we require a scaling up of infrastructure investment equiva-lent to 2 to 3 percent of GDP each year.[16]

Intellectual capital, the pride of America, is also diminishing, as America cedes technological leadership to China and other coun-tries in areas such as renewable energy and stem cell research. The energy system is in a deepening crisis. The power grid is outmoded, yet there is little advance in building a new state-of-the-art national transmission system. There is policy paralysis regarding many kinds of possible power generation: nuclear, coal plants with carbon capture and storage (CCS), offshore wind power, biofuels, gas shale, deepwater drilling, and many others.

The most serious threat is to our human capital. The quality of the labor force will be the most important single determinant of American prosperity in the decades to come. The evidence, there-fore, that America's public schools are falling behind those of the rest of the world in core attainments in reading, science, and math is a harbinger of a deepening crisis. There is now a systematic global comparison of scholastic performance of fifteen-year-olds carried out every three years as part of the Program for International Stu-dent Assessment (PISA), currently covering sixty-five countries. The 2009 results are chastening. On the one hand, the United States ranked only fifteenth in reading, twenty-third in science, and thirty-first in mathematics.[17] On the other hand, Shanghai, China, ranked number one in all three categories, and the fast-rising developing economies of Asia (including South Korea, Singapore, and Hong Kong) all ranked in the top ten, dramatically outperforming the United States. This is perhaps the starkest wake-up call in recent memory about our lagging educational performance and its implica-tions for the future, yet it made hardly a blip in the U.S. media.

There are other similarly stunning developments. The higher

educational attainment of the United States, once the world's un-challenged pacesetter, is falling behind. Currently, the United States ranks twelfth in the world in the proportion of twenty-five- to thirty-four-year-olds with at least an associate's degree (meaning a degree from a two-year college or higher).[18] Many other countries are enjoying a surge in college completion rates, especially in four-year colleges, which register the biggest returns to earnings, employ-ment rates, and job security. In the United States, more students are attending college, but the percentage completing a four-year bachelor's degree has stagnated since the year 2000.[19] After decades of enjoying the world's best-educated labor force, America's educa-tional credentials are now falling behind many countries' in Europe and Asia.

The Divided Workplace

Workplace conditions have also deteriorated during the past three decades. We derive most of our income and many of life's pleasures from productive work. A healthy workplace is key to a healthy so-ciety. Yet the overriding reality of the past thirty years has been a sharply widening gap in power, compensation, and job security between senior management and professionals, on the one hand, and the rest of the workforce, on the other. This has been an era of soaring CEO pay combined with a grinding squeeze on the wages and working conditions of production and clerical workers. Job se-curity has plummeted for relatively low-skilled workers (those with a high school diploma or less). The working class has been caught in the pincers of low-wage competition from abroad combined with the technological obsolescence of many traditional low-skilled jobs.

The top CEOs have cashed in as never before. As shown in Figure 2.5, the compensation packages of the top hundred CEOs soared from the mid-1970s onward. At the start of the 1970s, average top 100 CEO pay was roughly 40 times the average worker's pay. By the

Figure 2.5: Ratio of Top 100 CEO Compensation to Average Worker Compensation, 1970–2006

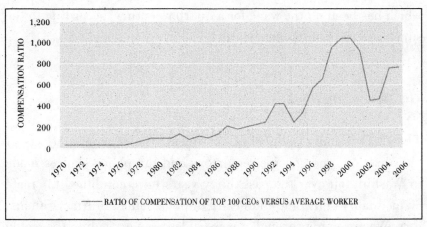

Source: Data from Database for "Income Inequality in the United States" (Saez and Piketty).

year 2000, it had reached 1,000 times the average worker's pay! The most important component of this compensation boom was the increased payment of stock options to CEOs and senior management teams.

While top CEO pay has been soaring, the median take-home pay of male full-time workers (adjusted for inflation) has stagnated since the early 1970s. This is shown in Figure 2.6. Incredibly, the median

Figure 2.6: Real Median Earnings of Full-Time Male Workers, 1960–2009 (in Constant 2009 Dollars)

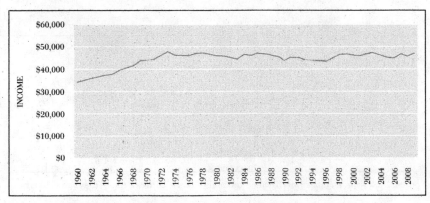

Source: Data from U.S. Census Bureau.

earnings of male full-time workers actually peaked in 1973. And it's not just earnings that have declined. So, too, has job satisfaction, which has been on the wane for a quarter century, according to the surveys of the Conference Board.[20]

The New Gilded Age

The CEO-friendly political environment, the economic effects of globalization, and specific regulatory and tax policy choices made in Washington over the past thirty years have combined to create an inequality of income and wealth unprecedented in American history. We are living through a new Gilded Age exceeding the gaudy excesses of the 1870s and the 1920s. The extent of riches at the top of the income and wealth distributions is unimaginable to most Americans, especially at a time when one in eight Americans depends on food stamps.[21]

The wealthiest 1 percent of American households today enjoys a higher total net worth than the bottom 90 percent, and the top 1 per-

Figure 2.7: Rising Income Inequality, 1913–2008

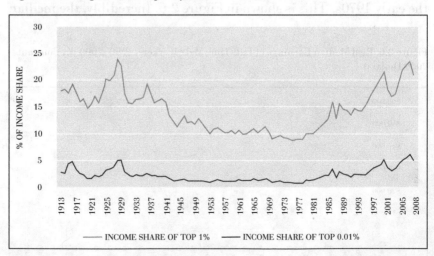

Source: Data from Database for "Income Inequality in the United States" (Saez and Piketty).

cent of income earners receives more pretax income than the bottom 50 percent.[22] The last time America had such massive inequality of wealth and income was on the eve of the Great Depression, and the inequality today may actually be greater than in 1929. As we see from the figure, the New Deal and post–World War II reforms led to a dramatic narrowing of income inequality. Economic growth was widely shared from the end of the war until the 1980s. Then all the economic benefits tilted toward the rich (see Figure 2.7).

Soaring income and power at the top has changed American society. Many of those at the top of the heap have come to look upon the rest of society with disdain. We have entered an age of impunity, in which rich and powerful members of society—CEOs, financial managers, and their friends in high political office—seem often to view themselves as above the law.

The recent cascade of corporate scandals has been unrelenting, often with close links between the scandal-ridden companies and powerful politicians. Dick Cheney went from being the CEO of Halliburton, a company involved in an endless tangle of bribery, contract violations, accounting frauds, and safety violations, straight to the vice presidency, where he used his high public office to coddle the oil industry. And Wall Street firms such as Goldman Sachs, Citigroup, and JPMorgan Chase not only were the central actors in the financial crisis of 2008 but were the very places to which Obama turned to staff the senior economic posts of his administration.

It's hard to know the ultimate cause of the breakdown in corporate truth telling and ethical business behavior in general. Dishonesty is a contagious social disease; once it gets started, it tends to spread.[23] Our "social immune system" has been deeply compromised. Perhaps we've become inured to hucksterism through a lifetime of watching the phony claims of advertisements, campaign commercials, and official military statements on Vietnam, Iraq, and Afghanistan. Perhaps the cause is the parade of CEOs who have cheated their own companies, their shareholders, and their customers, giving us the sense that everybody in corporate America is cheating. Perhaps the cause has been the repeated exposés of corporate lies in the drug and oil industries, financial rating agencies, investment banks, and military contractors.

When something goes wrong—a drug proves dangerous in follow-up tests, a drilling practice proves hazardous, or a paramilitary unit engages in murder or torture—the inevitable response is to lie first, cover up next, and acknowledge the truth only as a last resort, usually when internal documents are finally leaked to the public. I witnessed this at Harvard as well, when the U.S. government charged a colleague of mine with insider dealing on a federal contract. The university's response was to mobilize the PR machinery and fight the charges rather than to search for the truth.

Perhaps the ultimate cause is the nearly complete impunity of lying or costly failures in leadership. Almost nobody at the top pays a price for such behavior, even when the truth is eventually exposed. The bankers who brought down the world economy remain at the top of the heap, sitting across the table from the president in White House meetings or dining at state dinners as the president's guests of honor. Policy advisers such as Larry Summers, who led the U.S. government to deregulate the financial markets in the late 1990s, have been rewarded with lucrative positions on Wall Street and academia and then with renewed appointments at the top of government.

Those who are actually found guilty of violating the law typically get off with a slap on the wrist, if that. When Goldman Sachs was charged by the Securities and Exchange Commission (SEC) with stoking the subprime bubble through marketing of toxic securities under phony premises, the SEC agreed to a settlement of $550 million, a pittance compared to the firm's $13.4 billion income in 2009. When another creator of the subprime disaster, Countrywide Financial CEO Angelo Mozilo, was sentenced for fraud, the fine was $67.5 million, seemingly hefty until compared with Mozilo's 2001–2006 compensation, estimated at $470 million. The list is long. Wall

Street has acknowledged wrongdoing in one case after another, only to walk away with mild fines.[24]

Retracing Our Steps

America's problems may seem insoluble today, but that's mainly because the United States has gotten out of the practice of true social reform and problem solving. Once we start to diagnose our real ills and chart a course to solve them, practical problem solving will prove to be realistic after all. Despite all the challenges—budget deficits, financial scandals, lack of proper public education, corporate lying, impunity, antiscientific propaganda, and more—the U.S. economy remains highly productive and innovative. Even with the steep downturn after the 2008 crash, the average per capita income is around $50,000 per person, still the highest in the world in a large economy. There is no overall shortage of goods and services to go around. There is no deathly squeeze on food supplies, water, energy, or health care systems. There is a continued outpouring of new products.

Our challenges lie not so much in our productivity, technology, or natural resources but in our ability to cooperate on an honest basis. Can we make the political system work to solve a growing list of problems? Can we take our attention away from short-run desires long enough to focus on the future? Will the super-rich finally own up to their responsibilities to the rest of society? These are questions about our attitudes, emotions, and openness to collective actions more than about the death of productivity or the depletion of resources.

In the following chapters, we will retrace our steps as a nation. How did the world's leading economy reach such a position of despair, and apparently in such a short period of time? We will diagnose America's ills by studying four dimensions of the American crisis: economic (chapters 3 and 6), political (chapters 4 and 7), social (chapter 5), and psychological (chapter 8). By taking the economic, political, social, and psychological facets together, we can piece together an understanding of how America went from decades of consensus and high achievement to an era of deep division and growing crisis. That story will enable us to look forward toward solutions.

CHAPTER 3.

The Free-Market Fallacy

After decades of global economic leadership, America began in the 1980s to forget the basic lessons of economics, parroting slogans (typically about the wonders of the free market) while neglecting the art of economic policy. One of the most basic and important ideas of economics—that business and government have complementary roles as part of a "mixed economy"—has been increasingly ignored, to my amazement and consternation. This chapter aims to help make up the lost ground.

In this chapter I discuss the three main aims of an economy—efficiency, fairness, and sustainability—and show that the government must play an active and creative role alongside the private market economy to enable society to achieve them.

The Age of Paul Samuelson

Fortunately for me, I was well educated in the merits of the mixed economy during my student years (1972–1980), by intellectual giants who had done much to guide America's economy after World War II. The era of economic thought from the 1940s to the 1970s can be called the Age of Paul Samuelson, the economic genius at

MIT who personified the economics profession during the heyday of America's global leadership. More than any other economist of his time, Samuelson provided the intellectual underpinnings of the modern mixed economy created in the United States and Europe after the Second World War.

As a freshman at Harvard College, I studied from Samuelson's famed introductory textbook and his *Newsweek* columns, began a lifetime of reading his seemingly endless series of pathbreaking papers, heard wonderful stories about his scintillating intellect, and was able to attend his lectures or watch him in action at economics conferences. He was the undisputed doyen of American economic science and the first American winner of the Nobel Prize in Economic Sciences. He was also unfailingly kind and supportive to me as an aspiring young economist, as he was to generations of students.

His lifetime of remarkable scholarly output both established and epitomized five core ideas of modern mixed capitalism, which my fellow students and I imbibed in our introduction to economics:

- Markets are reasonably efficient institutions for allocating society's scarce economic resources and lead to high productivity and average living standards.
- Efficiency, however, does not guarantee fairness (or "justice") in the allocation of incomes.
- Fairness requires the government to redistribute income among the citizenry, especially from the richest members of the society to the poorest and most vulnerable members.
- Markets systematically underprovide certain "public goods," such as infrastructure, environmental regulation, education, and scientific research, whose adequate supply depends on the government.
- The market economy is prone to financial instability, which can be alleviated through active government policies, including financial regulation and well-directed monetary and fiscal policies.

Samuelson's great synthesis called on market forces to allocate most goods in the economy, while calling on governments to perform three essential tasks: redistributing income to protect the poor and the unlucky; providing public goods such as infrastructure and scientific research; and stabilizing the macroeconomy. This approach appealed enormously to me as a young student of economics and helped me understand the complementary responsibilities of the market and the government. I found the concept of the mixed economy to be compelling, and I still do after forty years.

The ideas of Samuelson and his great contemporaries, including Nobel Laureates James Tobin, Robert Solow, and Kenneth Arrow, did not arise from pure theorizing. Many aspects of the mixed economy were put into place during the New Deal, World War II, and the early postwar period. Pure theory helped those great economists account for what they observed in the economy, and their ideas, in turn, shaped further economic policies. Ideas and history thereby interacted in a dialectical process. Pivotal historical experiences such as the Great Depression and World War II guide economic theory, while economic theory helps to shape the next steps of history. This is the great drama and thrill of economics: with a deeper understanding of events comes the chance to help the world on its historic arc toward greater well-being.

Intellectual Upheaval in the 1970s

Little did I realize in my student days that a huge intellectual storm was about to hit the field of economics: the consensus over the mixed economy was about to be jolted. In 1971, the year before I entered college, the Bretton Woods dollar-exchange system collapsed, basically because America's inflationary monetary and budget policies during the Vietnam War era were destabilizing the world economy. The United States abandoned its monetary links with gold on August 15, 1971. Inflation soared worldwide as the major market economies searched for a new approach to the global monetary system. The situation was further complicated when the oil-exporting countries sharply raised oil prices in the midst of the global inflation. The surge of oil prices during 1973–1974 led to the combination of economic stagnation and inflation, christened the "Great Stagflation." The subject of stagflation became a major focus of my own early research.[1]

The crisis of the world economy during the 1970s proved to be a decisive break in U.S. economic and political governance. The optimism concerning the mixed economy was assailed. Within academia Samuelson's synthesis of market and government was under heated attack. Economics as an academic discipline was turned on its head by the ascendancy of a new school of thought led by Milton Friedman and Friedrich Hayek, one that deemphasized the mixed economy and played up the functioning of the market system. Though Friedman and Hayek were definitely not free-market zealots, as they supported a clear but limited role of government, they also expressed greatly increased skepticism about the role of government in the economy.

My preparatory economics education ended in 1980 with my PhD. I had entered Harvard as a freshman in 1972 during the Age of Paul Samuelson and joined the Harvard faculty as an assistant professor in the fall of 1980 at the start of the Age of Milton Friedman. That year, Ronald Reagan won the presidency on a platform of rolling back the role of government. Across the Atlantic, the United Kingdom's new prime minister, Margaret Thatcher, stood for the same. Together, Reagan and Thatcher launched a rollback of government the likes of which had not been seen in decades. Many of the measures of the Reagan presidency, notably the sharp cut in the top tax rates and the deregulation of industry, won support throughout the economics profession and the society.

The main effect of the Reagan Revolution, however, was not the specific policies but a new antipathy to the role of government, a new disdain for the poor who depended on government for income support, and a new invitation to the rich to shed their moral responsibilities to the rest of society. Reagan helped plant the notion that society could benefit most not by insisting on the civic virtue of the wealthy, but by cutting their tax rates and thereby unleashing their entrepreneurial zeal. Whether such entrepreneurial zeal was released is debatable, but there is little doubt that a lot of pent-up greed was released, greed that infected the political system and that still haunts America today.

The Case for a Mixed Economy

We need to understand precisely where the free-market ideology goes awry. A good starting point is the most basic functioning of the market economy, notably the law of supply and demand. It is when supply and demand stop functioning effectively that government must step forward.

In a competitive market, where there are large numbers of potential suppliers and consumers, the price of each good and service adjusts to balance the supply and demand. If at the current price firms want to supply more than is demanded by consumers, the price will decline, leading firms to cut back on their supplies and consumers to step up their purchases; if at the current price firms want to supply less than is demanded by consumers, the market price will rise, leading firms to increase their supplies and consumers to trim their purchases. When the balance of supply and demand is reached for each and every good or service, we say that the economy has reached "market equilibrium."

The key idea of Adam Smith, the late-eighteenth-century founder of economic science, is that the market equilibrium is reached without a central planner and that it has desirable results for the nation, notably in the forms of high productivity and wealth. With every firm and household pursuing its own self-interest, the resulting market equilibrium can almost miraculously lead to the well-being of all. Smith gave a famous and enduring name to the process by which the individual actions of millions of individuals and firms combine for the common good: the "invisible hand," encapsulating the paradox that self-interest in the marketplace can lead to the common good. As Smith famously declared:

> It is not from the benevolence of the butcher, the brewer, or the baker, that we expect our dinner, but from their regard to their own interest. We address ourselves, not to their humanity but to their self-love, and never talk to them of our own necessities but of their advantages [in supplying what we demand as consumers].[2]

In modern scientific terms, the invisible hand of the marketplace is called a *self-organizing system*. The idea is that a highly complex and productive system can create an orderly division of labor—and a benefit for the entire population—through the self-interested actions of the individual actors of the system. There is thus no need for a central power to move the society's resources here and there.

Smith brilliantly recognized that the self-organized market equilibrium is likely to result in a high level of productivity and therefore a high level of income and wealth of the population. In modern jargon, we say that the competitive market equilibrium is *efficient*, meaning that there is no waste of resources.[3] Well-functioning markets squeeze out waste in the use of resources. A wasteful firm is outcompeted by a more efficient, lower-cost firm. An artificial scarcity created by one business is undone by the entry of a competitor. And so on throughout the economy, until waste is squeezed from the system.

Why Markets Need Government

Unfortunately, free markets by themselves are not able to ensure the efficiency of the economy. Governments are needed to provide certain public goods, such as highways, that markets by themselves will either not provide or not provide to the right scale. Private markets work well when there are many suppliers and consumers, as is the case for goods and services such as clothing, furniture, automobiles, hotel services, restaurants, and the like. They begin to misfire when economic logic calls for a *single supplier,* for example to operate the police force, fire department, army, court system, highway network, or electricity distribution system.

In such cases, society basically needs just one supplier or at most a very small number, rather than many. We don't want competing armies or competing police and fire departments in our cities. Similarly, we need just one highway and power line from city A to city B, not several competing highways each offering the same route.

Free markets also fail when producers cause adverse spillovers to the rest of society, such as by polluting the rivers with toxic chemicals or emitting climate-changing carbon dioxide into the air from a coal-fired power plant. In such cases, the private economy tends to oversupply the goods in question, unless there are specific regulations or levies imposed on the offending actions. We say that the market needs "corrective pricing," such as a tax levied on the pollutant, in order to reduce negative spillovers.

Private markets fall short in the case of scientific research as well, where spillovers of knowledge occur. Scientists don't—and shouldn't—own the rights to their basic scientific discoveries. Imagine if Isaac Newton's estate held a patent or copyright on the gravity equation. The implication is that one of humanity's most important activities—scientific discovery—needs to be promoted in ways other than the pure profit motive. This is done through status (such as receipt of the Nobel Prize), financial support from philanthropists, government grants (for example, through the National Science Foundation and the National Institutes of Health), government prizes, and other nonbusiness approaches (such as volunteer work and open-source creations such as Linux and Wikipedia).

Free markets also need governments to help regulate the marketplace when information between buyers and sellers is "asymmetric." When sellers have inside information unavailable to buyers, fraud and waste are rife. In the lead-up to the 2008 financial crash, for example, Wall Street sold toxic assets to unsuspecting German banks, thereby extending the bubble and increasing its ultimate cost. In a different sphere, some doctors increase their fees by prescribing medical tests and procedures that are not needed, while patients and insurers are unable to second-guess the medical advice. In both cases, the implication is the need for government regulation: of securities markets to prevent financial fraud and of health care insurers to prevent medical fraud.

It's worth recalling that all great promoters of the market economy, including Adam Smith, John Maynard Keynes, Paul Samuelson, Friedrich Hayek, and Milton Friedman, were fully aware of the reality of public goods, environmental spillovers, and asymmetric information and therefore of the need for the government to be deeply engaged in public education, road building, scientific discovery, environmental protection, financial regulation, and many other activities. None ever denied a major role for government in a market system. That's true not only of Keynes and Samuelson, who are famous for their championship of the mixed economy, but also of Hayek and Friedman, who are known for their advocacy of unfettered markets. It is only the present-day free-market acolytes of Hayek and Friedman who neglect the key role of government in ensuring the efficiency and fairness of a market system.

Hayek noted in *The Road to Serfdom* that we should not confuse the opposition to central planning with "a dogmatic laissez faire [free market] attitude." The correct position, said Hayek, lies

in favor of making the best possible use of the forces of competition as a means of coordinating human efforts, not an argument for leaving things just as they are. It is based on conviction that, where effective competition can be created, it is a better way of guiding individual efforts than any other. . . .

Nor does it deny that, where it is impossible to create the conditions necessary to make competition effective, we must resort to other methods of guiding economic activity.[4] (Emphasis added.)

Hayek acknowledged, as had Adam Smith before him, "a wide and unquestioned field for state activity" in the economy. Indeed, Hayek reminds the reader of *The Road to Serfdom* that Adam Smith himself called on the government to provide those services that "though they may be in the highest degree advantageous to a great society, are, however, of such a nature, that the profit could never repay the expense to any individual or small number of individuals."[5] In other words, Hayek sides with Adam Smith in recognizing the importance of government provision of public goods.

Fairness and Sustainability

Though efficiency is a great virtue, it is not the only economic goal of interest to the society.[6] Economic fairness is also crucial. Fairness refers to the distribution of income and well-being, as well as to the ways that government treats the citizenry (including fairness in levying taxes, awarding contracts, and distributing transfers).

Most people would regard as unfair a market equilibrium in which some individuals are super-rich while others are dying of extreme poverty. In such a circumstance, most people would regard it as fair (or "just" or "equitable") for the government to tax the super-rich in order to provide basic resources for the poor such as food, shelter, safe water, and access to health care. Indeed, a solid 63 percent of Americans concur that "It is the responsibility of government to take care of people who can't take care of themselves."[7] The sentiment that government should help the poor who cannot help themselves has been an enduring value in American society.

The rule of law is also a matter of fairness. We demand equal treatment of citizens under the law. We expect that income transfers from the rich to the poor should follow due process, not an arbitrary levy or Robin Hood–style confiscation. The rebelling American colonists in 1776 did not object to taxation per se, but to taxation without representation.

Fairness entails not only the distribution of income within society at a point in time but also the distribution of income across generations, a concept that economists also call "sustainability." If the current generation depletes the earth's scarce natural resources, for example by using up its fossil fuel and freshwater aquifers, or acidifies the oceans through carbon dioxide emissions, or drives other species to extinction, it severely diminishes the well-being of the generations to come. Those future generations can't defend their interests today, since they've not even been born.

Sustainability, or fairness to the future, therefore involves the concept of *stewardship*, the idea that the living generation must be stewards of the earth's resources for the generations that will come later. That's a tough role to play. There is nothing natural or innate about it. We need to defend the interests of those whom we've never met and never will. Yet those are our descendants and our fellow humanity. Alas, it's a role that we've mostly ignored till now, to the increasing peril of all who will follow.

The Libertarian Extreme

A small number of Americans reject the very idea that government should promote fairness, or even efficiency for that matter, through the power of taxation. They hold that the only ethical value that matters is liberty, meaning the right of each individual to be left alone by others and by the government. In that philosophy, known as *libertarianism*, individuals have absolutely no responsibility to society other than to respect the liberty and property of others.

This extreme philosophy has been embraced by some of America's richest individuals, such as Charles and David Koch (combined net worth: $44 billion), who have used their great fortunes, based on an inheritance, to try to instill their libertarian views throughout the society.[8]

According to libertarians, America should be governed not by social responsibilities but by free-market forces and voluntary private contracts, with the government devoted solely to maintaining law and order, including the protection of private property. Taxes should be slashed to the minimum, as there is little or no legitimate role of government beyond the bare bones of the military, police, prisons, and courts.[9] Libertarians don't believe in levying taxes even to build roads and other infrastructure, believing instead that such investments should be left to the free market.

Libertarians argue that taxation is little more than government extortion. Most Americans disagree. Though we don't love paying taxes, we accept the *legitimacy* of taxes as long as they are properly voted into law and the revenue is used honestly and sensibly. In a 2009 Gallup survey, 61 percent of Americans declared the amount of income tax that they would pay that year as "fair," as opposed to 35 percent who called their income tax "not fair."[10]

Libertarians aim to absolve the rich of any social responsibilities toward the rest of society. As a school of thought, libertarianism is based on three kinds of arguments. The first is a moral assertion: that every individual has the overriding right to liberty, that is, the right to be left alone, free from taxes, regulations, or other demands of the state. The second is political and pragmatic: that only free markets protect democracy from government despotism. The third is economic: that free markets alone are enough to ensure prosperity.

Such an approach, while promising liberty, democracy, and prosperity, is a grand illusion. We know from both historical experience and economic theory that free markets alone cannot begin to ensure efficiency and prosperity; without government, we'd lack the highways, safe environment, public health, and scientific discoveries that make us productive. We know from historical experience that countries will not risk their democracies by levying taxes. Indeed, the heavily taxed countries of Scandinavia score higher than the United States on rankings of quality of governance and control of corruption. We also know from experience and moral tradition that although liberty is indeed an important value, it's not the only one that counts. If we have to choose between the liberty of a billionaire to avoid paying taxes and the needs of a poor and hungry child in need of food that would be supplied by those taxes (through food stamps, for example), most of us would choose the needs of the hungry child over the "liberty" of the billionaire to avoid helping the child.

When libertarians deride the idea of social fairness as just one more nuisance, they unleash greed. The kind of unconstrained greed that is now loose in America is leading not to real liberty but to corporate criminality and deceit; not to democracy but to politics dominated by special interests; and not to prosperity but to income stagnation for much of the population and untold riches at the very top. Fortunately, most Americans disagree with the harshness and extremism of the libertarian philosophy. Nonetheless, wealthy libertarians can gain the upper hand in real political decision making through massive lobbying, propaganda campaigns, and heavy campaign financing.

Achieving Society's Triple Bottom Line

The majority of Americans support the idea that America should aim for three goals—efficiency (prosperity), fairness (opportunity for all), and sustainability (a safe environment for today and the future)—rather than the single-minded libertarian objective of tax cuts and a shrinking government. Americans are eager to support effective public policies to achieve the three objectives. The question is how best to achieve those goals.

A free-market economy is not enough. A key lesson of economic theory and of two centuries of experience with market economies is that a *combination* of market forces and government actions is needed to achieve these three simultaneous goals. If we were to close down the government and leave everything to the marketplace, society could not achieve even one of the three core objectives. Only a mixed economy, one that is part business-led and part government-led, can achieve all three goals. Americans agree. According to a Pew Research Center survey, a solid majority of Americans, 62 percent to 29 percent, concur that the "free market needs regulation to best serve public interest."[11]

The marketplace does have some elements of basic fairness: hard work can produce a higher income; laziness is punished. A lifetime plan to study hard and get a good education produces an economic reward for the individual as well as a sense of fulfillment. But the fairness of the marketplace should not be exaggerated. Many people are simply unlucky. Market forces such as foreign competition may turn against them (such as when a technological change wipes out an industry in a gale of "creative destruction," as the economist Joseph Schumpeter called it). Others are born poor to parents who lack the education and skills to escape from poverty. Still others have disabilities and diseases that are no fault of their own. Some live in places hit by earthquakes, tsunamis, droughts, floods, or other hazards and depend on government to survive and recover. Whole regions of America and other countries have faced deep economic crises because of shifts in global market conditions that are far beyond anyone's control. In all of these cases, the marketplace can be brutally unsentimental, leaving the poor to starve or die from illnesses and neglect, unless society steps forward through government or charitable relief.

Just as there are many people who don't deserve their poverty, there are many others who don't deserve their wealth. Many great fortunes, such as the Koch brothers', are inherited. And of the fortunes that are ostensibly earned, many are not really earned at all. Wall Street bankers took home tens of billions of dollars in Christmas bonuses each year in the lead-up to the 2008 financial meltdown, just as they were driving their firms toward bankruptcy. Several of America's best-paid CEOs in the past decade led their companies into illegality, bankruptcy, or both.

Amazingly, even when Wall Street required government transfers to stay alive in 2009, the megabonuses persisted (and the White House looked the other way because Wall Street had financed Obama's 2008 campaign). Oil companies often owe their profits to bribery (like Halliburton in Nigeria), cushy government contracts, specially tailored tax breaks, the lack of environmental regulations, and the backing of the U.S. military in the Middle East, all of which occurs without any reimbursement from the oil industry, other than the campaign contributions that continue to flow.

Despite the claims of free-market advocates, virtually all societies throughout history have organized governmental means to ensure support for the poorest among them.[12] Most have also placed a special responsibility on the rich to pay their share. Until the last two centuries, however, the extent of poverty was so pervasive that there was often not much that society could really do for the poor beyond emergency relief (in the case of a famine, for example). Now, with our great affluence, we can do much more. Indeed, I argued in *The End of Poverty* that we can actually end extreme poverty once and for all in our generation if the rich will accept their share of the effort to help raise the education, health, and productivity of the poor.

Just as free markets do not guarantee fairness for the citizens of a generation, they do not guarantee sustainability for future generations. There are two reasons for this. The first is that much of any society's natural capital—the air, water, climate, biodiversity, forests, oceans, and the like—is the common property of the entire society (or even the world) and is therefore vulnerable to abuse unless it is properly managed through political choices. Right now, for example, the earth's atmosphere is a free "dumping ground" for carbon dioxide, which is dangerously changing the earth's climate. The world's major estuaries are a free dumping ground for chemical fertilizers that run off from millions of farms into the major rivers flowing to these estuaries and on to the open seas. Unless the world's governments agree to regulate the use of the environmental commons, private economic activity will inevitably undermine and eventually destroy these vital life-supporting ecosystems.

The second reason is the small matter of the market interest rate. Interest rates are positive because people are impatient, preferring present consumption to future consumption. The more impatient income earners are, the more today's income is used for current consumption and the less is used for saving, thereby driving up interest rates. Yet because of positive interest rates, profit-oriented resource holders (of timber, fisheries, oil, freshwater aquifers, and the like) tilt their production toward the present rather than the future, since $1 today is worth more than $1 in the future. This causes a deep tendency to eventual depletion of scarce resources, even the extinction of species, unless we pay attention and put our thumb on the scale to protect the environment. We need to say that yes, we are impatient, but we are also stewards of future generations whose views are not directly represented in the marketplace.

Like it or not, we have the fate of future generations in our hands. There is little within the logic of a free-market economy that forces us to take their interests seriously. True sustainability therefore requires that each generation protect the future even beyond its own shortsighted consumption preferences. We need to reflect not only on our personal wants and desires but also on our responsibilities as the planetary stewards. Innovations such as the National Park Service and the Endangered Species Act are examples of ways that we can prevent our own short-term temptations from endangering the well-being of later generations. We've still not faced that challenge squarely when it comes to long-term energy supplies, freshwater, and climate safety.

How Efficiency and Fairness May Reinforce Each Other

A few Americans, perhaps no more than 10 to 20 percent, believe that the market outcome is always fair. In this unforgiving view, if people are poor, it is their own fault. Most Americans don't believe this.[13] They know that circumstances matter. They remember the stories of their own parents or grandparents suffering through the Great Depression or through a tragic bout of illness that left them incapacitated and unable to work, of a factory in the town closing down, or of the impossibility of paying college tuition and therefore having to drop out of school and accept a low-paying job. Americans want the poor to make maximum efforts on their own behalf, but they also recognize society's responsibility to step in when the going gets too tough.

Specifically, most Americans subscribe to the view that market-determined gaps between the rich and poor should be softened by government. The rich should be taxed, and the poor should be helped. But how much should the government intervene? One common argument is that there is a *trade-off* between efficiency and fairness. If the rich are taxed and the poor are helped through transfers, the hard work of the rich is punished and the idleness of the poor is rewarded. The rich cut back on their effort—for example, by not opening a new business—while the poor use their windfall to support their leisure, for example by not taking an available job. The result, say the critics of income redistribution, is that society squanders much more than $1 of income for each $1 of government help that actually reaches the poor. Redistribution, they believe, should be severely limited, used to address only the most extreme problems of poverty and hunger.

Other societies, such as the Scandinavian social democracies, have for a long time taken a very different view. They believe that even extensive redistribution can and should be carried out by government and that such a redistribution can be accomplished with very little inefficiency. The rich will continue to work hard even if they are taxed relatively heavily, and the poor will use the government help to raise their productivity. Economic theory indeed supports the view that high tax rates can actually spur, rather than hinder, work effort, since more rather than less work effort is then needed to reach a specific target level of income (for example, to buy a house or to cover a tuition payment).

Let me underscore a basic point that is generally overlooked in the heated U.S. debate on this issue: in many circumstances, there is no trade-off at all between efficiency and equity because the two goals actually go hand in hand. Promoting fairness also promotes efficiency. Here's how.

In many cases, help for the poor is not simply an income transfer used for short-run consumption but is a government benefit that enables poor households to raise their long-term productivity. Some of the key government programs for poor households include help for nutrition of mothers and young children; preschool; college tuition; and job training. Each of these is a government-supported investment in "human capital" and specifically a way for a poor household to raise its long-term productivity. Taxing the rich to help the poor can then mean cutting lavish consumption spending by the rich to support high-return human investments by the poor. The outcome is not only fairer but also more efficient.

The need for public financing of education has been recognized by virtually all economists since Adam Smith, including the strong promoters of free markets such as Friedrich Hayek and Milton Friedman. They've understood that markets alone will not educate our young people, at least not enough of them. The situation has become even more serious today. With rising costs of education, the poor are likely to be left behind, and trapped in poverty, unless the government steps forward to help finance a quality education for all.[14]

Finding the Balance of Markets and Government

The proper balance between markets and government has been at the center of debate for generations, going back to Adam Smith's explanation of self-organizing markets. A fierce debate has been under way for more than two centuries. Here are five of my own conclusions regarding this debate, which I believe to be relevant for our times.

First, in productive sectors of many producers and consumers, and therefore where strong market competition applies, we should rely on market forces. This is Hayek's position, and it's a good one. Markets have several desirable attributes. They are decentralized, voluntary, and do not require the very difficult work of forging cooperation among a large number of people. They can cater to the distinct tastes of individual consumers. If markets suffice to get food from farms to urban tables, let us use markets. There is no need for central planning bureaus managing farm production, food processing, food transport, and food distribution. Profit-minded farmers, mill owners, shippers, and supermarkets will suffice. (And when government control of food production and distribution was tried in the Soviet Union, the result was a chronic shortage of basic food commodities.)

Second, we should turn to government to ensure the fairness and sustainability of market outcomes, including the broad distribution of income in the society. Market forces that cause wage levels to rise or fall can usefully direct workers to the sectors that need employment and away from those that do not, but the resulting distribution of income may be unjust. Many people can fall into destitution if they find themselves in sectors that face a sudden collapse of market demand or if they have skills that suddenly become obsolete. Or the generation alive today may be enticed to consume too many of nature's resources at great cost to future generations. The government should therefore use its powers to tax and transfer incomes, on a prudent and targeted basis, to help those who can't help themselves and to protect the well-being of future (still unborn) generations.

Third, we should recognize that the knowledge of science and technology is a public good that should be promoted actively by government alongside the private sector. Markets alone will not create the twenty-first-century knowledge society. America's huge interest in the accumulation and diffusion of knowledge calls for ample public spending on research and development, public education, e-governance, and open-source online materials, as complements to the market system of patents and copyrights. In this regard, patents and copyrights are double-edged swords. We use them to create a profit incentive to producers of knowledge, but we must also recognize that patents and copyrights create temporary monopolies that cause high drug prices, delays in research breakthroughs (when patented knowledge is a key input for further research), and an artificial digital divide of haves and have-nots.

Fourth, as economic life becomes more complex, we should expect the role of government to become more extensive. Therefore, expecting to find good twenty-first-century economic answers in a constitution that dates back to 1789 is unrealistic. The Founding Fathers were clever, to be sure, but the cleverest thing they realized is that Thomas Jefferson's famous aphorism that "the earth belongs to the living" means laws from a premodern age should not blindly bind us today. We need fresh thinking about our circumstances, especially at a time of rapid globalization, environmental threats, and a knowledge-based economy.

Fifth, we should appreciate that circumstances as to the appropriate role of markets and government differ across countries. There is no reason to expect that the United States, Europe, China, India, and others will or should make exactly the same choices about the roles of government and markets. History has shown that the emerging economies such as Brazil, China, and India should devote special government resources and policies to closing the technology gap, while countries in the lead (such as the United States) should devote special government resources to cutting-edge research and development. Thus, China and the United States each needs its own distinctive kinds of industrial policies, China's to facilitate rapid catching up and America's to facilitate scientific and technological leadership. In neither case would a naive free-market position be warranted.

A Market Economy? Yes—with Balance

To recap, the modern market economy is an amazing human contrivance.[15] In a highly decentralized way it engages the self-interest of billions of people in millions of businesses and more than 1 billion households around the world to organize the use of labor time, natural resources, and produced capital goods (such as machinery and buildings). Yet the market by itself is not equipped to achieve the triple bottom line of efficiency, fairness, and sustainability. The market system must be complemented with government institutions that accomplish three things: provide public goods such as infrastructure, scientific research, and market regulation; ensure the basic fairness of income distribution and long-term help for the poor to escape from poverty; and promote sustainability of the earth's fragile resources for the benefit of future generations. These are not simple or static tasks; they require the ingenuity and creativity of each generation to respond to the challenges of the times.

CHAPTER 4.

Washington's Retreat from Public Purpose

How did we get into the dreadful situation in which the federal government is in the lap of the corporate lobby? Why has the federal government stopped providing the public goods that Americans need to remain globally competitive in a fair and sustainable society? These are the puzzles we must solve in order to move forward. In the next four chapters we'll look at the role of globalization, domestic politics, social change, and even the media as contributors to this debacle. We'll see that many powerful currents have flowed together to tilt our politics away from the public good to special interests. As society understands what has happened, it will be in a position to turn the country toward its true democratic values once again.

From the New Deal to the War on Poverty

For roughly three decades, from the New Deal of the mid-1930s to the War on Poverty of the mid-1960s, the federal government steered the national economy as a relatively trusted and respected instrument of democratic power. The federal government led America through depression, war, and peacetime boom. The federal government conceived and financed the national highway system and the national power grid. Science and technology (S&T) initiatives created in Washington helped launch several of the most important technologies of the past half century: nuclear power, satellites, computers, the Internet, and much more. The federal government fought poverty and exclusion, culminating in the 1960s in Medicare for the elderly and civil rights legislation on behalf of minorities, women, and the disabled. When necessary, as in World War II, the government mobilized industry, putting it at the service of the nation. More often, it partnered effectively with industry in starting new industries (such as computers and the Internet) or expanding them (such as aviation and satellites). There was no question, however, about who was in the lead of the relationship.

Then, after three decades of active economic leadership, Washington gradually stopped steering. The public's support for collective action through federal policy making dissipated. The government stopped steering just as America faced growing challenges in the forms of globalization, the ecological crisis, and the massive rise of immigration. During the 1980s and onward, the instruments of federal power were increasingly handed over to vested corporate interests to be used for private advantage. The new corporatocracy was under way. And the economy, now guided by narrow interests, quickly became divided, unstable, and ultimately vulnerable to the kind of collapse that ensued in 2008.

The overarching reversal of Washington's role, from defender of the common man to the enabler of narrow interests, is the most important political change during the eight decades since the Great Depression in the 1930s. It is eye-opening today to recall the clarion words of Franklin D. Roosevelt in his second inaugural address, as he ushered in the era of government leadership in the economy:

[G]overnment [is] the instrument of our united purpose to solve for the individual the ever-rising problems of a complex civilization. Repeated attempts at their solution without the aid of government had left us baffled and bewildered.[1]

Those sentiments are no longer recognizable. America had already begun to change fundamentally by 1981, when Ronald Reagan proclaimed:

In this present crisis, government is not the solution to our problem; government is the problem. . . . It is my intention to curb the size and influence of the Federal establishment.[2]

He not only curbed the government's steering of the economy but also, wittingly or not, turned the levers of power over to the highest bidder. Fifteen years after Reagan came to power, Democratic President Bill Clinton made the handover of power to the corporate sector a bipartisan reality when he declared, "The era of big government is over."[3] Clinton was especially the enabler of Wall Street power, which gained enough leeway to win tens of billions of dollars per year of bonuses and cost the world tens of trillions of dollars of financial losses in the great crash of 2008. After Clinton, the United States no longer had a center-right Republican Party and a center-left Democratic Party, but rather two center-right parties whose heated differences on the surface mask a common agenda at the core. Washington's obeisance to the rich while squeezing the poor has so far proved to be bipartisan and durable. Yet the results are so meager for the broad public that its death knell will also toll.[4]

The Rise of Public Spending

The rise of the federal government's economic role from the New Deal onward is well captured by a single key statistic: the size of civilian (nondefense) federal spending relative to national income (Figure 4.1). From around 3 percent of GDP in 1930, the civilian budget rose to 8 percent of GDP by 1940 under the aegis of the New Deal.[5] By 1950, the share of federal civilian spending had reached 10 percent of GDP. Civilian spending gradually ascended to around

Figure 4.1: Civilian Federal Spending as a Percentage of GDP, 1930–2010

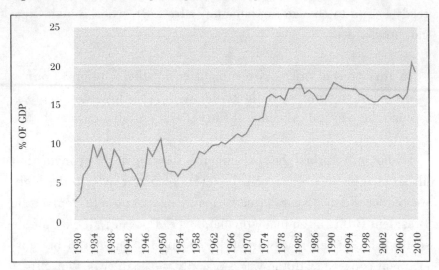

Source: Data from Office of Management and Budget Historical Tables.

12 percent of GDP by 1970 and 16 percent of GDP by 1980, where it stayed roughly unchanged until the 2008 financial crisis. (The 2008 crisis ushered in a spike in spending that may or may not prove to be temporary, depending on the budgetary choices we make.) The long-term rise in spending occurred in every high-income country in the world, in fact more in Europe than in America. The long-term rise in public spending relative to GDP reflects the deep need of every modern society for a mixed economy rather than any specific twists and turns of U.S. politics.

Figure 4.2 displays the allocation of civilian spending between "mandatory" programs such as Social Security and Medicare, where the benefits are written into law, and "discretionary" programs such as NASA's space missions and U.S. energy research, where the spending has to be approved annually by Congress.[6] Up until 1980, both the mandatory and the discretionary parts of the budget had an upward ascent. Since 1980, the mandatory spending has risen slightly while the discretionary spending has been cut as a share of GDP. Therein lie many of the crises of poor governance today.

The federal programs brought in by the New Deal and then ex-

Figure 4.2: The Trajectory of Civilian Spending as a Percentage of GDP, 1962–2010

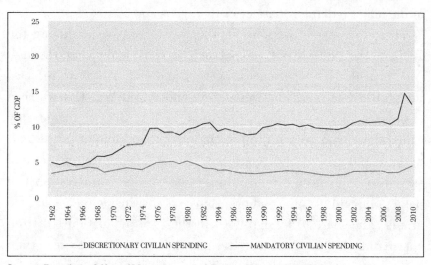

Source: Data from Office of Management and Budget Historical Tables.

tended during the 1940s to 1960s include several kinds of activities: construction of physical infrastructure (roads, bridges, electricity, dams), regional development (such as in the Tennessee Valley), increased provision of public services (health and education), retirement and disability pensions (Social Security), support for science and technology, public administration, income security (unemployment insurance), transfers to the poor (food stamps), and others. Almost none of those programs existed before 1933, when Roosevelt assumed the presidency in the depths of the Depression.

Roosevelt's New Deal policies generated enormous controversies in their day, with many of Roosevelt's fervent opponents decrying the rising role of government in the economy, much as libertarians call for a scaling back of government today. Nonetheless, after the United States had passed through the Great Depression in the 1930s and World War II in the first half of the 1940s, American society coalesced around a new vision of the economy. Democrats and Republicans alike agreed that a new and larger federal government was needed to ensure that the U.S. economy would stay out of depression and keep the nation secure in the postwar era. During the 1940s through the 1960s, the public consistently supported the expansion of the major federal initiatives of the 1930s and 1940s.

There are several reasons for this era of consensus during the 1940s to the 1960s. First, the nation as a whole had passed through two "near-death" experiences together and emerged as an increasingly united society. The Depression and World War II were rites of passage for the Greatest Generation, as Tom Brokaw memorably called those who grew up in the Depression and fought in the war. Second, and less widely recognized, the 1924 Immigration Act had served to reduce the flow of immigrants, so that immigration was not a political lightning rod or a source of dissension on social programs. The share of foreign-born in the U.S. population fell from approximately 15 percent of the population in 1924 to less than 5 percent of the population by 1970, when it started to rise because of revisions to immigration law.[7]

Third, simply and crucially, the government was viewed as highly competent and representative of broad national interests. It had nursed the nation through the Great Depression; it had led the nation to victory in World War II; it had led to the creation of postwar institutions including NATO and the European Coal and Steel Community (eventually to become the European Union) and to the recovery of Japan; it had helped the economy recover from the end of the war more swiftly than anyone imagined. Government was widely trusted and seen as a guarantor of national prosperity. It was not seen as a tribune of special interests, and particularly not the interests of the rich, who paid stiff income taxes, with top tax rates soaring to 80 percent or higher after 1940.

The apogee of government leadership of the economy was reached in the mid-1960s, immediately following John F. Kennedy's assassination. Lyndon B. Johnson declared war on poverty in early 1964 and launched an astonishing array of legislative initiatives in 1965, including: the Voting Rights Act of 1965, the Elementary and Secondary Education Act of 1965, the Water Quality Act of 1965, the Higher Education Act of 1965, the Federal Cigarette Labeling and

Advertising Act of 1965, the Solid Waste Disposal Act of 1965, the Motor Vehicle Air Pollution Control Act of 1965, and, most important in terms of size of outlays, the Social Security Amendments of 1965, which ushered in Medicare for the elderly and Medicaid for the indigent. The War on Poverty had its most lasting effect on two groups, the elderly and African Americans. Medicare and the expansion of Social Security effectively ended the persistent high poverty among those over sixty-five. In 1959, the elderly poverty rate stood at 35.2 percent; it fell to 25.3 percent by 1969 and just 9.7 percent by 2007. African American poverty rates fell from 55.1 percent in 1959 to 32.2 percent in 1969 and 24.5 percent in 2007.[8]

One more crucial factor made possible the surge in social programs during the period of the 1960s: the availability of *existing* government revenues to pay for them. Up until the mid-1960s, politicians could enact new social programs without having to raise taxes as a share of national income for a simple but powerful reason: the federal tax system that emerged from World War II and the Korean War (1950–1953) was able to collect 18 percent to 19 percent of GDP in revenues and therefore to support a roughly equivalent level of spending; as defense spending declined after the Korean War, nondefense spending had room to expand.[9]

The Great Reversal

As of the mid-1960s, most political observers expected a continued ascendancy of social programs in the service of promoting prosperity and fighting poverty. Few guessed at the time that the great consensus on the role of government in the economy would soon begin to unravel, and that a rival economic strategy calling for small government and privatization of public functions would surge to the forefront by 1980. Deep social cleavages surrounding the civil rights movement were the first wedge in the national consensus. I describe those in the next chapter. Yet economic shocks also played a role in undermining the public's confidence in Washington.

The rise of inflation at the end of the 1960s and a series of major economic upheavals of the 1970s shook the faith of the public in the ability of government to steer the economy and to fight poverty at a modest cost to society. The two most important events were the collapse of the post–World War II global exchange-rate system in 1971 and the sharp increases in oil prices in 1973–1974 and again in 1979–1980.[10] Rather than see the events of the 1970s as temporary aberrations requiring specific problem solving, conservative politicians, with Reagan as spokesperson, argued that they were signs of fundamental failures of the public sector and its role in the economy.

President Jimmy Carter's one term, 1977–1981, proved to be the transition in every way.[11] Big Labor lost its political influence reflecting the rise of Sunbelt power and that region's antipathy to organized labor.[12] The 1978 Revenue Act began the process of cutting capital gains taxation that would be greatly extended during the Reagan years. The tax measure "discarded historic principles of interclass equity and methods of promoting business investment" and was "not simply a triumph of capital, but of financial capital, which was assuming a prominent role in U.S. politics."[13] Japan's exports to the United States in steel, automobiles, and electronics goods surged, giving the United States a first taste of the tough competition that would arise in the new era of globalization.

Carter also began the processes of deregulation (notably in airlines, trucking, and finance) that would become a hallmark of the Reagan years and after. Many of Carter's forays into deregulation (for example, in transport) proved to be successful, but the process of deregulation got out of hand in the years that followed, especially in the financial sector. And tellingly, Carter lost his effort to reform the energy sector, tripped up by the power of the oil and gas sector to block his initiatives in alternative energy sources. By 1981, the country was set for a major transformation favoring the Sunbelt, financial capital, wealthy Americans, and Big Oil.

All of this tumult gave an extraordinary opening to the new philosophical assertion that it was "big government" itself rather than new and specific challenges (energy, the exchange rate, and so forth) that constituted the major barrier to prosperity. This was an odd assertion. The major problems that had been experienced were macroeconomic in nature: the collapse of the gold-based exchange system, the budget deficits caused by the Vietnam War, and the oil price shocks. They did not, evidently, relate to the size of government (other than the Vietnam War) as much as to shifts in the world economy.

The assertion that big government had destabilized the economy was doubtful on its face, but Reagan uttered his ideas with such conviction and charm that an unhappy public was ready to vote him into office. Had the evidence been brought to bear, the flimsiness of the claim would have been exposed. Federal tax revenues as a share of GDP were nearly constant from the mid-1950s onward at 17 percent to 18 percent of GDP. Total federal spending as a share of GDP had increased slightly, from around 18 percent of GDP in the late 1950s to around 20 percent of GDP in the late 1960s and 21 percent of GDP in the late 1970s.

There was no evidence then—or now, looking back—that the shocks of the 1970s had much if anything to do with the War on Poverty, social programs, infrastructure investment, science and technology, community development, Medicare, Social Security, or other government programs. Yet the chaos created by the oil price shocks, the new floating exchange rate regime, and lax monetary policies by the Federal Reserve reverberated into budget politics. Suddenly tax cutting, shrinking civilian government, and rolling back welfare policies became the vogue and the diagnostic basis for policy change. There was no turning back. However dubious was the interpretation of the economic mayhem of the 1970s, a political reality had resulted: government lost its aura of competency. Probably this alone was fatal to the economic consensus that had guided the country for almost forty years.

The Reagan Revolution

The political coalition that put Reagan into office was determined to create a lasting legacy of a smaller federal government ("to curb the size and influence of the federal establishment"), and in this it partly succeeded. There were four main instruments of the Reagan Revolution: tax cuts on higher incomes, restraints on federal spending on civilian programs (at least relative to the growing economy), deregulation of key industries, and outsourcing of core government services. All four of these major policy changes took hold in the 1980s and are still in place today.

At the aggregate level, the Reagan Revolution did not shrink the federal public administration, but it probably did stop it from expanding. The federal civilian bureaucracy had 2,109,000 full-time-equivalent civilian employees in 1981, the same in 1988, and nearly the same over the next twenty years, with an expected 2,101,000 full-time-equivalent civilian employees in 2011.[14]

In terms of taxation, total federal revenues as a share of national income in 2007, before the financial panic, stood at 18.5 percent, virtually unchanged from the start of the Reagan administration. Total spending in 2007 stood at 19.6 percent of GDP, slightly lower than the 21.7 percent of GDP in 1980. Civilian spending was 13.9 percent of GDP in 2007, down slightly from 14.8 percent of GDP in 1980.

The larger shift from Reagan onward was across the categories of domestic spending.[15] As we saw in Figure 4.2, discretionary civilian spending declined from 5.2 percent of GDP in 1980 to around 3.6 percent of GDP in 2007 (before a temporary recession-related boost). Mandatory spending, mainly transfer programs to individuals such as Medicare, Medicaid, Social Security, and veterans' benefits, grew slightly, from 9.6 percent of GDP in 1980 to around 10.4 percent of GDP in 2007. Thus the Reagan Revolution set into motion a squeeze on government investments in areas such as education, infrastructure, energy, science and technology, and other productivity-enhancing areas, while leaving mostly untouched the growth of transfers to individuals for health care and retirement.

Demonizing Taxation

The deepest political impact of the Reagan era was the demonization of taxes. Taxes are rarely popular, especially in the United States, a country that was founded on a tax revolt. Taxes not only take money out of pockets; they are widely seen by Americans as a denial of freedom itself. The standard libertarian line is that since government collects around a third of national income, it's as if Americans are indentured to the government, even its slaves, during January through April of each year. Accurate or not, the anti-tax sentiment is ingrained in the American political discourse.

Reagan's main target was to reduce the top marginal tax rates on rich taxpayers. The history of the top marginal tax rates is shown in Figure 4.3. The federal income tax is a recent invention, just one

Figure 4.3: The Top Marginal Personal Income Tax Rate, 1913–2009

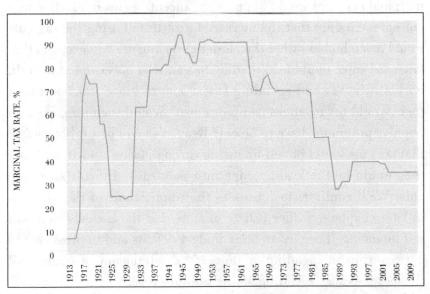

Source: Data from Tax Policy Center (Urban Institute and Brookings Institution).

century old. At the start, the highest marginal tax rate was a very modest 7 percent, but within a few years, and due to America's entry into World War I, the top marginal tax rate soared to 77 percent in 1918. In the 1920s, the conservative administrations of Calvin Coolidge and Herbert Hoover brought the top rate back down to 25 percent, where it stood at the time of the Black Tuesday stock market crash on October 29, 1929, that marked the onset of the Great Depression.

With the New Deal, the top marginal tax rate rose to 63 percent, and then it rose further during World War II, to reach 94 percent by 1945. It remained near this stratospheric level until the 1960s, when tax cuts during the Johnson administration reduced it to 70 percent in 1965. It remained around that level until the Reagan Revolution. A series of tax cuts at the center of the Reagan agenda reduced it in steps to 28 percent by 1988. It is a mark of the lasting legacy of Reagan that the top marginal tax rate has not again reached even 40 percent since then. Obama entered office with the top rate at 35 percent.

Reagan argued for tax cuts on three major grounds: that lower marginal tax rates would improve the incentives for innovation and entrepreneurship; that the increased growth following the tax cuts would mean higher rather than lower government revenues; and that lower tax rates would lead the way to a smaller government overall, on both the tax and spending sides. The message was contradictory. Would tax revenues go up or down? Would spending, even on popular programs, have to be cut? Reagan's team had it both ways: that tax cuts would be self-financing through faster growth and that they would be the leading edge into politically difficult spending cuts. We'll continue to return to the implications of the tax cuts in later chapters. Suffice it here to state that the tax cuts were not self-financing. They led to large budget deficits and to pressures to cut government spending on domestic discretionary programs, all the more because spending on the military rose.

Cutting Civilian Outlays

It was also an overt goal of Reagan and his supporters, almost as important as the tax cuts, to cut the size of civilian government outlays while simultaneously boosting military spending. Civilian programs were viewed as wasteful, unnecessary, and lavish transfers to the undeserving poor. One of Reagan's lasting images was the "welfare queen," a larger-than-life individual, always imagined as an African American woman, who bilked the federal welfare programs by registering for benefits under multiple aliases. Whether such a figure truly existed was much debated, but the wildly popular idea that welfare fraud was rampant led to a surge of public support for cutting or eliminating many income support programs. The War on Poverty thus became a war on the poor.

The broadest indicator of the post-1980 change is the share of national income devoted to the provision of public goods and services in several categories. Figure 4.1 showed the overall civilian budget of the federal government relative to GDP. We can see that the Reagan Revolution achieved one of the first things it set out to accomplish: an end to the rising trend of civilian outlays as a share of GDP. The civilian budget rose from around 5 percent in 1955 to a peak of 14.9 percent of GDP in 1981. Then the increases stopped. Total civilian spending remained in the range of 13 to 15 percent of GDP thereafter, settling at 13.9 percent of GDP in 2007, the year before the financial crash and the rise in stimulus spending.

Spending on "physical resources," mainly infrastructure, was sharply curtailed, falling by half, from around 2 percent of GDP to around 1 percent of GDP.[16] The accumulated backlog of unmet infrastructure needs has soared as a result, to more than $2 trillion (roughly 15 percent of GDP), according to the American Society of Civil Engineers, which keeps track of America's infrastructure performance and needs.

Another area that was sharply cut was education, job training, and employment programs, all vital areas of investment in human capital, especially in the context of globalization. Most education spending is at the state level, but the federal role is extremely important to preschool, higher education, and job training and placement. The federal education programs were curtailed in the 1980s, and overall public spending in this area fell from 0.85 percent of GDP in 1981 to 0.50 percent of GDP in 1988 and then rose very slightly to 0.53 percent of GDP in 2007, the year before the crisis.[17]

One of the most consequential decisions of the Reagan administration was to dismantle the research and development program on alternative energy supplies begun by Jimmy Carter. When Americans wonder why we are far more dependent on oil in 2010 than in 1973, at the time of the first oil embargo, and why we are drilling in dangerous deep-sea reserves, they should look first at Figure 4.4, showing the outlays on energy R&D. Jimmy Carter declared the energy crisis the "moral equivalent of war." The free-market Right mocked Carter's call for a national energy strategy and cleverly and unfortunately repackaged Carter's call to arms with its acronym, MEOW.

Carter substantially boosted R&D on solar energy, biofuels, coal-to-liquid-gas, and other technologies. R&D spending roughly

Figure 4.4: Federal Energy Research and Development as a Percentage of GDP

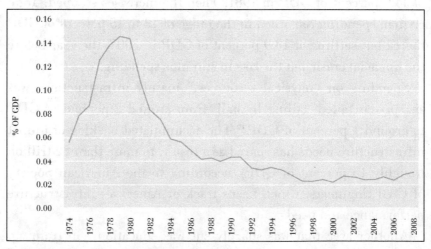

Source: Data from International Energy Agency Data Services.

tripled from 1974 to 1980, rising from $2.9 billion to $9 billion (expressed in constant 2009 dollars).[18] When Reagan came to office, he dismantled what he found, driving R&D back to around $3 billion, with much of that really directed at dual-use military technologies of nuclear power. Symbolically, he ultimately removed the solar panels that Carter had installed on the White House roof, vividly indicating the end of the drive for renewable energy. We are now paying the price, a quarter century later, for Reagan's actions.

The Great Deregulation

The free-market ideologists of the Reagan Revolution despised regulation as an intrusion on private property and more pragmatically saw government regulation as an obstacle to short-run profitability. Bureaucrats were seen as meddling in the genius of the market and standing between business and a gusher of profits. Since the early 1980s, the underlying conceptual reasons for the regulation— including externalities, asymmetric information, principal-agent problems, outright fraud, and risks of self-fulfilling market panics— have been downplayed as unimportant or unworthy of attention compared with the benefits of granting more entrepreneurial discretion as soon as possible.

The biggest deregulation blunders were in financial markets and environmental regulation, both areas in which markets do not function efficiently on their own. The Great Depression had taught the country of the need for thorough financial regulation to curb fraud and excessive leveraging of risk. Yet the Reagan administration unleashed a process of dismantling that regulation. The first step was the Garn–St. Germain Depository Institutions Act of 1982, which deregulated savings and loan institutions and set the course for the massive savings and loan crisis a few years later. From the 1980s onward, financial deregulation became a bipartisan political gift to Wall Street, which amply rewarded politicians with jobs and generous campaign funds. Some of the key measures included the dismantling of barriers between commercial banking and investment banking and the decision at the end of the Clinton administration to keep derivatives unregulated. The disdain for regulation led Alan Greenspan to believe that financial institutions would police their own risks, a blunder that ended up costing the world economy trillions of dollars.

Tough environmental regulations on air and water pollution introduced in the 1960s and 1970s were also partially rolled back after 1980. James Watt, Reagan's secretary of the interior, slashed funding for regulatory agencies within the Interior Department and championed mining and oil production on federal wilderness lands. Environmental regulations certainly did not disappear after 1980, but their application has remained inconsistent, conflict-ridden, and limited by aggressive claims of private property rights asserted by libertarian groups within the Republican Party.

Another aspect of deregulation, which has had profound but underrecognized consequences, was the deregulation of the media, especially TV. Until the 1980s, television networks had a mandate to serve the public good through public-interest programming, a fair balance in reporting, and access to the airwaves through the so-called Fairness Doctrine. This mandate was completely eliminated in the wave of deregulation. TV station owners became interested in one overriding goal: making profits through advertising and mass viewership. The fragile ability to promote public education and awareness was abandoned. The arrival of our media-saturated age was given a major boost.

The Privatization of Public Services

The general belief of the Reagan administration, sustained through several administrations till now, was that private providers of services should replace direct government provision, even when the government is financing the services. Thus, the government has massively stepped up the contracting of military services such as base operations, judicial services such as management of federal prisons, and social services, including health care, education, and income support. In each of these areas, private companies on contract to the government now provide the services that were once provided directly by the government. As with deregulation, tax cuts, and limits on government spending, the outsourcing phenomenon has been a bipartisan strategy since it was unleashed in the Reagan administration.

As the public has discovered during the course of the Iraq and Afghanistan wars, private contractors now implement an astounding array of military activities. This form of contracting is treacherous, as it is highly vulnerable to abuse: favoritism in allocating contracts, kickbacks, nonperformance of contracted services, over-invoicing, and more.

The notion that the private provision of public services will automatically deliver more value for money than the direct government provision of services is built on a series of confusions. Most of the services in question are public goods, so that private competition is inherently lacking. Government outsourcing is therefore tantamount to converting a public monopoly to a private monopoly, with no competition regarding the quality of services. Nor does the free-market ideology acknowledge the pervasive abuses of the contracting process. Contractors are often selected fraudulently as the result of bribes or on political grounds in return for campaign contributions. Congress routinely pays for expensive weapons systems that are opposed by the Pentagon, because local military contractors win the political backing of their congressional delegations.

The End of Government as National Problem Solver

The final legacy of the Reagan Revolution is the most important of all. Since the early 1980s, Washington has stopped serving as a national economic problem solver. From the 1930s to the 1970s, when a major national problem presented itself, the federal government tried to solve it. That included reducing unemployment in the 1930s, winning the war in the 1940s, building the national infrastructure in the 1950s, fighting poverty in the 1960s, and confronting environmental and energy threats in the 1970s. It was taken for granted that major economic problems required policy leadership and federal engagement.

How different our national life has been during the past thirty years. By declaring government to be the problem and not the solution to America's economic ills, Reagan inaugurated a new mind-set as well as a new set of policies. If you are an average citizen, don't expect Washington to address your concerns. If you are a special interest, however, come take a seat at the regulatory table; the regulations will be expunged or rewritten to suit your needs. As new challenges—including globalization, climate change, financial instability, and soaring health care costs—have come along, special interests rather than the national interest have been at the political center stage.

Reagan's Bad Diagnosis and the Meager Results

The proof of a bold diagnosis is whether it leads to a useful prescription. Reagan's diagnosis that the federal government needed to be reined in led to sharp cuts in marginal tax rates, widespread deregulation and privatization of government services, and essentially a ceiling on tax revenues at around 18 percent of GDP. On all relevant indicators, the period from 1981 to 2010 proved to be no better, and was generally much worse, than the period from, say, 1955 to 1970, before the onset of the terrible decade of the 1970s. (The same conclusion applies if we limit the third interval to 2008, on the eve of the Obama administration.) As we see in Table 4.1, economic conditions deteriorated in the 1970s on many fronts: the unemployment rate, growth of earnings, budget deficit, and inflation.

Table 4.1: Economic Performance, 1955–2010

Indicator	1955–1970	1971–1980	1981–2010
Top marginal tax rate	82.3%	70.0%	39.3%
Federal revenues as % of GDP	17.7%	17.9%	18.0%
Growth in GDP	3.6%	3.2%	2.8%
Growth in GDP per capita	2.2%	2.1%	1.7%
Growth in total employment	1.7%	2.7%	1.1%
Average unemployment rate	4.9%	6.4%	6.3%
Change in income inequality: share of income earned by top 1%	–2.0%	0.6%	10.9%
Change in national poverty rate	–9.8%	0.5%	0.3%
Growth in earnings for full-time male workers	2.9%	0.5%	0.2%
Budget balance as % of GDP	–0.7%	–2.4%	–3.0%
Inflation rate	2.3%	7.7%	3.2%

Source: Tax Policy Center; Office of Management and Budget Historical Tables; U.S. Census Bureau; Saez and Piketty Data Set on Income Inequality; U.S. Bureau of Economic Analysis.[19]

The Reagan prescription aimed to reverse the trends of the 1970s. In this, it mostly failed. The period from 1981 to 2010 had much lower top marginal tax rates, but that prescription had little overall benefit for the economy. Economic growth declined, as did employment growth. The unemployment rate averaged more than 6 percent. Inequality soared, with the share of household income accruing to the top 1 percent rising from 10 percent in 1980 to 21 percent in 2009.[20] Earnings stagnated. The deficit widened. Only inflation showed a marked improvement compared with the 1970s. The conclusion is really unmistakable: the Reagan Revolution failed to put America back on its previous path of growth, high employment, and shared prosperity.

CHAPTER 5.

The Divided Nation

The retreat of government after 1980 partly reflected Reagan's incorrect diagnosis that "big government" had caused the economic crises of the 1970s. Another cause was globalization, as I will explain in the next chapter. A third factor was the rise of social tensions in America that made it more difficult to acknowledge, and act upon, shared principles and values. From the 1980s till now, America has seen itself as a tensely divided society, and we've dissipated tremendous national energies on our social divisions rather than focusing on the important values that unite most Americans and that can and should be the basis of economic policies.

Our era's social cleavages are well known to any American: red states versus blue states; suburbs versus urban centers; rural versus urban; whites versus minorities; fundamentalist versus mainline religious denominations; conservatives versus liberals; and Sunbelt versus Snowbelt.[1] These divisions are real. Americans have very diverse views about many important matters, from their religious preferences to cultural standards to attitudes about social justice. And as with most things in life, "Where you stand depends on where you sit" (or reside, to be more accurate). Being a white suburban southerner creates a different reality from that of an urban African American northerner, with a different set of cultural attitudes, social norms, and political views.

For a time, these divisions were muted by the circumstances facing America. During the 1930s and 1940s, Americans were "in it together," first in the Great Depression and then in World War II. These epochal events were a great crucible of consensus building. The Cold War period created a sense of shared risks and responsibilities as well, meaning that Harry Truman, Dwight D. Eisenhower, Kennedy, and Johnson all could feel, at least until 1965 or so, that they were presiding over a society that shared certain touchstones. This feeling of consensus began to unravel in the early 1960s and by the 1980s was lost.

There were innumerable reasons for this, far too many to trace in detail. Here are some. The ebbing of Cold War tensions, ironically, created an environment in which smoldering social tensions could be acknowledged rather than suppressed under a veneer of consensus. The rapidly changing role of women in society—itself the result of World War II, birth control, and economics that pulled women into higher education and the workforce—created new social divisions and eventually contributed to the "culture wars" of the 1960s and onward. The Vietnam War divided the country between hawks and doves, a division that would persist in later conflicts. The counterculture movement of the 1960s pitted traditional households against more experimental lifestyles. Changing sexual mores unleashed controversies that continue to today.

I'll focus on four more trends that I believe have also played a deep and lasting role and are even more directly related to the changes in Washington. The first is the civil rights movement, which led to major advances in the economic and social conditions of African Americans but also to a political backlash among some white Americans, notably in the South. The second is the rise of Hispanic immigration, another source of ethnic division. The third, and perhaps deepest, change is the demographic and economic rise of the Sunbelt, which brought new regions and values to the forefront of American politics. Finally, the suburbanization of America, including the residential sorting of Americans by class, contributed to polarized politics.

Civil Rights and Political Realignment

The civil rights movement marked the moment in which political power shifted from the Snowbelt to the Sunbelt. I had a visceral glimpse into the changing social and political landscape by virtue of growing up in Detroit, Michigan, in the 1960s. My father was a labor lawyer and local civil rights leader, and our house was a meeting place for progressive politics. We knew full well the tensions of the time. Yet nothing prepared my family or the Detroit community for the devastation of the rioting in African American neighborhoods in 1967. Dozens of people died, the city burned, and Detroit began a downward spiral into poverty and abandonment. The riots were followed by massive white flight to the suburbs and an astonishing political backlash. The segregationist governor of Alabama, George Wallace, found a surge of support in working-class neighborhoods in his third-party run for the presidency in 1968 and won the 1972 presidential primary in Michigan.

It is here, I believe, that one must start the narrative of the anti-government and anti-tax revolt that culminated in Reagan's election in 1980. The civil rights movement caused a nearly immediate and decisive political realignment throughout the country. The South, solidly Democratic for a century after the Civil War, suddenly flipped to the Republican Party. The Deep South and the Southwest (which together constitute the Sunbelt) were now politically ascendant in that they could deliver a Republican president (first Richard Nixon in 1968, then Reagan in 1980, George H. W. Bush in 1988, and George W. Bush in 2000), ushering in an era in which white opposition to federal programs had an underlying racial component. Before the civil rights era, federal social spending was mainly for white voters. Federal support for farmers, home owners, and retirees introduced in the 1930s to 1950s overwhelmingly benefitted the majority white community and was precisely designed that way. When Social Security was introduced in the 1930s, it excluded farmworkers and therefore most of the poor African American population in the South.[2]

With the success of the civil rights movement and the rise of antipoverty programs in the 1960s, federal benefits increasingly flowed to minority communities. The political reaction was a sharp turn of many white voters away from government's leadership role.[3] This backlash was amplified by repeated overreaching by liberal leaders. Ending discrimination was broadly acceptable to the white working class, but affirmative action was a step too far for many whites. Desegregation of neighborhood schools was acceptable, but busing children long distances was another step over the line. Nor did it help that the civil rights era was cut in two by race riots and a surge in urban violent crime.

The emergence of white evangelical Christians as a solid Republican voting bloc also has a racial background. Up until the late 1970s, white evangelical voters divided their loyalties between the two parties. It was in the late 1970s, mainly in reaction to intensified federal pressure to desegregate religious schools, that the white evangelicals moved en masse into the Republican fold.[4] The swing of these middle-income white voters to the Republican Party made an enormous difference in the emergence of Republican presidents for twenty of twenty-eight years between 1980 and 2008.

The Hispanic Immigrant Surge

The rapid rise of the Hispanic population in the United States created yet another huge source of political and ethnic division, pushing white voters toward a philosophy of low taxation and retrenchment of the federal government. In 1965, the United States adopted the

Immigration and Nationality Act of 1965. This legislation, which ended quotas on national origin introduced in the Immigration Act of 1924, decisively changed America's demography. Figure 5.1 shows the remarkable dip in the share of foreign-born population in the United States after 1924 and then the sharp rise beginning after 1965. As of 1970, the Hispanic population in the United States was an estimated 10 million, equal to around 5 percent of the U.S. population, and heavily concentrated in California and Texas. By 1990, under the liberalizing provisions of the 1965 act, the Hispanic population had doubled, to 22 million and 8.6 percent of the population, and by 2009 the Hispanic population had doubled again, to 48 million and 15.7 percent of the population, with sizable communities in the Southwest, Florida, New York, New Jersey, and the Northwest.[5] Hispanic votes have become decisive in key national and state elections, including the 2008 presidential election, in which Hispanics voted overwhelmingly for Obama.

The surge in Hispanic immigration exacerbated racial tensions and put immigration policy back at the forefront of national politics, feeding directly and powerfully into the growing anti-tax sentiments of the 1970s and afterward. The national tax revolt movement

Figure 5.1: Foreign-Born Percentage of U.S. Population, 1850–2010

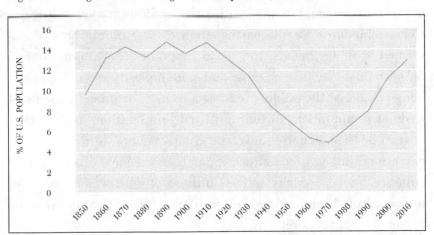

Source: Data from U.S. Census Bureau.

began most vividly in California's referendum on Proposition 13 in 1978. California's tax revolt was strongly influenced by the surge in the state's Hispanic population and the opposition in much of the white community to the added property taxes being levied to provide schooling for an increasingly Hispanic student population.[6]

It is important to understand the special animus attached to illegal immigration. The political backing for programs that assist the poor (for example, with health care, education, income support, food stamps, and other programs) depends entirely on there being a sense of shared community among the members of the society. That sense of community is hard enough to achieve in America's ethnically and religiously divided communities. It is nearly impossible to achieve when the borders are open to illegal inflows. With a vast, impoverished world of literally hundreds of millions if not billions of people who are eager to enter the United States, middle-class and working-class American taxpayers understandably believe that the fiscal demands on their checkbooks will be essentially without bounds if America fails to secure its frontiers. The animus is probably less toward specific groups, e.g., Hispanics, than it is toward the sense of unfairness of working very hard and then being called upon to support perfect strangers who number in the millions and rising.

This sentiment needs to be taken seriously. Social transfer programs must go hand in hand with a clearer immigration policy and clearer standards for the participation of new immigrants (documented or undocumented) in social programs. Washington has so far been unable to take up these questions honestly and directly and has squandered the public's trust as a result. Fortunately, the fiscal costs of immigration, including illegal immigration, are nowhere near as adverse as anti-immigrant groups believe. Millions of illegal immigrants pay federal taxes, partly in the hope of an eventual amnesty. Social Security collects billions of dollars per year from undocumented immigrants, and millions of illegal immigrants file personal income tax returns.[7]

The Sunbelt Overtakes the Snowbelt

The civil rights movement and the surge in immigration not only divided Americans according to race and ethnicity but also helped to change the geography of political power. For a century after the Civil War, American national power was centered in the North, especially in the Northeast and Midwest. Almost all American presidents hailed from the North. Industry, too, was concentrated in the North, as was great wealth. The South lagged for many complex reasons beyond the obvious one of defeat in the Civil War: an agrarian rather than industrial economy, low technological skills, poor public education, and the burdens of tropical diseases such as yellow fever, malaria, and hookworm. All those factors meant that economic power remained concentrated in the North.

Then came the great political change. Between 1900 and 1960, the Snowbelt states provided every U.S. president but one. But between 1964 and Obama's election in 2008, the Sunbelt states provided every one![8] The civil rights movement created a stark dividing line between the Snowbelt and Sunbelt presidential eras. Starting with Nixon, Republican candidates garnered the bulk of the South's electoral votes. Until Obama, only two Democratic candidates (Carter and Clinton), both from the Sunbelt, were able to shake loose even a few electoral votes in the now strongly Republican region. Northern Democrats tended to face a wall of southern white middle-class opposition, making them nearly unelectable. (Lower-income white voters tended to remain in the Democratic Party column.)

The rise of the Sunbelt to presidential power in the 1960s and afterward was far more than merely a civil rights backlash, however. It also reflected the gradual rise in economic power of the South after World War II, especially as electrification, air-conditioning, public investments in infrastructure (such as western dams and large-scale water projects), and greatly improved health care and education all made possible the migration of industries such as textiles and apparel from the high-cost, highly unionized Northeast to the low-cost, nonunionized Sunbelt. The shift of industries from the Snowbelt to the Sunbelt was, in many ways, a dry run of the later transfer of industry from the high-wage United States to the low-wage Asia. As the Sunbelt economy boomed and the U.S. population (including both native-born Americans and Hispanic immigrants) increasingly settled in the Sunbelt, political power necessarily gravitated to the South. Figure 5.2 shows the remarkable rise of the Sunbelt relative to the Snowbelt along three crucial dimensions: the share of population, the share of national income, and the share of total congressional seats (which also tracks the share of electoral votes for presidential elections).

On all three dimensions, the Sunbelt was far smaller than the Snowbelt in the 1940s to 1960s but rapidly caught up and overtook the Snowbelt by 2000. Political power has followed suit with the rising share of population and income.

Here is a funny thing about the rise of the Sunbelt anti-government political power: it created Sunbelt power without necessitating a nationwide swing in values. The shift in the Sunbelt's demographic and economic weight was enough to give rise to a new national political orientation. Let me explain through a simple numerical illus-

Figure 5.2: The Rise of the Sunbelt, 1940–2010

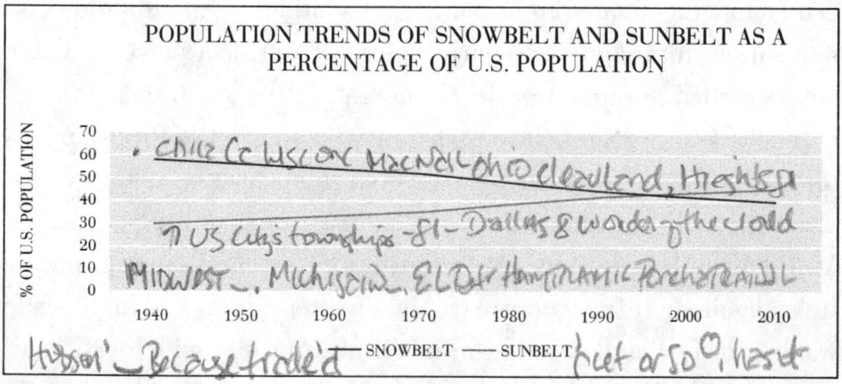

Source: Data from U.S. Census Bureau.

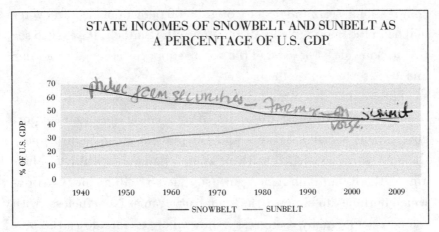

STATE INCOMES OF SNOWBELT AND SUNBELT AS
A PERCENTAGE OF U.S. GDP

Source: Data from U.S. Census Bureau.

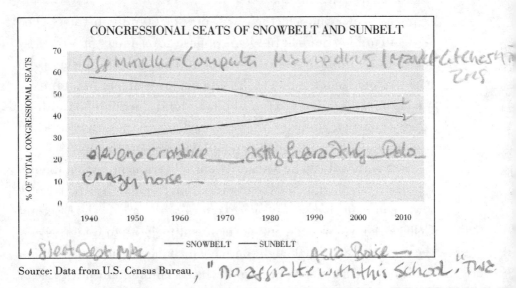

CONGRESSIONAL SEATS OF SNOWBELT AND SUNBELT

Source: Data from U.S. Census Bureau.

tration how powerful a role demographic shifts can play in national politics.

Suppose that Snowbelt voters support federal government social programs by a 70–30 margin, while Sunbelt voters oppose those programs by a 70–30 margin. To keep things simple, also suppose that there are 100 million voters in all, initially divided as 60 million in the Snowbelt and 40 million in the Sunbelt. Sixty percent of congressional seats and hence (roughly) 60 percent of electoral votes will be in the Snowbelt and 40 percent in the Sunbelt. It's easy to see that nationwide 54 percent of the voters support the social programs and 46 percent oppose them.

Suppose now that a random mix of 20 million northerners move to the Sunbelt. Of those migrants, 70 percent (14 million) support government social programs and 30 percent (6 million) oppose them. Assume as well that there is no change of political values among the 100 million Americans, so that a 54–46 majority nationwide continues to support the social programs. Nonetheless, with the new demography, Congress is now likely to vote down the programs. Here's why.

In the "new" Sunbelt, there will now be 60 million voters. The "old" 40 million Sunbelt residents oppose government programs by a vote of 28 million versus 12 million. The "new" residents (who have arrived from the Snowbelt) support government programs by a margin of 14 million to 6 million. In total, therefore, 34 million voters of the new Sunbelt (57 percent) will oppose government social programs and 26 million (43 percent) will support them.

The South will still be a majority anti-government region, though less decisively than before the in-migration from the North. Yet now it will command *a majority of seats in Congress* and in the Electoral College and will elect an anti-government majority to Congress and the presidency. Even though there is no change in national opinion (which is still a majority in favor of the social programs), the rise of the Sunbelt population by itself is enough to shift Washington from a pro-government majority to an anti-government majority. Demography is not quite destiny, but it plays a major role.[9]

Sunbelt Values

With the rise of the Sunbelt came new and deep cultural cleavages in American politics. Well before the 1960s, state and local politics in the South had long resisted a large role of government in the local economy. After all, this was the home of "states' rights" and the losing side of the Civil War. Moreover, the anti-Washington sentiment was a reflection of the long-standing traditional resistance of southern white voters to funding public goods in a population with a significant African American minority. With the rise of the Sunbelt, that anti-government fervor gained weight, indeed an effective majority, in national politics. Anti-Washington sentiments came easy to a region that had long harbored deep historic resentments against the federal government, sentiments newly stirred by the civil rights movement, immigration, and the cultural upheavals of the 1960s.

The South is also the bastion of fundamentalist Christianity: 37 percent of southerners count themselves as evangelical Protestants, and 65 percent are Protestants, including mainline and evangelical denominations.[10] This compares with just 13 percent of northeasterners who count themselves as evangelical Protestants and 37 percent as Protestants of any denomination. With Sunbelt presidents backed by powerful evangelical constituencies, the evangelical cultural agenda right to life, prayer in the schools and other public facilities, anti–birth control, anti–gay marriage, antievolution school curricula, and so forth—came to national prominence and supercharged the country's cultural cleavages.

The culture wars opened on many fronts. In addition to the civil rights movement, urban riots, and rising crime rates, the 1960s had ushered in the counterculture of drugs, sexual liberation, the surge of women's rights, and the beginning of gay rights. The cumulative effect of these cultural upheavals, packed into just a few years and capped by increasingly intrusive social regulation such as cross-city busing, affirmative action, and Supreme Court–led legalization of abortion in 1973, led to a sense among religious conservatives that liberals aimed not just to fight poverty and discrimination but also to dictate a new social order. The culture pot was set boiling. Sunbelt conservatives rose up against an activist federal government that they believed threatened traditional Christian values.

Suburban Flight

The civil rights era and racial unrest in the cities in the 1960s also accelerated another massive geographical trend: the flight to the suburbs by affluent white households. Suburbanization was already under way in the 1950s, before racial politics came to the forefront. The rise of the automobile, combined with the postwar baby boom and the return to normalcy in the 1950s, spurred the surge in suburbanization. Then came a dramatic white flight to the suburbs in the 1960s and afterward, reflecting both social and economic forces. The social forces consisted mainly of the desire of many whites to live in homogeneous white neighborhoods. The economic forces consisted mainly of the search by affluent (and mainly white) households for quality schooling for their children.[11]

More affluent households increasingly sorted themselves into higher-priced affluent suburbs that supported better public schools based on higher tax collections. The influx of affluent households into favored suburbs raised property prices and priced out working-class households, which had to choose among less desirable urban and suburban locations. The poor were generally left to the low-rent and least desirable locations in the inner cities. Thus, Americans sorted themselves by class and race to produce today's residentially divided America.

The economic ramifications of the suburban-urban divide were stark, in that school financing diverged between poor inner cities and affluent suburbs. Residential sorting became a crucial way in which educational and income inequalities were propagated from one generation to the next. In order to avoid a prolonged poverty trap, federal and state financial support for very poor school districts became more important than ever.

The political ramifications were equally stark: the affluent suburbs turned more Republican, and the poorer urban areas turned more Democratic. Congressional districts thereby became "safer" for Republicans or Democrats, with fewer swing districts as a result.

In the safe districts, dominated by one of the political parties, the real political competition comes not in the November elections but during the primaries, tending to pull the Republicans in safe districts more toward the right and the safe Democrats more toward the left. We should remember, though, that big corporate money has pulled both parties to the right. The overall effect is a very conservative Republican Party and a Democratic Party that is generally centrist (or even right of center in districts where campaign financing looms especially large).

Still a Consensus Beneath the Surface

One possible reading of this chapter is that the search for a new economic consensus in America is a fool's errand. After all, the country is deeply riven by cultural, geographical, racial, and class differences, all of which have become deeper in recent decades. The Tea Party seems to represent the latest ratcheting up of the ongoing battles between liberals and conservatives, northerners and southerners, whites and minorities. How, in these circumstances, can there possibly be a new set of shared values? I think this view of a nation in a fundamental and irreconcilable divide is wrong. There is much more consensus than meets the eye.

The real issue about consensus is not whether Americans can agree on everything important to their lives—clearly the answer to that is no—but whether Americans can agree on a set of national economic policies to promote overall efficiency, fairness, and sustainability. Here, then, are some things on which Americans broadly agree.

They agree that there should be equality of opportunity for American citizens. They agree that individuals should make the maximum effort to help themselves. They agree that government should help those in real need, as long as they are also trying to help themselves. And they broadly agree that the rich should pay more in taxes. These core values can form the basis of a broad and effective consensus on the basic direction of economic policy.

In 2007, the political scientists Benjamin Page and Lawrence Jacobs found that 72 percent of Americans agreed that "differences in income are too large," and 68 percent rejected the notion that the distribution of income and wealth is fair.[12] Large majorities agreed that government "must see that no one is without food, clothing, or shelter" (68 percent); agreed that "government should spend whatever is necessary to ensure that all children have really good public schools they can go to" (87 percent); "favor own tax dollars being used to help pay for . . . early childhood education in kindergarten and nursery school" (81 percent); "favor own tax dollars being used to help pay for retraining programs for people whose jobs have been eliminated" (80 percent); and agreed that "it is the responsibility of the federal government to make sure that all Americans have health care coverage" (73 percent).[13]

In the Page and Jacobs data, no less than 95 percent agreed with the general principle that "one should always find ways to help others less fortunate than oneself." The proportion agreeing with the proposition that government "should redistribute wealth by heavy taxes on the rich" climbed from 35 percent in 1939 to 45 percent in 1998 to 56 percent in 2007. It is plausible that the realities of America's massive increase in income inequality have contributed to the rising sentiment for redistributive taxation.

Such egalitarian views have recently been confirmed in surveys by the Pew Research Center.[14] Eighty-seven percent agreed that "our society should do what is necessary to make sure that everyone has an equal opportunity to succeed." Sixty-three percent concurred that "it is the responsibility of government to take care of people who can't take care of themselves." Yet, as always, primary responsibility in America is pushed back to the individual. Only 32 percent agreed that "success in life is pretty much determined by forces outside of our control," and only 33 percent subscribed to the view that "hard work offers little guarantee of success." In the American ethos, the government should help when necessary, but the individual can and should remain the principal author of his or her own fate.

The flip side of the view supporting public responsibility toward the poor is an equally strong consensus that big business has been allowed to run away with the prize. Though the public overwhelmingly recognizes the importance of private business to the economy, it also overwhelmingly concurs that "there is too much power concentrated in the hands of a few big businesses" (77 to 21 percent in April 2009) and that "business corporations make too much profit" (62 to 33 percent in April 2009).[15] There is also a consistent public majority in favor of raising tax rates on the rich.

Surveys have also shown a continuing high importance accorded to the natural environment. Americans are environmentally conscious, even if their federal government is not. In the Pew survey, 83 percent of Americans agreed that "there needs to be stricter environmental laws and regulations to protect the environment."[16] In June 2010, a *USA Today*/Gallup poll found that by a margin of 56 to 40 percent, Americans favor legislation to "regulate energy output from private companies in an attempt to reduce global warming." An ABC News/*Washington Post* poll similarly found that by a margin of 71 to 26 percent, Americans agree that the federal government should "regulate the release of greenhouse gases from sources like power plants, cars and factories in an attempt to reduce global warming."[17] In a January 2011 Rasmussen survey, respondents said that renewable energy is a better long-term investment than fossil fuels by a margin of 66 to 23 percent.[18] Environmental protection and economic growth are generally accorded a roughly equal priority, though the young prioritize the environment and older Americans prioritize economic growth. If anything, the environment tends to edge out growth as the overall top priority.

There would also be many fewer disagreements if the electorate was helped to be better informed. Many studies and surveys have found that the public often has very little knowledge of the specifics of income distribution in America, and how public policies can actually affect it. Americans greatly overestimate federal spending on "giveaway" programs such as foreign aid or "welfare" for poor families (now known as Temporary Assistance for Needy Families). They often see these programs as a dominant part of the budget, when in fact they constitute a very small fraction of spending.

One of the greatest and most interesting confusions involves the real burdens and benefits of federal taxes and transfers. The red states of the Sunbelt tend to be the great opponents of federal taxation and spending, no doubt partly the legacy of southern resentment of federal rule. The residents of these states generally don't realize, however, that they are the leading net beneficiaries of today's federal taxes and transfers. The millionaires and billionaires live in the blue states—California, New York, Connecticut, New Jersey—and their income taxes support the Medicaid, disability, and highway programs of red state residents.

As we can see in Table 5.1, precisely those states in the lead of attacking federal programs are the ones that would cut off their own livelihoods and well-being if the federal government were to shut down. The table ranks states according to the federal spending each state receives per dollar of federal taxes that the state's residents pay to Washington. A ratio greater than 1 signifies that the state's residents are net recipients of federal spending paid by taxes of other states, while a ratio less than 1 signifies that on net the state's tax payments are going to the benefit of the residents of other states. Of the ten largest net-recipient states, Obama carried only two, New Mexico and Virginia, in the 2008 election. Of the ten largest net-paying states, Obama carried all. The paradox is that the states that currently lead the anti-tax revolt are actually the largest net recipients of federal spending. This is a fact that their citizens do not understand.

Table 5.1: Federal Spending per Dollar of Tax Payments, by State

	Federal Spending per Dollar of Tax Payments	State Rank	Obama's Share of the Vote
Top Ten Recipient States			
New Mexico	$2.03	1	57%
Mississippi	$2.02	2	43%
Alaska	$1.84	3	38%
Louisiana	$1.78	4	40%
West Virginia	$1.76	5	43%
North Dakota	$1.68	6	45%
Alabama	$1.66	7	39%
South Dakota	$1.53	8	45%
Kentucky	$1.51	9	41%
Virginia	$1.51	10	53%
Top Ten Net-Paying States			
Colorado	$0.81	41	54%
New York	$0.79	42	63%
California	$0.78	43	61%
Delaware	$0.77	44	62%
Illinois	$0.75	45	62%
Minnesota	$0.72	46	54%
New Hampshire	$0.71	47	54%
Connecticut	$0.69	48	61%
Nevada	$0.65	49	55%
New Jersey	$0.61	50	57%

Source: Data from the Tax Foundation (2005) and CNN Election Center (2008).

Toward a New Consensus

At first appearance, America is hopelessly divided. Yet, on a closer view, what unites Americans is still greater than what divides us.

Our politics feel divisive not because of a raging battle in middle America but because there is a vast gap between (1) what Americans believe; (2) what the mass media tell us Americans believe; and (3) what politicians actually decide, no matter what Americans believe. Even with their differences according to region, class, race, and ethnicity, Americans are generally moderate and mostly generous in spirit, though the media tend to emphasize and even promote the extremes. And the politicians vote along with the rich and the special interests. We thereby end up with a very biased view of our own country. America can be much better than it is today if public policies begin to follow American values, not the values that corporate-driven media pretend to be American values.

For that to happen, though, the public will have to exercise a new and higher level of political responsibility. Special interests dominate our politics not only because they have more money but also because much of the general public has disengaged itself from public deliberations. Yes, the politicians and corporate interests typically strive to keep the public in the dark, but much of the public allows this to happen by not working hard enough to stay informed.

CHAPTER 6.

The New Globalization

Globalization has been the unmet economic challenge of the past forty years. Reagan was not only wrong about blaming big government for America's ills; he was even more mistaken in neglecting the true gathering storm of the 1970s and 1980s. Starting around 1970, the United States and the world began to be buffeted by three global changes: the technological revolution of computers, the Internet, and mobile telephony ushered in by the digital electronic age; the history-changing rise of Asia within the world economy; and the newly emerging global ecological crises. These three changes are the cause of massive and ongoing shifts of incomes, jobs, and investments all over the world, including in the United States. The changes are so vast and pervasive that active direction by the federal government is absolutely required to ensure that the burdens and benefits of globalization are shared widely among the American population and that America's global competitiveness is maintained.

Every generation faces novel challenges to combine efficiency, fairness, and sustainability. Two hundred years ago in Western Europe and the United States, the main challenge was to promote and humanize the first industrial revolution; 150 years ago, the main challenge was to create a safe and livable urban environment as large industrial cities began to explode in population; 75 years ago, the main challenge was to surmount the Great Depression. Our main challenge is to harness the new globalization. We must find new ways to live efficiently, fairly, and sustainably in a very crowded and tightly interconnected world.

The New Globalization

The essence of globalization is that all parts of the world are now linked through trade, investment, and production networks (wherein a final product such as a computer, mobile phone, or automobile is the result of production processes in many countries, often a dozen or more). In a way, globalization has been going on for several thousand years. Han China exported silks to the Roman Empire in return for gold and Syrian-made glass two thousand years ago. Christopher Columbus and Vasco da Gama initiated the economic linkage of all parts of the world at the end of the fifteenth century by discovering sea-based routes linking Europe with Asia and the Americas, discoveries that Adam Smith deemed to be "the two greatest and most important events recorded in the history of mankind."[1] Still, even with this long history of global trade, there is something qualitatively different about the globalization of our day, different enough to describe our era as a new globalization.

What is new is that a combination of breakthrough technologies and changes in geopolitics has created a far more intensive set of economic interconnections than ever before. The most important technologies of the new globalization are those of information, communication, and transportation. The new globalization is the globalization of the digital age. With computers to store and process information, the Internet and mobile telephony to transmit it instantly and seamlessly around the world, and containerized ocean transport and worldwide air travel to provide low-cost global trade, the world's economies have become more tightly interlinked than

ever before, with a global division of labor that is vastly more sophisticated and intricate than anything in the past. In the nineteenth century, and indeed up to 1950, industrial production was
based on the shipments of a few raw materials from various parts of
the world to a manufacturing site in Europe, the United States, or
Japan. Today, production at all stages of the value chain, from raw
materials to final packaging, occurs in a complex network of sites,
often linking dozens of production facilities in far-flung regions of
the world.

The lead protagonist of the new globalization is the multinational
company (MNC), with operations straddling more than one country
and sometimes a hundred or more. Among America's MNC giants
(ranked by foreign assets in 2008) are General Electric, Exxon-
Mobil, Chevron Corporation, Ford Motor Company, ConocoPhillips,
Procter & Gamble, Wal-Mart Stores, IBM, and Pfizer Inc.[2] These
companies often have half or more of their global workforce outside the United States. In 2010, for example, GE employed 133,000
workers in the United States and 154,000 overseas in more than
sixty countries, with more than half of its $155 billion in revenue
($83 billion) earned outside the United States.[3] Another key indi-
cator of the rising role of globalization in the U.S. economy is the
share of corporate profits received from outside the United States, as
shown in Figure 6.1. While the data are fraught with measurement
difficulties, there is no doubt that corporate profits are increasingly
internationalized. The national income accounts suggest that more
than 25 percent of corporate profits have come from abroad in recent years, up from around 5 percent in the 1960s.[4]

In addition to the pivotal advances in information, communications, and transport technologies, changes in geopolitics have
played a key role in the emergence of globalization. The first great
event was the independence of Europe's former colonies after World
War II. Independence provided the political foundations for subse-
quent economic development. Then, starting in the 1960s, several
developing economies in Asia, most notably Hong Kong, Taiwan,

Figure 6.1: Foreign Profits as a Percentage of Total Corporate Profits, 1948–2010

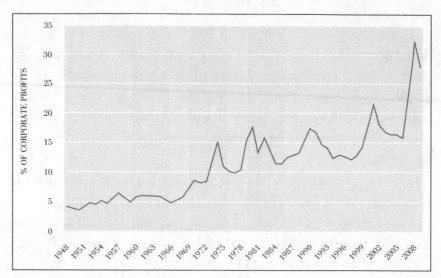

Source: Data from U.S. Bureau of Economic Analysis.

and South Korea, began to join the global market-based trading system, especially by welcoming foreign investments from the United States, Europe, and Japan and hosting export-oriented production facilities in specially designated export-processing zones. Then, in 1978, the biggest change of all occurred: the People's Republic of China, with around 1 billion people at the time (and 1.3 billion today), opened its economy to global trade, finance, and foreign investment. In 1991, India followed suit. By now virtually all of the world is linked through trade, finance, and production.

The main economic implication of globalization is that a tremendous and rapidly expanding range of sophisticated economic activities that once were carried out only in the United States, Europe, and Japan can now be carried out even more profitably in China, India, Brazil, and elsewhere. Goods and services that were once produced in the United States and Europe are now produced in developing countries around the world and then exported to the high-income economies as intermediate or final products. As the production of a widening range of goods and services is relocated to the emerging economies, U.S. employment and incomes are subjected to tremendous upheaval.

In 1985, merchandise trade between China and the United States was balanced at $3.9 billion in each direction, a level equal to 0.09 percent of U.S. GDP that year. By 2009, China's exports to the United States had soared to $296.4 billion, equal to 2.1 percent of U.S. GDP and roughly 19 percent of the value added (output minus inputs) of U.S. manufacturing. U.S. exports had also increased substantially, to $69.5 billion. China's merchandise exports to the United States are overwhelmingly manufactured goods (around 98 percent) and span a remarkable breadth of sectors.[5] More than half, however, are concentrated in a few key sectors: computers, telecommunications equipment, television sets, other electronics, textiles, apparel, footwear, furniture, and toys. The United States lost around 2 million jobs in those sectors between 1998 and 2009.[6]

The new globalization is fundamentally changing the world economy and global politics. In 2010, China overtook Japan as the second largest economy in the world, when converting both countries' national incomes into a common currency using market exchange rates. (If we compare national incomes according to purchasing power rather than market exchange rates, China overtook Japan as early as 2001.) Most likely, China will overtake the United States within the next two decades and perhaps by 2020 using purchasing-power-adjusted measurements. This is, of course, changing not only trade and investment patterns but geopolitical patterns as well. China is looming ever larger in global diplomacy, as more and more countries in the world see China as their major trade and financial partner. It's fair to say that more than two hundred years of North Atlantic dominance of global politics is coming to an end as power shifts from the Atlantic to the Pacific and Indian oceans. China is also looming ever larger as a voracious importer of the world's natural resources, such as oil, coal, copper, and soybeans, and has also recently overtaken the United States as the largest emitter of climate-changing greenhouse gases.

The Tendency to Underestimate the New Globalization

Despite this economic drama, the greatest of our time, America's politicians and even academics have consistently underestimated the effects of globalization, looking inward for explanations of events when the major drivers are global. America is so used to being the center of attention, the "number one country," that it hasn't been able to fathom the magnitude of global changes taking place around it.

The underestimation goes back to the 1970s, when the United States first started to slip from its post–World War II preeminence. The 1970s were a repeated international comeuppance to the United States. First, the U.S.-centered international monetary system collapsed in 1971 as the nation abandoned its pledge to convert foreign-owned dollars into gold at the fixed price of $35 per ounce. Two years later, oil prices began to soar, both because of the newly organized power of Middle East producers and because global economic growth began to hit up against the depletion of traditional petroleum supplies. Then, in 1975, the United States lost the war in Vietnam, putting into perspective the limits of U.S. conventional military power. Fourth, in the second half of the 1970s, Japan began to penetrate U.S. consumer markets in automobiles and electronic appliances, showing dramatically that America's vaunted technological leadership could be rapidly overcome through technology transfers to Asian industries combined with Asian-based innovations.

These international realities should have become the focus of U.S. politics by the end of the 1970s. They did not. The U.S. debate turned almost entirely on domestic issues. Rather than focusing on the various new international dimensions of the U.S. economic crisis of the 1970s—monetary policy, resource scarcity, foreign competition—the Reagan "diagnosis" put all of the focus on cutting the size of the federal government, as if this were in the least responsive to the challenges of rising competition from abroad.

How Alan Greenspan Misjudged Globalization

As Federal Reserve chairman from 1987 to 2006, Alan Greenspan presided at the Fed during the rise of the new globalization. Yet, like Reagan, he basically misunderstood or neglected this crucial phenomenon on repeated occasions. By treating the United States as a closed economy, he continually overlooked the severe risks of his own policies and thereby helped stoke several financial crises, including the megameltdown of 2008.

Greenspan was fixated on a key point: that as much as he pushed down interest rates to spur consumer spending and housing purchases, U.S. inflation remained low. He considered this a miracle of U.S. productivity, that the economy had a new growth potential because of a surge of innovation in the "new economy" of information technology. His staff repeatedly demurred, saying that such a surge of productivity could not be found in the data. Greenspan persisted, however, insisting that low inflation could be explained only by the elusive productivity miracle.

He missed the real point, and with serious adverse consequences: inflation was being held down not by a productivity miracle but by the surge of consumer goods that were arriving from China. As U.S. consumers increased their demand for consumer goods, China scaled up its supply, setting up factories almost overnight to take advantage of the voracious U.S. appetite. The more Greenspan put his foot on the monetary accelerator, the more he stoked a runaway consumption and housing binge. His policies were therefore a core part of America's excess spending, which led up to the financial crash of 2008.

Had Greenspan been correct that America was enjoying a productivity boom, the country would have been experiencing a surge of growth of GDP, wages, and employment. National output would have been running ahead of consumption spending. Savings rates would have been rising. Of course, the opposite was occurring: America's GDP growth was sluggish; wages were stagnant; and employment was flagging. Although manufacturing employment was relatively stable from 1990 to 1998 at around 17.2 million workers, between 1998 and 2004 the floor fell through the labor market, with a loss of 3.2 million manufacturing jobs.[7] All of these adverse outcomes suggest that it was imports from abroad, rather than a productivity surge, that was the main reason for low inflation. The Federal Reserve's easy monetary policy succeeded in creating manufacturing jobs, but in China, not in the United States.

The Fed's policies did create around 1 million U.S. jobs in construction between 2002 and 2006, but they proved to be evanescent.[8] With the Fed's foot to the monetary pedal, U.S. interest rates hit rock-bottom levels, causing the demand for mortgages to soar. Wall Street began to securitize mortgages and sell them off to other financial pools such as pension funds, foreign banks, and insurance companies. As everybody now knows, the lucrative fees earned by everybody involved in packaging securities led to the collapse of lending standards—and ethical standards—in the mortgage sector.

There are two lessons here. The first is that monetary policy cannot solve America's employment problem. Greenspan tried again and again, through cheap credits, and Ben Bernanke is doing the same. This is a hopeless, self-defeating strategy. Temporary jobs in construction can be created through a Fed-led housing bubble, but when the bubble bursts we are left with the reality that America's manufacturing employment has fallen further under the weight of foreign competition and America's lack of global competitiveness. The second lesson is that ignorance or neglect of globalization repeatedly comes back to haunt us. Unless we focus on the reality that the United States is now tightly integrated into the global economy and connected with more than 6 billion other people in a worldwide production network, we'll keep failing to restore prosperity in a meaningful and sustainable manner.

Long-Term Effects of the New Globalization

The new globalization played a role in the recent boom-bust cycle in America, but its effects go even deeper. The integration of China, India, and other emerging economies into the global economy is causing a fundamental shift in income distribution, employment, investment, and trade. Even our domestic politics are being massively affected. I will focus on three overarching effects of the new globalization, each of which is globally transformative. These may be called the convergence effect, the labor effect, and the mobility effect.

The *convergence effect* refers to the fact that the new globalization provides the conduit for today's emerging economies to leapfrog technologies, and thereby to rapidly narrow the income gap with the rich countries, and notably with the United States. When production systems are globalized, the developing countries learn rapidly about cutting-edge technologies coming from Europe, Japan, and the United States. China has made massive efforts not only to upgrade its production systems based on the advanced technologies imported from abroad, but also to master the imported technologies through learning by doing. One key government strategy has been to insist that foreign investors desiring to enter the Chinese market do so in a joint-venture partnership with a Chinese counterpart. The Chinese partner quickly masters the imported technologies and then branches out on its own. This process of deliberate and targeted technology transfer (or absorption, as it might be better described) helps account for China's remarkable record of economic growth and technological upgrading. China's growth has averaged around 10 percent per annum since 1980, enough to raise GDP twentyfold between 1980 and 2009.

The *labor effect* refers to the fact that China's opening to global trade in 1978 was tantamount to bringing hundreds of millions of low-skilled workers into a globally integrated labor pool. The world's total supply of relatively low-skilled workers thereby soared, pushing down the wages of low-skilled workers around the world. Of course, that didn't happen all at once. At the start of China's opening to global trade, most of China's potential manufacturing workers were still peasants on farms in the rural areas of the country. They lacked the education, skills, complementary technologies, business capital, and physical proximity to ports to be much of a threat to apparel workers in North Carolina. Yet, over time, their skills were raised by a determined educational push led by the Chinese government and by the efforts of the ambitious and hardworking Chinese themselves.

The technologies and capital to employ these new industrial workers were mostly imported from abroad, as foreign investors set up operations in China's coastal cities that were designated "special economic zones." The physical proximity to the new work was created as around 150 million Chinese workers left the countryside and migrated to the cities, where they could find better employment in the new manufacturing enterprises.[9] Thus education, skills, technology, capital, and physical proximity came together in places such as Shenzhen, China, the coastal city that lies just north of Hong Kong, which grew from a small fishing village of some 20,000 residents in 1975 to around 9 million residents in 2010.[10]

The *mobility effect* refers to a basic asymmetry of globalization: the difference between internationally mobile capital and immobile labor. When capital becomes internationally mobile, countries begin to compete for it. They do this by offering improved profitability compared with other countries, for example, by cutting corporate tax rates, easing regulations, tolerating pollution, or ignoring labor standards. In the ensuing competition among governments, capital benefits from a "race to the bottom," in which governments engage in a downward spiral of taxation and regulation in order to try to keep one step ahead of other countries. All countries lose in the end, since all end up losing the tax revenues and regulations needed to manage the economy. The biggest loser ends up being internationally immobile labor, which is likely to face higher taxation to compensate for the loss of taxation on capital.

Income Inequality and the New Globalization

In principle, the new globalization can ultimately be beneficial for the entire world. The rising productivity of China, India, and other emerging markets, and the falling transportation and communications costs worldwide, can raise incomes around the world.[11] Clearly, the emerging economies can win in a big way, as they are able to boost productivity through technology inflows, attract internationally mobile capital, and raise real wages as workers are hired in new export industries. This success has been borne out in practice. Globalization has permitted China, India, and some other emerging economies to achieve the fastest economic growth rates in history.

The high-income countries, including the United States, Europe, and Japan, can also be winners. The newly emerging economies produce a wide variety of low-cost goods and services that we desire, and in turn we can export a wide variety of goods and services to the emerging economies. Sectors that have strong economies of scale will benefit from the expanded reach of the global market. This includes high-tech companies engaged in cutting-edge innovation (such as pharmaceutical companies and information technology companies) that make profits by creating and marketing information-based products and services. Google, Microsoft, Apple, Amazon.com, and others fit this mold. Trade can therefore allow for more specialization, increased innovation, and an expanded overall array of goods available to consumers in high-income countries.

Yet the gains are likely to be distributed unevenly within the high-income economies. High-skilled (and therefore high-income) workers are likely to benefit straightaway, while low-skilled (and therefore low-income) workers are likely to feel the pressure of tougher competition from abroad. For all broad segments of society to benefit from globalization, therefore, the winners have to help compensate the losers. High-income earners who enjoy a surge in income and wealth resulting from globalization should pay more in taxes to finance increased income transfers and public investments (for example, for job retraining) for those who are the losers.

It is even possible that the whole world will end up losing from globalization if the surging income in the emerging economies leads to global environmental calamity—if China's growth, for example, results in such a large increase in carbon dioxide emissions from coal use that global climate change accelerates catastrophically. Achieving the benefits of globalization therefore requires active international cooperation as well as internal cooperation.

Notice that internationally mobile capital (for example, a U.S. hedge fund that invests in China or a U.S. apparel company that may relocate abroad) gains in three ways from the rise of China. First, with the sudden, sharp boost of productivity in China arising from the inflow of technology (the convergence effect), major new investment opportunities in China that offer high rates of return are created. Second, with the surge in the global labor supply (the labor effect), wage levels around the world are bid down, leaving more corporate revenues as profits. Third, with governments around the world cutting corporate taxes and easing regulations to compete for internationally mobile capital, companies are enjoying a sharp fall in taxation.

All three effects favor U.S. corporate investors, but all three jeopardize U.S. workers. As U.S. business investments have shifted to the emerging economies, U.S. wage and employment growth has slowed. Similarly, the massive expansion of the global labor pool due to the inclusion of workers from China and India has put downward pressure on U.S. wages. And the race to the bottom in corporate taxation and regulation has led the U.S. government to cut corporate tax payments while cutting government programs that benefit workers (e.g., job training).

The winners include not only the owners of physical capital (who can shift operations abroad) and financial capital (who can invest funds abroad) but also owners of human capital, who can export skill-intensive services to the emerging economies. This includes Wall Street bankers, corporate lawyers, high-tech engineers, designers, architects, senior managers, and others with advanced degrees and who work in high-tech fields. Finally, athletes, performing artists, and brand-name products are all given a boost by an expanded global market. Many U.S. and European brands are now enjoying booms by expanding into the emerging economies, where hundreds of millions of consumers with rapidly rising incomes are eager to follow in the path of their Western counterparts.

Among American workers, the biggest losers by far are those with a low level of education. This is because most of the new entrants to the global labor market in China and India also have a high school diploma or less. These emerging-economy workers enter labor-intensive export sectors such as apparel cutting and stitching, shoemaking, furniture making, electronic appliance assembly, and standardized manufacturing processes such as plastic injection. As the prices of these globally traded labor-intensive products are pushed down, the wages of low-skilled workers in the United States are also pushed down. U.S. firms in those sectors also shift their operations to China, leaving their own workers unemployed or having to accept sharp cuts in wages to remain employed.

One of the key realities of the new globalization is the ever-expanding range of competition between U.S. and emerging-economy workers. Half a century ago, American workers did not have to fear much competition from abroad, least of all from low-wage countries. Transport and logistics costs were simply too high for American firms to source in Asian low-income countries. Moreover, most of those countries were closed to investment from the United States. Yet as transport, communications, and logistics costs began to fall, and as those economies opened to trade and investment, some low-tech industries could relocate factories abroad. As costs fell further, it became possible for even high-tech industries, such as computer and other advanced machinery manufacturing, to relocate just parts of the value chain—for example, final assembly operations—abroad. As costs fell still further, due mainly to the Internet, it became possible to shift back-office jobs, such as accounting and human resources operations, from the United States to India (favored over China because of its English-speaking workers), all enabled by the Internet. Now American workers compete directly with their counterparts in the emerging economies without companies' needing to shift physical capital, only to have online connectivity.

A key result of the new globalization has therefore been a huge change in income distribution in the United States. Capital owners have been the big winners, enjoying a rise in pretax returns and a cut in the tax rates levied on them. Workers with low educational attainments have tended to lose, as they are directly in the line of competition from the emerging economies. And the federal government has exacerbated these trends. First market forces raised the incomes of the rich, and then the government, caught up in a race to the bottom with counterparts, cut both personal and corporate income taxes, thereby giving an added boost to the rich, while turning around to slash public spending for the poor.

Throughout the high-income economies, governments have cut the effective average tax rate (EATR) on corporate income, and the spread in effective tax rates across countries narrowed as well. Both the decline of EATRs and the narrowing of the spread of EATRs are shown in Figure 6.2 for nineteen high-income countries, including the United States. The careful statistical study from which this figure is taken demonstrates that "increased capital mobility (FDI) has a negative impact on the corporate tax rate."[12]

The effective U.S. corporate tax rate shows the same decline as in

Figure 6.2: Effective Average Tax Rate in High-Income Countries, 1979–2005

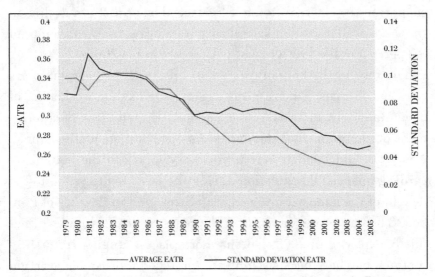

Source: Data from Alexander Klemm, "Corporate Tax Rate Data," Institute for Fiscal
Studies, August 2005.

other high-income countries. America's EATR declined from 30 to
40 percent during the 1960s to less than 30 percent from the mid-
1970s onward, and is currently under 20 percent (Figure 6.3). One
part of that decline reflects the greater ability of U.S. companies to

Figure 6.3: U.S. Corporate Taxes, 1950–2010

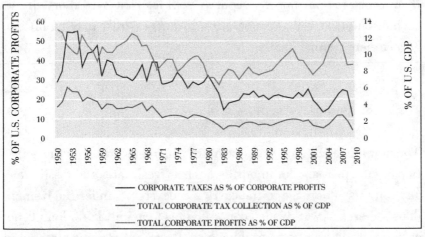

Source: Data from U.S. Bureau of Economic Analysis.

hide their profits in offshore tax havens, with the implicit or explicit support of the Internal Revenue Service. The upshot is a decline in the share of GDP paid in federal corporate taxes, from an average of 3.8 percent in the 1960s to just 1.8 percent in the 2000s.[13]

The race to the bottom exists not only in falling corporate tax rates but in many other aspects as well, such as the weakening of labor standards, financial sector deregulation, and lack of enforcement of environmental standards. As one consequential example, New York and London were in a dramatic race to the bottom regarding financial deregulation during the past twenty years, to the delight of the financial firms on Wall Street and in the City of London. The end result was to feed the massive financial bubble that finally exploded in 2008. Dozens more places, ranging from Dublin to Dubai, have been slashing corporate tax rates and converting themselves into destinations for tax evasion.

There is one overarching solution to the race to the bottom: international cooperation. All countries are suffering from the decline in corporate tax rates and the downward pressures on financial, environmental, and other regulatory standards. By banding together to set minimum international norms, such as a common approach to eliminating tax havens and a common standard of financial and environmental regulation, all countries can gain. Of course, with their overweening power, corporate lobbies routinely short-circuit such attempts at global cooperation by successfully playing off one government against another.

The Depletion of Natural Resources

The new globalization poses one more enormous problem: the depletion of vital primary commodities such as freshwater and fossil fuels, and long-term damage to the earth's ecosystems under the tremendous stresses of worldwide economic development. For a long time, economists ignored the problems of finite natural resources and fragile ecosystems. This is no longer possible. The world economy is pressing hard against various environmental limits, and there is still much more economic growth—and therefore environmental destruction and depletion—in the development pipeline. The explosive growth of production in China, India, and other emerging economies is already pushing world prices of food and feed grains, coal, oil, and countless other primary commodities sky-high, indicating an era of much greater scarcity and resource depletion. The surge in primary commodity prices in recent years, including fuels (oil, gas, and coal), minerals (copper, aluminum, iron ore, and others), and cereal grains (wheat, maize, rice, and others), is shown in Figure 6.4. The commodity price indexes are divided by the U.S. GDP price deflator to obtain inflation-adjusted indexes for each commodity group. It was only the steep economic downturn in 2009 that brought commodity prices down from their 2008 peaks.

The scarcity problems may be even more serious in areas where market prices are not available to warn us of impending environmental crises. This is the case of climate change, deforestation, loss of biodiversity, land erosion, and many kinds of large-scale pollu-

Figure 6.4: Primary Commodity Prices (Inflation-Adjusted), 1992–2010

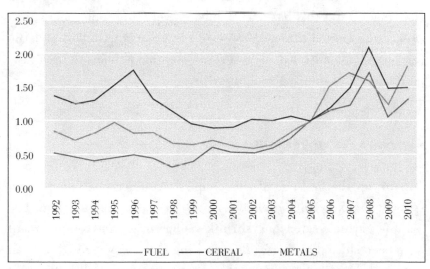

Source: Data from International Monetary Fund World Economic Outlook, 2011.

tion. In all those cases, unprecedented environmental destruction is under way and getting worse, but without market signals in place to guide us back to sustainable technologies and business practices.

The issue of environmental sustainability is a huge one that could take us too far afield here. I earlier tried to provide an overview of the interconnected and complex challenges in my book *Common Wealth*. In the current context, though, I would like to emphasize that America's sustained prosperity will require solutions to the rapidly encroaching resource pressures.

There are two main obstacles to a sustainable trajectory. First, the scientific and technological know-how to deploy more sustainable technologies (such as massive supplies of low-carbon energy from solar power) still needs large-scale research and development. Second, we need to overcome the power of corporate lobbies in order to impose regulations and market incentives that will steer markets toward sustainable solutions. So far, the corporate lobbies of the polluting industries have blocked such measures.

Free-market economists, once again including Hayek and Friedman, have recognized the need for public action to protect the natural environment. And Americans have consistently agreed, expressing strong environmental sentiments on a wide range of environmental challenges.[14] Yet this basic truth has not yet found political expression in the United States because of the power of Big Oil and Big Coal. In chapter 10, I'll suggest some possible policies to break the hammerlock of these special interests.

America's Failed Response to the New Globalization

To sum up the findings of this chapter, America has failed to respond effectively to the challenges of the new globalization. The manufacturing sector has shrunk as factories and employment have been shifted overseas. The working class, especially, has been squeezed. Economic policies did not exactly stand still but in fact responded perversely: taxes on the rich were cut; the manufacturing sector was allowed to decline in the face of growing foreign competition; employment in construction was temporarily spurred by easy money from the Fed and subprime lending, but that expedient lasted only until 2007, when the subprime bubble burst. The 2008 financial crisis was therefore a crisis of utterly mismanaged globalization. The United States had responded to the long-term loss of manufacturing competitiveness by the temporary expedient of a housing boom. When the boom was followed by a collapse, U.S. unemployment soared and the emptiness of U.S. short-termism was exposed for all to see. What is remarkable is that even after the collapse of the bubble, Washington was still unable to come up with any long-term, serious responses to America's waning competitiveness, instead turning again to the very same policy mix that had failed previously: easy money, tax cuts, large budget deficits, and, starting in 2011, cuts in government outlays on education, infrastructure, science, and technology, the very areas in which the United States needs to invest to regain its long-term competitiveness.

CHAPTER 7.

The Rigged Game

Here's the conundrum: A healthy economy is a mixed economy, in which government and the marketplace both play their role. Yet the federal government has neglected its role for three decades. Just when the government was needed to chart a course through the twists and turns of globalization, it went AWOL. Or, more accurately, it turned the levers of power over to the corporate lobbies. America's economic failures are therefore at least as much political as economic. This chapter examines the politics of America's corporatocracy, a political system in which powerful corporate interest groups dominate the policy agenda.

We can see how the corporatocracy arose as the confluence of four big trends. First, the American political system has weak national parties and strong political representation of individual districts. This allows special interests to have a great say in politics through local representatives. Second, the large U.S. military establishment after World War II created the first of the megalobbies, the military-industrial complex. Third, big corporate money finances America's election campaigns. And fourth, globalization and the race to the bottom have tilted the balance of power toward corporations and away from workers. Add up these trends, and we have the perfect political storm, in which Washington has been overrun, and overtaken, by the lobbies. The wealth/power spiral has continued to amplify the political disaster.

The main aim of this chapter is to explain how America's money-drenched political system works today. Another is to shake us from a lazy habit: the unexamined notion that decisions made in Washington reflect the will of the American people and the public's underlying values. The public has its main say on one day every two years: election day. The choice is between two political parties that cynically ignore their constituencies the very next day in order to carry out policies aimed at the rich and powerful rather than the voters.

The voters have a significant unmet responsibility, to be sure, in pulling Washington back to a true democracy. Yet most voters are poorly informed, and many are easily swayed by the intense corporate propaganda thrown their way in the few months leading to the elections. We have therefore been stuck in a low-level political trap: cynicism breeds public disengagement from politics; the public disengagement from politics opens the floodgates of corporate abuse; and corporate abuse deepens the cynicism.

America's Weak Party System

Political scientists distinguish between majoritarian and consensus electoral systems. Majoritarian systems tend to have just two or three major parties, and elections generally produce a clear winning party at the polls. The winning party (or perhaps a two-party coalition) governs while the losing party is out of government. Consensus systems have electoral rules that produce a large number of parties, and several parties generally govern as part of a broad coalition.[1]

The main reason for America's majoritarian character is the electoral system for Congress. Members of Congress are elected in single-member districts according to the "first-past-the-post" (FPTP) principle, meaning that the candidate with the plurality of votes is the winner of the congressional seat. The losing party or parties win no representation at all. The first-past-the-post election tends to produce a small number of major parties, perhaps just two, a principle known in political science as Duverger's Law.[2] Smaller parties are trampled in first-past-the-post elections.

There are two major implications of America's FPTP system. First, in a two-party system, the swing votes are near the center of the income distribution and political ideology. Both parties attempt to woo the middle class and independent (nonparty) voters. The poor are typically not wooed and are often not even mentioned in the campaigns, since they are rarely the swing votes. During the three presidential debates in 2008, the words "poor" and "poverty" were not uttered a single time (neither by the candidates nor by the questioners). The opinions and needs of the poor are represented only in districts that have a high rate of poverty.

In European proportional systems, on the other hand, winning more national votes among the poor means winning more parliamentary seats overall. The poor may be represented by their own party or may have a strong hold on a center-left labor party. Even if the poor are disbursed throughout the country, they still form a powerful voting group.[3]

These basic differences show up in systematic differences in social spending according to the voting system. Proportional systems are likely to support higher social spending and more redistribution toward the poor. Consider, for example, the share of public-sector social outlays in GDP in 2007 across three electoral systems (first-past-the-post, proportional, and a mix of the two) in a sample of fourteen high-income countries. The FPTP countries (the United States, the United Kingdom, and Canada) have an average social outlay of 19.9 percent of GDP. The proportional countries rank at the top of the list, with an average outlay of 28.1 percent. The mixed voting systems are in the middle, with an average social outlay of 24.6 percent. This correlation is not proof that the FPTP voting system causes the lower level of social outlays, and even within the group of FPTP countries, U.S. social spending is very low, but the pattern certainly suggests that FPTP systems tend to neglect the needs of the poor.

The second implication of America's FPTP system is the lack of strong party discipline within the two national parties. In proportional systems, the national parties almost always stick together in parliamentary votes. In parliamentary FPTP systems such as those in the United Kingdom and Canada, the governing party or parties also stick together on major votes, since a failure on a major policy vote usually triggers a new national election or at least the fall of the government.

In America's FPTP system, by contrast, in which Congress and government are separate branches and the government does not fall when it loses a legislative vote, national party discipline is limited and fragile. Members of Congress prioritize local interests over national interests, since Congress is elected locally. A strong national party leader may occasionally achieve party discipline in Congress, but party ranks are easily broken when interests conflict across districts.

A stable national majority coalition in Congress is therefore hard to achieve and sustain.[4] Moreover, congressional procedures give tremendous leeway to individual members to delay legislation and block appointments to executive departments and regulatory agencies. In the Senate, a minority of forty-one senators is usually enough to stop legislation favored by the majority, via the filibuster. Congressional power is fragmented, veto power is rife, and special interests are very well represented and able to penetrate the legislative process.

To pass economic legislation, the president must inevitably run a minefield of local interests. Though the president wields considerable power over the executive departments and agencies and limited influence over regulatory processes, the White House cannot be assured of passing a program or budget through Congress. Each major budget vote is an adventure on its own, with the president winning some and losing many.

With weak national parties and with elections to Congress in single-member districts, the main local industries and wealthy constituents in each district are likely to have great sway over each representative. In a coal-mining district, the representative is likely to vote in support of coal interests (and against anti–climate change legislation) irrespective of party or overall ideology. Military bases, mines, major factories, financial markets, and other major industries in the district are all likely to define the voting behavior of members of Congress. Congress is therefore a maze of special interests. Passing national legislation means forming coalitions of local interest groups and trading off favors across these groups. This kind of politics naturally gives enormous weight to narrow interest groups.

The power of special interests is exacerbated by yet another unusual feature of American politics: nonstop campaigning. Due to an outdated choice made in the 1789 Constitution, the United States has a national election every two years, which is by far the shortest election cycle of any high-income democracy. Between 1960 and 2009, Sweden had fifteen national elections; the United Kingdom had twelve; the United States had twenty-five.[5] The two-year cycle between congressional elections means that the United States is always in campaign mode and members of Congress are consumed by the need to fund-raise for the next election. Special interests are always at the ready to trade campaign financing for votes on crucial issues.

The Rising Power of Big Money

The large and growing role of big money in politics is the grim political reality of our times. It is the key to understanding the expanding tentacles of the corporatocracy. Campaign costs, especially to cover expensive media spending, have soared, as we see in Figure 7.1, which shows the estimated total campaign spending on each federal election since 1998, as estimated by the Center for Responsive Politics. These costs include direct spending by the candidates,

Figure 7.1: Total Federal Spending by Election Cycle (in Constant 2008 Dollars), 1998–2010

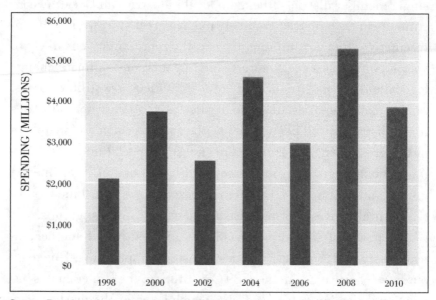

Source: Data from Center for Responsive Politics.

spending by the political parties, and direct spending by third-party groups for media and marketing. The overall upward trend is a rise in campaign spending of around $450 million per each two-year election cycle.[6] Even a nonpresidential federal election cycle now costs around $4 billion. Though this amount is not huge relative to the size of the country, about $50 per household, the rich are the predominant funders and thereby win the predominant political influence as a result. Public funds could easily replace the private contributions (and would account for a mere 0.13 percent of the federal budget), but the rich certainly don't want to lose their leverage, and therefore they aggressively block any greater role of public financing.

Lobbying outlays, as shown in Figure 7.2, are also soaring by roughly $200 million per year, at levels comparable to the campaign spending, also above $5 billion during the election cycle of 2009–2010 (the annual lobbying outlays should be added across the two years of the election cycle to compare them with campaign contribu-

Figure 7.2: Total Lobbying Outlays (in Constant 2008 Dollars), 1998–2010

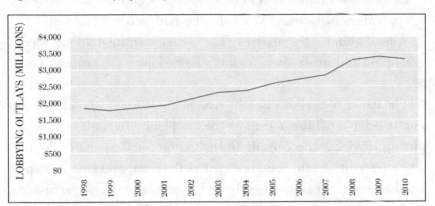

Source: Data from Center for Responsive Politics.

tions). Some of these outlays are essentially campaign contributions disguised as spending on lobbyists. Corporations pay the lobbying firms, which then channel the funds to campaigns through their staffs' contributions to the campaigns and through the funding of issue campaigns linked to candidates. Lobbyists also earn kudos by hiring the family members of politicians and by keeping lucrative jobs in wait for politicians, military brass, and regulators, to be taken up once they leave office.

In his excellent recent book on corporate lobbying, *So Damn Much Money*, Robert Kaiser summarizes the record this way:

By 2007, everyone in the system took it for granted that a high percentage of members and staff would eventually pass through the revolving door, because so many already had. A 2007 directory of Washington lobbyists listed 188 former members of the House and Senate who were registered to lobby. A study done by Public Citizen, an advocacy group, found that half the senators and 42 percent of House members who left Congress between 1998 and 2004 became lobbyists. Another study found that 3,600 former Congressional aides had passed through the revolving door. Appointees from the executive branch followed the same path. In early 2008 the Center for

Responsive Politics, a watchdog group, identified 310 former appointees of George W. Bush who had become lobbyists or Washington representatives. The center identified 283 former Clinton administration officials who had done the same.[7]

The list of top sectors in lobbying is like a who's who of bad corporate behavior. Table 7.1 shows the total lobbying outlays by sector during 1998–2011, according to the Center for Responsive Politics. The top sectors are the same ones where the economy is in the deepest trouble, and for reasons directly tied to regulatory failures: finance, health care, transport, agribusiness, and others. Each has landed remarkably cushy federal contracts, subsidies, tax breaks, and lax regulation and oversight. It should also be no surprise that finance, real estate, health care, and pharmaceutical companies rank among the lowest in public approval in Gallup polls, in all cases receiving "net negative" rankings by the public (in the August 2009 survey).[8]

Table 7.1: Lobbying by Sector (1998–2011)

Sector	Total Lobbying Outlays, 1998–2011 (USD Billion)
Finance, Insurance, and Real Estate	$4.5
Health	$4.5
Miscellaneous Business	$4.5
Communication and Electronics	$3.7
Energy and Natural Resources	$3.3
Transportation	$2.4
Other	$2.3
Ideology/Single-Issue	$1.5
Agribusiness	$1.3
Defense	$1.3
Construction	$0.5
Labor	$0.5
Lawyers and Lobbyists	$0.4

Source: Data from Center for Responsive Politics.

These industries epitomize the destructive policies produced by the corporatocracy, and the public knows it.

America's Two Right-of-Center Parties

Every recent president has been caught in the same web of campaign financing and well-heeled special interests. Every candidate draws funds from the same sources, and all must hone their policy positions accordingly. Even as politics heats up in shouting matches on the air, the real range of policy prescriptions is shockingly narrow. For all the times that Obama has been accused by the right wing of dragging America to socialism, the actual content of Obama's policies is often nearly indistinguishable from his predecessor's. For all of the talk about the logjams in Washington, what have been the real differences between Bush and Obama?

- Bush wanted tax cuts for 100 percent of households; Obama campaigned on tax cuts for 95 percent of the households but, when the deadline approached in December 2010, agreed to extend tax cuts for all.
- Bush supported large deficits, in order to maintain low taxes and high military spending; Obama also supported large deficits, mainly as a macroeconomic stimulus.
- Bush bailed out the banks and the auto companies; Obama continued those policies.
- Bush supported immigration reform but was blocked by his own party; Obama favors immigration reform but is blocked by both parties.
- Bush favored nuclear power and deep-sea oil drilling; Obama favors nuclear power and deep-sea oil drilling.
- Bush filled his White House with Goldman Sachs and Citigroup executives; Obama has done the same.

There are, of course, several reasons for these very narrow differences. Most important, each party pulls its campaign contributions from the same sources and therefore does not deviate far from the core messages of the corporate sector and high-net-worth individuals. America has thereby been pulled to a "median" that is politically far to the right of center and to the right of the public's true values. On issue after issue, Washington politics back the special interests rather than broad public values.

We can consider America's political system today to be not so much a true democracy as a stable *duopoly* of two ruling parties, whose members shout at each other from time to time but which both basically stand for many of the same things when it comes to issues touching the interests of business, the rich, and the military. Both parties are instruments of powerful businesses and the rich. Rather than aiming for the median voter, as in the textbook two-party election theory, both parties actually aim to the *right* of center to attract high-income campaign contributors. For the Republican Party, this is easy and natural. For the Democrats, who ostensibly represent the needs of the poor, it means party leaders such as Presidents Clinton and Obama, who relentlessly side with Wall Street and the rich and just as relentlessly apologize to their base.

The overpowering role of money in politics has led to a fairly stable bipartisan consensus among politicians (though not necessarily the broad public) on five major points of policy in the past thirty years that reflect a fidelity to vested interests. These are low marginal tax rates for the rich, as sponsored by campaign contributors; the contracting of public services to well-connected private interests; the neglect of the budget deficit when voting on tax and spending issues, leaving the debt to future generations; the favoring of large military outlays, even as domestic spending is squeezed; and the lack of serious long-term budget planning. These five policy biases have been maintained through the thick and thin of presidents since Reagan.

The famous "triangulation" of Obama and Clinton with conservative positions is designed less to win centrist voters than to fill campaign coffers with corporate funds. Corporatocracy, the over-representation of corporate and wealthy interests, is the essential feature of the duopoly. Campaign financing and lobbying are the key elements that keep the system intact.

The compromises made with the rich are consistently out of line with public opinion. The public desires to tax the rich more heavily, cut military spending, and develop renewable energy alternatives to oil. The outcome instead is tax cuts for the rich, unchecked military spending, and a continued stagnation in alternatives to oil, gas, and coal.

Both parties have consistently downplayed the importance of budget balance in favor of other political objectives. Reagan's supply-side advisers argued that tax cuts would spur enough growth to pay for themselves. Obama's stimulus supporters have argued something analogous: that deficits in the midst of a downturn have little or no longer-run cost, and even that deficit cutting in a recession is not feasible. These are both magical arguments without any empirical support but lots of ideological fervor. More important, they are arguments of convenience, allowing each party to favor its constituencies with short-term benefits (more tax cuts or spending increases) while downplaying the buildup of debt that will inevitably ensue. There have been only two short-lived exceptions to the chronic neglect of budget deficits. The first was George H. W. Bush, who broke his 1988 campaign pledge of "no new taxes" in order to reduce the budget deficit in 1990. The second was Bill Clinton, who pushed a modest hike in the top income tax rate (from 31 to 39.6 percent) and agreed to Republican-led budget cuts that helped move the budget to a temporary surplus at the end of the 1990s, albeit one that was quickly reversed under George W. Bush.

The duopoly also applies to foreign policy. Both parties view the Middle East and its greater neighborhood (stretching from the Horn of Africa and Yemen in the west to Afghanistan in the east) as the core theater of U.S. foreign policy, with the primary concern the continued flow of Middle East oil to the world economy. Carter enunciated a military doctrine that any threat to the flow of Middle East oil would be viewed as a security threat to the United States. There have been marginal differences in military proclivities between the two parties, with Bush Jr. being the most trigger-happy of recent presidents, but the differences should not be exaggerated. Obama not only retained Bush's secretary of defense but also expanded the war in Afghanistan while drawing down troops in Iraq. As the author and former army colonel Andrew Bacevich makes clear, the core U.S. military doctrine—based on the global projection of force—has remained constant on a bipartisan basis for more than forty years.[9]

The final feature of the two-party duopoly during the past three decades has been the willful neglect of longer-term thinking in government. The only place where even a modicum of long-term budgeting takes place is the Congressional Budget Office, which provides a nonpartisan budget "score" of legislative proposals, usually on a ten-year time horizon, though occasionally longer. But this budget score is a far cry from systematic thinking about long-term issues: infrastructure, budget balance, education, energy policy, and climate change. It is hard to think of a single recent case in which the U.S. government, led by either party, has produced a quantitative assessment of any long-term challenge and then followed through with a considered policy reform based on that assessment. For decades, Washington has been improvising through the repeated alternations of power.

The Four Big Lobbies

The corporatocracy is a quintessential example of a feedback loop. Corporate wealth translates into political power through campaign financing, corporate lobbying, and the revolving door of jobs between government and industry; and political power translates into further wealth through tax cuts, deregulation, and sweetheart contracts between government and industry. Wealth begets power, and power begets wealth.

Four key sectors of the American economy exemplify this feedback loop. The military-industrial complex is perhaps the most notorious example. As Eisenhower famously warned in his farewell address in January 1961, the linkage of the military and private industry created a political power so pervasive that America has been condemned to militarization, useless wars, and fiscal waste on a scale of many tens of trillions of dollars since then.[10]

The second powerful lobby is the Wall Street–Washington complex, which has steered the financial system toward control by a few politically powerful Wall Street firms, notably Goldman Sachs, JPMorgan Chase, Citigroup, Morgan Stanley, and a handful of other financial firms. The close ties of finance and Washington paved the way for the 2008 financial crisis and the megabailouts that followed, through reckless deregulation followed by an almost complete lack of oversight by government. Wall Street firms have provided the top economic policy makers in Washington during several administrations, including the likes of Donald Regan (Merrill Lynch) under Reagan, Robert Rubin (Goldman Sachs) under Clinton, Hank Paulson (Goldman Sachs) under Bush Jr., and several Wall Street–connected senior officials under Obama (including William Daley, Larry Summers, Gene Sperling, and Jack Lew).

The third sector is the Big Oil–transport–military complex that has put the United States on the trajectory of heavy oil import dependence and a deepening military trap in the Middle East. Since the days of John D. Rockefeller and the Standard Oil Trust a century ago, Big Oil has loomed large in American politics and foreign policy. Big Oil teamed up with the automobile industry to steer America away from mass transit and toward gas-guzzling vehicles driving on a nationally financed highway system. Big Oil has consistently and successfully fought the intrusion of competition from non-oil energy sources, including nuclear, wind, and solar power. Big Oil has been at the side of the Pentagon in making sure that

America defends the sea-lanes to the Persian Gulf, in effect ensuring a $100 billion–plus annual subsidy for a fuel that is otherwise dangerous for national security. And Big Oil has played a notorious role in the fight to keep climate change off the U.S. agenda. Exxon-Mobil, Koch Industries, and others in the sector have underwritten a generation of antiscientific propaganda to confuse the American people.

The fourth of the great industry-government tie-ups has been the health care industry, America's single largest industry today, absorbing no less than 17 percent of GDP. The key to understanding this sector is to note that the government partners with industry to reimburse costs with little systematic oversight and control. Pharmaceutical firms set sky-high prices protected by patent rights; Medicare, Medicaid, and private insurers reimburse doctors and hospitals on a cost-plus basis; and the American Medical Association restricts the supply of new doctors through the control of placements at American medical schools. The result of this pseudo–market system is sky-high costs, large profits for the private health care sector, and no political will to reform.

Recent Case Studies of Corporatocracy

Now it's time to see the corporatocracy at work, to understand how the lobbies dominate policy making at the expense of the nation and contrary to the expressed opinions of the American people. I will explore these workings in four recent case studies.

Case 1: The Extension of Tax Cuts for the Rich
During the 2008 campaign, President Obama said he would support a rollback of the Bush-era tax cuts on the richest 5 percent of taxpayers but sustain the Bush tax cuts for the remaining 95 percent of the population. His campaign pledge to tax the rich involved little more

than a rise in the marginal tax rate from 35 percent to 39.6 percent on households with incomes above $250,000. Despite all the sound and fury on tax policy, there was in fact little difference between John McCain and Obama, a difference in essence of 4.6 percentage points on the highest incomes.

Even more tellingly, when push finally came to shove in 2010 on whether to extend the Bush tax cuts even for the rich, Obama rather quickly sided with the Republicans in favoring an across-the-board extension of the Bush-era tax cuts, including for the richest households. The two-party duopoly held firm, despite the crying need for more revenues to stanch the hemorrhaging of red ink.

It might be supposed that public opinion had forced Obama's hand, but this is patently not the case. In the months leading up to the Obama-Republican agreement to extend tax breaks for the rich, the broad public supported a rollback of the tax breaks at the top. According to the Pew Research Center, a consistent majority of Americans from September 2004 to December 2010 called for repealing the Bush tax cuts on the wealthy or repealing the tax cuts altogether (see Table 7.2).

At the moment of truth during the lame-duck session of Congress in December 2010, only one-third of the public actually supported the extension of the tax cuts for the richest Americans, and nearly 60 percent opposed it. The minority viewpoint prevailed. The political system paid no heed to the public.

Obama and his top advisers have known from the start of the administration about the deep contradictions between Obama's tax policies and his activist objectives on education, science, and infrastructure. They promised low taxes to get elected and have held to the line. In private the top advisers routinely acknowledge the need for higher tax revenues but declare that they are politically infeasible. Rather than explaining the basic truths to the public and defending a truly defensible position, they instead pander to the public and especially to their rich campaign contributors. Obama aims to

Table 7.2: Attitudes About Ending the Bush Tax Cuts

	September 2004	October 2006	October 2007	October 2008	July 2010	September 2010	December 2010
Keep all tax cuts	27%	26%	24%	25%	30%	29%	33%
Repeal some or all of the tax cuts	59%	62%	61%	62%	58%	57%	58%
Of which:							
Repeal tax cuts for the wealthy and keep others	31%	36%	31%	37%	27%	29%	47%
Repeal all tax cuts	28%	26%	30%	25%	31%	28%	11%

Source: Richard Auxier, Pew Research Center for the People & the Press, "Taxed Enough Already?," September 20, 2010, and Pew Research Center, "Mixed Views on Tax Cuts, Support for START and Allowing Gays to Serve Openly," December 7, 2010.

raise perhaps $1 billion for the campaign war chest for 2012, which will require a political environment highly favorable to wealthy campaign contributors.

The proof of this pandering is the behavior of key advisers after they leave office. No sooner had Office of Management and Budget (OMB) Director Peter Orszag left the White House than he wrote about the need for higher tax revenues as a share of GDP, a position he never took publicly while OMB director.[11] The head of the Council of Economic Advisers, Christina Romer, also called for tax increases—once she had left office:

> Finally, the President has to be frank about the need for more tax revenues. Even with bold spending cuts, there will still be a large deficit. The only realistic way to close the gap is by raising revenue.[12]

It's a funny thing about being frank. We spend billions of dollars every two years to elect politicians who in turn bring top academic experts to Washington. Is that merely so that the experts can then hide the truth from the American people until those experts leave office and begin to write the truth once again?

Case 2: The Health Care Reform Debacle
The health care reform effort also exemplified the power of special interests. Obama worked very hard to make some progress in this area, and he achieved some progress, but at huge costs to public morale and huge sacrifices to corporate power. When the administration began its legislative efforts in early 2009, it decided not to put forward a plan, on the grounds that the last attempt to prepare a health plan, in Clinton's first year of office, had gone down to defeat. A plan, it was argued, would leave too many hostages to the lobbyists' whims.

Obama was determined to avoid a confrontation with two key corporate sectors, the health insurers and the pharmaceutical industry.

If he put forward a plan that would really control costs, for example, or that introduced government competition into the insurance market (through the so-called public option), the private insurance industry would bolt. Therefore, from the start, Obama winked at the industry and assured its lobbyists that there would be no heroics on the critical cost and competition issues. He did not say as much to his constituents and the general public, who were told repeatedly that cost control was central and that a public option was very much on the table. Similarly, Obama negotiated an early truce with the big pharmaceutical companies, assuring the industry that the United States would not explore new methods of drug pricing. This too was never clearly articulated to the public.

The entire health care debate then took on a surreal air for the next fifteen months. Obama could not table a plan because the outlines of the implicit agreement with industry ran counter to the views of much of his own party, and indeed a majority of the public at large. During 2009, the public repeatedly indicated in opinion surveys that it backed the option of a government-run plan to compete with private plans. According to CBS/*New York Times* polls, the margin was 66 percent to 27 percent in favor of the public option in June–July 2009; in a Pew survey, it was 52 percent to 37 percent.[13] Obama aimed to keep supporters of the public option satisfied by assuring them that such a policy was still on the table, while not explaining clearly to the public the outlines of the actual White House understandings with private industry.

The situation was even murkier because the costly part of the proposal—subsidies to expand health care coverage—meant additional annual outlays of around 1 percent of GDP in the latter years of this decade, but paying for this through tax increases on higher incomes was very unpopular with politically powerful groups. Eventually a hodgepodge financing package was cobbled together, including some planned future cutbacks in Medicare spending that are unlikely to be implemented when the time comes, as well as some modest increases in payroll taxes on high-income households and excise taxes on high-premium private insurance plans held mainly by high-income households. (Revenues from the latter two sources are expected to raise around 0.1 percent of GDP in fiscal year 2015, 0.2 percent of GDP in fiscal year 2018, and 0.3 percent of GDP in fiscal year 2021.)[14]

In the middle of the health care debate I asked a leading congresswoman about the miserable state of the health care legislation. She literally put her head in her hands and declared "The lobbies, the lobbies." It felt to me like the final scene of *Heart of Darkness*, in which Kurtz mutters, "The horror! The horror!"

The health care debate, indeed, exposed once again that U.S. politics are narrowly channeled in a very deep groove of special interests.[15] Lost throughout the fifteen months of debate were the public's trust and a coherent reform effort. By failing to put forward a coherent plan during the entire process, Obama left the public on the sidelines. He stumped energetically for "health care reform," but few people (including myself) were able to keep track from week to week of what was actually in the reform legislation of the moment. Nor was the public honestly apprised of the merits and likelihood of key changes, such as a public option, systemic change for cost controls, or the various potential means of financing expanded coverage. The administration and Congress turned to their favorite experts along the way, but America lost the chance to hear systematically from the expert community about the merits and demerits of various alternative proposals. In short, we were told to avert our eyes to the "sausage making" on Capitol Hill but then forced to eat the sausage, like it or not.

Case 3: The Energy Policy Stalemate

America desperately needs a coherent energy strategy, since the country is being hemmed in on three sides: the global scarcity of oil; the intensifying competition over supplies in unstable regions of the world; and the environmental risks of a continued rapid rise in fossil fuel use. The president came into office promising to break the logjam on climate change and to set a new course for U.S. energy security. Yet after more than two years in office, his progress on creating a new overall framework has been minimal. Bits and pieces of policies are coming into place—such as R&D for renewable energy, new funding for nuclear power, and modest funds for intercity fast rail—but there is no overarching strategy or clarity. When I asked Larry Summers to explain the administration's plan to reduce carbon emissions by 17 percent as of 2020, as Obama announced in late 2009, he responded, "We don't plan in America." That may be true, but we also don't achieve our energy and environmental objectives either.

Why don't we plan an energy policy when it is so manifestly evident that we need one? Here, too, corporate power is the key reason. I witnessed this during another meeting at the White House, this time with the former energy "czar" Carol Browner. I thought that perhaps she would be interested in promulgating an energy plan. That did seem, after all, to be her assignment. Our conversation made it clear that she had a quite different role, almost purely dedicated to managing the corporatocracy. Rather than discuss energy policy with me, Browner went through a long list of senators, noting the special demands that each senator was making in return for a promised vote for anti–climate change legislation. One senator wanted special provisions for the auto industry; the next wanted more favorable benefits for states involved in offshore drilling; the third wanted special provisions for nuclear power; and on went the interminable list. Rather than a national policy, Browner was designing a grab bag of special perks in order to get a shell of a policy. In the end, the entire process failed; Big Oil and Big Coal torpedoed the legislation.

Case 4: The Financial Lobby Bailouts and Bonuses

The financial saga has been equally illuminating. The 2008 financial crash resulted from a confluence of forces: deregulation, monetary mismanagement, and reckless irresponsibility by the top management on Wall Street, who lusted after profits with sheer disregard for their shareholders, workers, and clients. Behind it all, of course, were the astounding wealth and power of Wall Street, which epitomizes the translation of big bucks into power, power to achieve a massive bailout when the going got tough in 2008.

Not only was Wall Street bailed out, but the corporate leadership was allowed to continue to rake in megabonuses even as the firms were on Washington's life support systems. During 2009, I exchanged views on several occasions with Larry Summers about the need to rein in the egregious bonuses, which had no merit in market forces or morality. He staunchly defended the administration's "hands-off" position—hands off in the peculiar sense of giving the bailouts but then leaving the CEOs alone to pocket them. Absurdly, after the Treasury pumped tens of billions of dollars of bailout funds into AIG, Summers claimed that he couldn't find a way to stop the company from paying megabonuses to the very traders who had caused the disaster: "We are a country of law. There are contracts. The government cannot just abrogate contracts. Every legal step possible to limit those bonuses is being taken by Secretary Geithner and by the Federal Reserve system."

Suffice it to say that the limits were never found. The extraordinary political power of Wall Street arises from many quarters. The top decision makers such as Rubin, Paulson, Summers, Rahm Emanuel, Orszag, Jack Lew (Orszag's successor at the Office of Management and Budget and a former Citigroup executive), Daley, and countless others have one foot in Wall Street and one in Washington. Wall Street was, of course, one of Obama's main campaign financiers. Obama's campaign was properly renowned for mobilizing Internet-based donations from small donors, but it is still the case that 65 percent of his donations came from individuals who gave $200 or more and 42 percent came from individuals who gave $1,000 or more. Obama depended on the heavy-hitter campaign contributors from Wall Street and elsewhere just like other more traditional candidates.[16]

The links of Wall Street and Washington go far beyond the White House, the Fed, and the Treasury. The industry has established a remarkable army of lobbyists carefully detailed by the Center for Responsive Politics.[17] During 2009–2010, the financial services industry (including banks, investment firms, insurance companies, and real estate companies) "commissioned 1,447 former federal employees to lobby Congress and federal agencies," including an astounding "73 former members of Congress, accounting for 47 percent of the 156 former members who have reported lobbying in the time period." These seventy-three former members included "17 former congressional members [who] served on the Senate or House banking committees." Moreover, "at least 42 financial services lobbyists formerly served in some capacity in the Treasury Department; and at least seven served in the Office of the Comptroller of the Currency, including two former comptrollers."[18]

Case 5: The Proliferation of Tax Havens
The globalization of capital markets has also made it far easier for companies to hide their profits in offshore tax havens. This is part of the "race to the bottom." The use of tax havens has soared in the past thirty years, and what was once a dodge for wealthy individuals avoiding the IRS has become a systematic vehicle for hiding corporate income from taxation. Yet what is even more notable is that the IRS is often a willing handmaiden to these practices. A recent report on Google pulled the curtain back just a bit on these practices.[19]

Google is an American-based corporation with earnings all over the world. Its main capital is its intellectual property (IP), specifically its powerful search engine. Under the U.S. tax code, the allocation of Google's earnings around the world should reflect the reality that its core IP is U.S.-based. Specifically, when a Google foreign subsidiary sells search-engine services to a foreign client, the foreign subsidiary should transfer the bulk of those earnings back to the U.S. headquarters in the form of internal royalty payment for the use of the intellectual property. For allocating incomes among Google's international operations for U.S. tax purposes, the internal transfers should take place at a royalty rate that mimics an arm's-length commercial transaction between unrelated firms.

Google instead found friends in the IRS. In 2006, Google and the IRS reached a secret agreement whereby a wholly owned Google subsidiary could keep the revenues and profits abroad. Specifically, Google was allowed to license its IP at a noncommercial rate to a foreign subsidiary called Google Ireland Holdings. Google's foreign operations pay IP royalties to Google Ireland Holdings, which thereby books almost all of Google's profits earned in Europe, the Middle East, and Africa. Specifically, Google's operations for those three regions are headquartered in Dublin in another entity called Google Ireland Ltd. Google Ireland Ltd. takes in around 90 percent of Google's $12.5 billion in revenues from those markets and then channels the profits to Google Ireland Holdings as royalty payments. The last step of this wonderful chain is that Google Ireland Holdings, despite its name, is based in Bermuda, where it avoids taxation on the billions of dollars of royalties paid to it.

There are many other tax shelters for the super-rich, including the so-called carried interest provisions for hedge fund managers. A typical hedge fund manager receives as compensation a fraction of the assets under management and of the profits earned on the portfolio, for example the standard 2 and 20 rule, meaning 2 percent of assets and 20 percent of profits. Under an obscure IRS rule, the profit earnings are not treated as ordinary income for the manager, taxable at 35 percent, but rather as capital gains, taxable at 15 percent.[20] Incredibly, this provision has survived the recent public outcry over Wall Street behavior, a remarkably vivid testament to the power of hedge fund campaign financing to smooth over any inconveniences of noxious tax rules.

We in the public are of course innocents in this remarkable process. How many people aside from the tax lawyers and their clients know of the "Double Irish" tax shelter or many other gimmicks like it? And which advocates of "free markets," as they hail the technological wonders of Google (an admiration I share), realize that Sergey Brin's ingenious work in creating Google's search engine was supported by the National Science Foundation?

Google's tax dodge exemplifies a vast system of corporate tax havens and tax shelters that operate with the connivance and support of the Internal Revenue Service. A recent report of the Government Accountability Office (GAO) on the subject makes frightening reading.[21] Of the 100 largest public traded U.S. corporations, 83 reported operating in tax havens, and often in several simultaneously. A Congressional Research Service study suggested that tens of billions of dollars of revenues are lost per year as a result of shifting corporate profits out of the United States through transfer pricing and similar means.[22]

Whose Opinion Really Counts?

One of the most interesting insights about money in politics has come from studies examining how congressional votes are linked to the attitudes of constituents. Larry Bartels has studied how the votes of senators align with the survey attitudes of their constituents when divided into high-income, middle-income, and low-income groups. The results are clear, if not totally surprising:

> For Republican senators there is no evidence of responsiveness to middle-income constituents, much less low-income constituents. The views of high-income constituents, however, seem to have received a great deal of weight from Republican senators [on the issues studied]—almost three times as much . . . as for Democrats. Meanwhile, Democrats seem to have responded at least as strongly to the views of middle-class constituents as to the views of high-income constituents—though, once again, there is no evidence of any responsiveness to the views of low-income constituents.[23]

The point is that even when translating the wishes of constituents into congressional votes, money counts and the poor are effectively dispossessed. This is more than a congressman aiming for the middle or the median voter. It is, instead, catering disproportionately to those who will finance their campaigns. At least the Democrats evidence some responsiveness to the middle of the income distribution.

We can see the results of this representation bias in case after case: the "temporary" tax cuts for the rich are extended; the unpopular war in Afghanistan continues; the public option for health care is dropped; alternative energy technologies are left undeveloped; the largest banks get megabailouts and use them to continue to pay outrageous subsidies. In all of these cases, public opinion has run strongly against the decisions made by the bipartisan congressional majority in Washington.

The Role of Corporate Spin

The power of the corporatocracy is supported not only by campaign financing and lobbying, but also by relentless public relations spin. A number of studies in recent years have deconstructed the ways in which key sectors—military contractors, oil and coal, health care insurers, and Wall Street— use public relations firms and disinformation campaigns to disguise the damage they are doing to society. Major corporate media outlets, led by Rupert Murdoch's vast News Corporation empire of newspapers and television networks, aid and abet the process. Murdoch himself is a personal investor in the oil sector (together with former Vice President Dick Cheney) as well as other industries, so the PR interest is often direct personal gain as well as corporate gain.[24]

In many recent cases where industries are causing environmental and public health damage, such as acid rain from coal-fired power plants, ozone depletion from CFCs, and climate change from fossil fuel use, industry lobbyists have deployed slick, well-funded public relations campaigns to spread antiscientific propaganda in order to forestall federal regulations. Big Oil and Big Coal are the most notorious abusers, and *The Wall Street Journal* has been the most consistent enabler of antiscientific propaganda. The main strategy has been for the industry lobby to sow confusion in the public mind by making it appear that well-established scientific findings are in fact open to major doubt and scientific dispute. Industry has shown time and again that it is possible to find people with a PhD in their title to sign off on just about any fraudulent scientific claim, if the fee is right. And experience has shown repeatedly that a poorly informed public is highly vulnerable to manipulation by a determined corporate lobby.

Climate change is the latest example of this relentless corporate assault on science. ExxonMobil, Koch Industries (the largest privately owned oil company in the United States), News Corporation, and other companies have conspired for years to spread unscientific nonsense about climate change, mainly around the theme that human-induced climate change is not yet an established scientific consensus. Several dogged journalists such as Ross Gelbspan and researchers such as Naomi Oreskes have laid bare the web of big corporate money that funds this ongoing PR effort. To a trained eye, the PR effort is rather pathetic: egregiously antiscientific and even puerile in its misuse of basic facts. Yet for a confused public, it works. Around half of the American people deny the reality of human-induced climate change despite the overwhelming scientific consensus that human actions have already dangerously disrupted the climate, with a lot more damage to come.

The Corporate Sector Continues to Win Big

The main thing to remember about the corporatocracy is that it looks after its own. There is absolutely no economic crisis in corporate America. Consider the pulse of the corporate sector as opposed to the pulse of the employees working in it:

- Corporate profits in 2010 were at an all-time high.[25]
- CEO salaries in 2010 rebounded strongly from the financial crisis.[26]
- Wall Street compensation in 2010 was at an all-time high.
- Several Wall Street firms paid civil penalties for financial abuses, but no senior banker faced any criminal charges.
- There were no adverse regulatory measures that would lead to a loss of profits in finance, health care, military supplies, and energy.

The creation of America's rich class (those in the top 1 percent, with incomes above $400,000 per year) and super-rich class (those in the top 0.01 percent, with incomes above $8 million per year) has been the thirty-year achievement of the corporatocracy. We can now see the tools of the trade. It began with globalization, which pushed up capital income while pushing down wages. These changes were magnified by the tax cuts at the top, which left more take-home pay and the ability to accumulate greater wealth through higher net-of-tax returns to saving. CEOs then helped themselves to their own slice of the corporate sector ownership through outlandish awards of stock options by friendly and often handpicked compensation committees, while the Securities and Exchange Commission looked the other way. It's not all that hard to do when both political parties are standing in line to do your bidding.

CHAPTER 8.

The Distracted Society

Most attempts to explain the current economic crisis put the spotlight on reckless financial deregulation, and a few link the disastrous regulatory choices to the corrupted politics of Washington. Very few put a spotlight on the citizenry as well. It is easy, and right, to blame our politicians and greedy CEOs. The public knows the score and detests it. Yet at the end of the day, Americans have elected their leaders. Americans have allowed themselves to be manipulated by corporate propaganda. And Americans have behaved in a very shortsighted way with their own budget management, falling dangerously into debt and eventually into bankruptcy. Tens of millions of Americans are repeatedly overconsuming today and regretting it tomorrow: whether by overeating, overborrowing, overgambling, excessive TV viewing, or indulging in yet other addictions.

Just as Washington has abandoned any long-term economic steering, households have abandoned clear thinking regarding their personal budgets. They tend to be inconsistent about the federal budget as well, poorly informed and often contradictory in position. Voters regularly support middle-class tax cuts and government spending increases while simultaneously professing deep concern over the budget deficit. They also sometimes give the rich a free pass, such as by supporting cuts in the inheritance tax on the wealthy. Voters are easily enticed by promises of higher short-term income, seemingly without concern for the long-term consequences.

To understand such behavior and attitudes, we need to plow more deeply into our psyches to get a grip on our behavior both as consumers and as citizens. To retake political power from the lobbies, to establish meaningful solutions for America, we will need to take the long view. Yet taking that long view is exceedingly difficult, especially when much of the economy is working overtime to encourage us to succumb to temptation. The purpose of this chapter is to understand our psychological fragilities as thinkers, planners, and decision makers. By getting our heads cleared of deceptions, we can help to rebuild the economy as well.

The Psychology of Affluence

When a society is poor, consumer behavior is relatively straightforward. Consumers know what they need: food, shelter, and clothing. Local producers strive to meet those needs. Impoverished households can't save very much if anything, since they depend on their incomes to stay alive, but when poor households exceed the subsistence threshold, they start to save in order to guard against disasters in the leaner years.

It's when the society gets much richer and basic needs are met that consumer behavior becomes trickier. In high-income countries such as the United States, we can no longer properly speak of a consumer's "needs" in the case of the middle class and the rich but only of a consumer's "wants." Economists pretend that those wants are real, stable, and based on deeply held preferences, almost a birthright. Brand managers and advertising executives know much better. A successful business not only manufactures products, it also manufactures wants. Businesses now spend an estimated $300 billion on advertising each year to create and manipulate consumers' demands.[1]

In real sweat-and-blood decision making, consumers buy things out of intense cravings, whims, addictions, confusions, come-ons, and quests for status. They may try to save, for example, but temptations often get the best of them. The problems of irrationality are actually multiplied by our affluence. The truly poor know what they need to stay alive: food, shelter, clothing, safe water, and health care. Affluent consumers may not have a clear idea ahead of time what will make them happy. Should they consume or save? Should they try to keep up with the Joneses across the street or with a work colleague or their favorite celebrity? Should they buy that new product just flashed across their TV or computer screen?

A considerable amount of American consumption spending is not for the enjoyment of consumption per se, but to show off wealth, status, or sexual allure. In the famous phrase of the economist and social critic Thorstein Veblen, this is "conspicuous consumption," that is, consumption whose main purpose is to impress others rather than to be enjoyed by oneself.[2] The phenomenon is very familiar from the animal world, where evolutionary competition leads males of a species to develop remarkable "ornaments" in order to rise in the pecking order and thereby attract the females. This so-called sexual selection has resulted in the male peacock's brilliant plumage and the elk's large antlers.

Conspicuous consumption is therefore akin to an arms race between two rivals. Most or all of the investments end up wasted as useless arms (or antlers or yachts). The economic arms race ends up as the proverbial "rat race," in which everybody works to the point of exhaustion merely to keep up with others. Herein lies at least one reason why the good Lord commanded that everybody take the Sabbath off. If we had to do so on our own, we'd have to worry whether our neighbor-competitor would also do the same. More likely than not, we'd both end up working through the weekend. It's a similar reason why many European governments (but not yet that of the United States) prevent this kind of "self-exploitation" by mandating a minimum of four weeks' paid vacation each year for all workers.

A related but distinct kind of "social consumption" occurs when specific consumption goods are necessary for an individual to be part of a desired social group. An example might be the purchase of a Harley-Davidson to ride with the motorcycle gang; a smartphone to be part of a social network; or a house in the suburbs to have wealthy neighbors and excellent local public schools. The last kind of consumption, however, is not merely about signaling or status; having wealthy neighbors facilitates other crucial outcomes, such as sending one's children to a good school.

In America, the most important kind of social consumption by far is housing. The choice of a residence may have little to do with the house per se but quite a bit to do with the neighbors and neighborhood that come along with the house. America's neighborhoods, as we have noted, are very strongly sorted by income, race, and ethnicity. Since public schools in America, unlike in many other parts of the world, are financed heavily by local property taxes, living in an affluent neighborhood is vital to being part of a good school system. Households are willing to spend extra on a given quality of land and house to buy into an expensive neighborhood in order to be able to send the kids to a high-quality school. The cycle is reinforcing: the affluent move into a neighborhood, bidding up prices; this induces other affluent households to move in, squeezing out the poor, who are left to fend in poor neighborhoods with poor schools and poor networks to the labor market.

The end result of all this consumption is a society running furiously to stay in place. The overwork by each member of society puts a burden (a negative externality) on others, who must also run hard to keep up. Consumers also run because others are running, with everybody finding themselves in a race they'd rather do without.

The Technologies of Mass Persuasion

Mainstream economists are stuck with an entirely antiquated view of consumer behavior. Even though they know full well that the relentless quest for more consumer goods no longer brings major benefits of well-being, they still treat the quest for greater personal consumption as the be-all and end-all of human happiness. The rise of the gross national product, of which 80 percent is consumption spending, is still taken as the bellwether of economic efficiency. Though this focus on consumerism does not feel funny to economists, it comes as a shock to the psychologists, sociologists, and philosophers who are also observing American society in action.

To understand this phenomenon, we must turn to the enticements of modern media, especially TV. For more than a century, incessant waves of commercial advertising, public relations campaigns, and official propaganda have remolded our psyches to want more and more consumption. The technologies of mass persuasion have become ever more encompassing. The first half of the twentieth century was first the age of newspapers and then of radio and movies. The second half was the great age of television. Now we are fully digital and wired, multimedia, spending hours each day in front of many different kinds of screens that are sending nonstop messages to buy, spend, borrow, and buy some more. These messages are driven by a highly professional and highly effective public relations, marketing, and advertising industry.

The modern discoverer of our unconscious impulses, Sigmund Freud, was an uncle (actually a double uncle) of the founder of modern public relations, Edward Bernays. Bernays was a marketing genius who correctly foresaw how the basic processes of public manipulation (which he called "engineering consent") could operate in similar ways across a wide range of social persuasion, whether promoting the sales of cigarettes, political candidates, or even a military coup (in Guatemala in 1953). The art was hidden manipulation of the public's unconscious urges combined with the public's tendency to run in herds.[3]

The stark reality today is the vastly increased powers of the digital technologies that advertisers, politicians, campaign advisers, and lobbyists use to prey upon us. In the 1910s to 1930s, Bernays relied mainly on newspapers, publicity stunts, and word of mouth. His dark arts of manipulation depended heavily on getting black-and-white photos into the press.

Then, beginning in the 1940s, came the exceptional powers of television, which atomized the population by sending it home from the town square. With unprecedented speed for a new technology, Americans reoriented their lives around the television set. In 1950, 9 percent of households had a television. By 1960, the number had already reached an astounding 87 percent, the fastest adoption of a major new technology in history.[4] And from the start, Americans devoted a remarkable proportion of their discretionary hours to the TV screen, reaching three to four hours per person per day by the 1960s, of which around one-third was devoted to commercials. Now the opinion manipulators have readily at hand the combination of television, the Internet, video, billboards, newspapers, magazines, special events, and other traditional outlets. It has been estimated that the average two- to seven-year-old sees an average of 13,900 TV ads a year and an eight- to twelve-year-old sees 30,100.[5]

We were, of course, forewarned early on about the manipulative power of the TV screen, by George Orwell in the 1940s, Vance Packard in the 1950s, the economist John Kenneth Galbraith and the media guru Marshall McLuhan in the 1960s, and the linguist Noam Chomsky in the past two decades. Joe McGinniss told us in 1968 that the image makers were now "selling the president" through television-based election campaigns.[6] Yet, despite those warnings, Americans have continued to "buy the president" and whatever other products are on sale on the tube.

The amount of time now spent with electronic media is staggering. In a 2004 survey, eight- to eighteen-year-olds were in front of a TV screen roughly three hours per day; a DVD or movie, another hour; computers, video games, and handheld devices, another two hours; and audio consoles, another hour. That left twenty-three minutes per day for reading. Taking into account multitasking (using two or more media simultaneously), total media time averaged an astounding eight hours, thirty-three minutes per day.[7] Our kids increasingly inhabit a virtual electronic world, much of it suffused with nonstop messaging and advertisements. Parents are only marginally less hooked, watching an average of three to four hours of television per day.

Of course, not one of those ads or expensive multimedia campaigns is telling us to buy less and save more. None are warning us to look skeptically at the thirty-second campaign spots designed to capture our vote. No advertisement is warning us to be aware of our susceptibility to bright colors, nice slogans, beautiful faces, suggestive gestures, and emotion-laden slogans. None teaches the public to ignore the pseudoscience that pours forth daily from corporate-financed PR campaigns. And certainly no advertising spot tells us to turn off the TV and read a book, go for a walk, or volunteer at a soup kitchen. The reason is obvious: there is no money in such messages. The $300 billion in advertising is mobilized instead to elect a candidate or sell a product, paid for by somebody who expects a commercial return on investment.

The effects of television go far beyond the direct message of the advertisements.

TV also shifted the center of gravity of society from the public park and the bowling alley to the privacy of our own homes, as couch potatoes in front of the giant screen. Over time, the single screen in the living room migrated into separate TV screens in each bedroom. Families retreated from other families, and then family members eventually retreated from one another. The political scientist Robert Putnam, in *Bowling Alone*, his magisterial account of the decline of civic engagement, found that time in front of the TV screen is the most powerful single characteristic accounting for the long-term decline in the time devoted to civic activities.

The cross-national evidence is highly suggestive: TV watching is bad for your social health (and your personal health as well). TV eats away at the social capital. Countries whose citizens watch more television have lower levels of social trust and higher levels of political corruption. The inverse relationship between TV viewing and social trust, which is statistically significant, is shown in Figure 8.1(a), which shows the estimated hours of TV watched per adult, varying from around 167 minutes per day by the Swiss to an astounding 297 minutes (5 hours per day) by Americans. There is a group of relatively low-watching countries (Switzerland, Finland, Sweden, Norway, the Netherlands), a group of medium-watching countries (France, Germany, Japan, Spain, Italy), and then the United States. We see that hours of TV watching are strongly inversely correlated with the level of social trust (as measured in the World Values Survey). Similarly, a high measure of perceived corruption (as measured by Transparency International) is positively associated with heavy TV-viewing hours, as we see in Figure 8.1(b). Italy, for example, scores very high on both measures, a fair reflection of a country long governed by a media owner with a seemingly endless trail of corruption charges, while the citizens of Scandinavian countries are low TV viewers with very high levels of social trust. The United States, fortunately, lies a bit below the best-fit line in this case. De-

Figure 8.1(a): Relationship Between Television Viewing and Social Trust

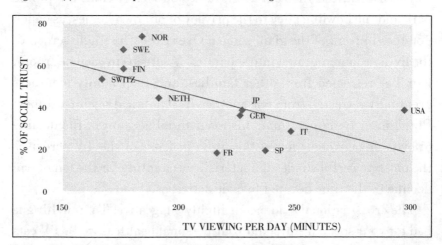

Source: Data from World Values Survey Databank and the RTL Group.

Figure 8.1(b): Relationship Between Television Viewing and Corruption Perception

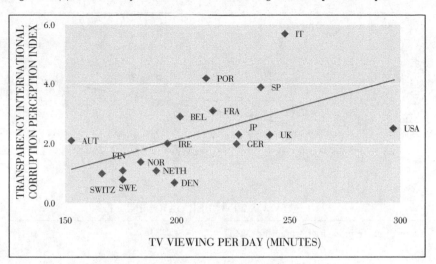

Source: Data from Transparency International and the RTL Group.

spite America's remarkably heavy TV viewing, the corruption level is judged to be only moderate in comparison with the others. (Perhaps this is because much of America's corruption is in effect legalized through corporate lobbying and campaign financing.)

Heavy TV viewing also appears to be bad for one's mental and physical health. We know from opinion surveys that heavy TV watchers report being less happy on average and indeed unsettled by their heavy TV viewing. Heavy TV viewing therefore seems to fit the pattern of psychological addiction rather than a healthy consumption behavior. There is also a not-surprising positive correlation between TV-viewing hours and obesity, shown in Figure 8.2. This correlation probably reflects, in part, a direct causal link from sedentary behavior (heavy TV watching) to obesity. It may also reflect a higher tendency of TV watchers to have the junk-food diets promoted in TV ads. Perhaps there is also a psychological linkage in play, in which overeating and excessive TV watching both reflect a loss of self-control.

The correlations between heavy TV viewing and the adverse social and personal outcomes are, of course, very far from causal

Figure 8.2: Relationship between Television Viewing and Obesity

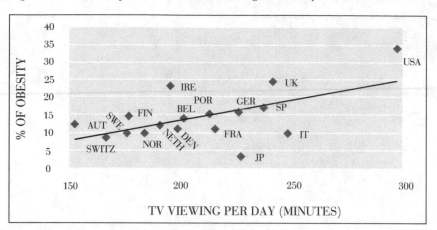

Source: Data from the RTL Group and OECD.

proofs. Heavy TV viewing would be only one of several factors determining complex social outcomes. Still, the relationships are suggestive and worrisome.

The relentless streams of images and media messages that confront us daily are professionally designed to distort our most important decision making processes. We are encouraged to act on impulse and fantasy instead of reason. And we need to understand that the difficulty of maintaining our balance in a media-rich economy is even greater than we might have supposed even ten or fifteen years ago. The advances in modern neurobiology and psychology have revealed a level of human vulnerability that would have surprised even Freud and Bernays.

The problem is not just that we are a bundle of rational and irrational motives that operate without our conscious knowledge and therefore are vulnerable to unconscious manipulation. Uncle Freud and nephew Bernays knew that, and generations of research psychologists have since confirmed it time and again, by showing how our decisions are influenced by the slightest changes in mood, setting, or unconscious cues as manipulated by the experimenter. The newly understood fact is that we are also biological "works in progress," even into our later years. Our brains, and hence personalities, decision making capacities, and values, are subject to extensive and continued neural rewiring over time. We are not just what we eat. We are also what we see and hear, since these literally change our brains, minds, and future judgments.

This constant reshaping of our brains, and our deep vulnerability to manipulation, require us to understand just how strange our advertising-laden economy really is. We've learned more and more that human beings are vulnerable to manipulation, yet we've also fostered a vast advertising and PR industry designed to prey on those weaknesses. The neuroscientists give us four reasons why advertising and mass consumerism should concern us even more than we might suppose.

First, our brains are malleable. Scientists use the term "neuroplasticity" to describe the fact that our brains are continually being rewired depending on the kinds of stimuli that we receive and the ways that we choose to behave. Meditation can help us gain calm. TV watching can reduce that sense of calm, especially among young children. Second, animal behaviorists emphasize the importance of "super-normal stimuli," meaning simple cues of color, sexual stimulation, or some other sensory information that can trigger highly complex behavior. Harvard psychologist Deirdre Barrett has convincingly extrapolated from the remarkable animal findings to argue that humans too are biologically configured to respond powerfully to particular cues.[8] The food industry entices us with the fatty foods and refined sugars that we naturally crave. Marketers easily lure us into buying cars, beer, and cigarettes through the sexually provocative poses of models selling these products. These are well-known lures, of course, but we've opened the floodgates through the ubiquity of advertising. Third, our vulnerability to addiction makes it easy for the marketers to hook young children into a lifetime of consumption and overconsumption. We are a society of pushers, not the drug gangs, but many of the biggest names in advertising. Fourth, many of our decisions are unconsciously made. We are often not even aware of why we've made a purchase or latched on to a particular product. The brain is easily "primed" by sights, smells, and stimuli of which we are not even aware, inducing us to buy products for reasons that are even obscure to the purchaser.

When I reflected on such issues twenty or more years ago, I regarded the problems of consumer addictions and "irrationalities" to be serious social issues but not serious macroeconomic issues. Addictions were for social workers and drug enforcement officials to deal with. Macroeconomics, I reasoned, is about the preponderance of behavior, not about the oddities and painful exceptions. I no longer accept that division of labor between psychology and economics. Within one generation, Americans have displayed a shocking array of addictive behaviors (smoking, overeating, TV watching, gambling, shopping, borrowing, and much more) and loss of self-control. These unhealthy behaviors surely have reached a macroeconomic scale and raise deep questions about our well-being in an era of relentless advertising and excess. Have we actually created a world that is programmed to undermine our very balance as individuals? Our society is addicted to overconsumption and household debt. It is addicted to a miserable diet that has led to a staggering 33 percent obesity rate. It is addicted to television itself, with individuals spending four to six hours per day in front of the tube and indications that they are unhappy as a result.

The Marriage of Mass Media and Hypercommercialism

The astounding fact of America's media system is that it has become a juggernaut out of social control, one that is partly responsible for carrying America to the abyss. The media juggernaut has taken over our living rooms, our national politics, even the battlefields. It is yet another of the runaway factors that are destabilizing American society. The media, major corporate interests, and politicians now constitute a seamless web of interconnections and power designed to perpetuate itself through the relentless manufacture of illusion. The media peddle illusions, and those illusions lead to even more addictive behaviors, including the fixation on the media itself.

Many observers have documented how America took a distinctive course in the TV age, thereby opening itself to maximum long-term vulnerability to the dark arts of propaganda, both corporate and official. Most consequentially, at the start of the TV era the government decided to hand the TV networks almost entirely to the private sector, based on an advertising-led model of broadcasting. In 1934, Congress rejected the alternative approach of a mixed public-private system when it passed the Communications Act of 1934.

For several decades, the federal government, largely through the Federal Communications Commission (FCC), maintained at least some regulatory control on private broadcasters to enforce some public-spiritedness and competition.[9] As in so much of American society, however, the corporate-owned media escaped the grasp of public regulation during the 1980s and 1990s, so that by the beginning of the twenty-first century, the media stood unchallenged by government and indeed had become a full-fledged propaganda partner with Washington.

One key stop on the journey of the private sector's complete takeover of the airwaves came in 1996, with the Telecommunications Act signed into law by President Clinton. Yet again, Clinton proved that corporate empowerment is bipartisan, without much difference between the Republicans and the Democrats. The new act effectively undid the remaining barriers to media concentration in TV and radio and unleashed a wave of corporate mergers, creating the mega–media companies. As of today, the media giants include Disney, Comcast, Westinghouse, Viacom, Time Warner, and News Corporation.

The media and the politicians now live in splendid symbiosis. The airwaves promote corporate products, consumer values, and the careers of friendly politicians. The politicians promote media deregulation, low taxes, and freedom from scrutiny of performance and public service.

Measuring Hypercommercialization

Though I can't prove that America's mass-media culture, ubiquitous advertising, and long hours of daily TV watching are the fundamental causes of its tendency to let markets run rampant over
social values, I can show that America represents the unhappy extreme of commercialism among the leading economies. To do this,
I have created a Commercialization Index (CI) that aims to measure the degree to which each national economy is oriented toward
private consumption and impatience rather than collective (public)
consumption and regard for the future. My assumption is that the
United States and other heavy-TV-watching societies will score high
on the CI and that a high CI score will be associated with several of
the adverse conditions plaguing American society.

I include six items in the Commercialization Index, each item
designed to measure a distinct aspect of the public-private or
current-future dimensions of social choice. In each case a higher
score signifies a higher degree of commercialization:

- The national consumption rate (private plus government consumption as a share of GDP)
- The average hours worked per year by a full-time employee (low
  leisure time, high orientation to market consumption)
- The national nonvoting rate (lack of public participation)
- Private health care spending as a percentage of total national
  health care spending (health care as a private good rather than
  a public good)
- Private education spending as a percentage of total national
  education spending (education as a private good rather than a
  public good)
- Private consumption spending as a percentage of national (private plus public) consumption (private consumption as the
  dominant form of consumption)

To keep things simple, each of these measures is scaled from 0 to 1, with 1 being the most commercially oriented score. Each country's overall Commercialization Index score is calculated as the simple average of the six component measures. The overall ranking and the six components are shown in Table 8.1.

The United States is by far the most commercialized country in the sample, followed by Switzerland. America ranks first in one of the six variables (the share of private health care spending) and second in three of the remaining five. Generally, the rankings on the various components of the index are highly correlated across the countries. Australia, Canada, New Zealand, the United Kingdom, and the United States tend to rank high on most dimensions of commercialization. The Scandinavian social democracies—Denmark, Norway, and Sweden—tend to rank low on all dimensions.

Highly commercialized societies like America are more likely to leave the poor behind. A high CI score is strongly associated with a high national poverty rate (measured by the OECD as the share of households below 50 percent of the median income), as we see in Figure 8.3. A high CI is also associated with a low level of development aid to poor countries, measured by official development assis-

Figure 8.3: Relationship Between Commercialization Index and National Poverty Rate

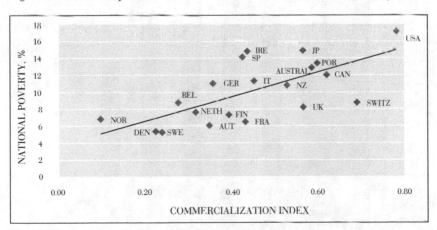

Source: Data from the RTL Group and OECD.

Table 8.1: Commercialization Index

Country	CI Score	National Consumption Rate	Average Annual Hours Worked	National Nonvoting Rate as % of Total	Private Consumption Spending as % of Total	Private Health Care Spending as % of Total	Private Education Spending as % of Total
United States	0.90 (1)	88% (3)	1,681 (8)	58% (2)	79% (2)	54% (1)	32% (2)
Australia	0.56	76%	1,713	17%	76%	33%	28%
Austria	0.35	74%	1,581	24%	71%	23%	11%
Belgium	0.26	76%	1,550	14%	66%	27%	6%
Canada	0.60	76%	1,699	46%	71%	30%	26%
Denmark	0.20	78%	1,536	17%	61%	16%	8%
Finland	0.39	82%	1,697	32%	65%	26%	3%
France	0.42	81%	1,554	45%	69%	22%	9%
Germany	0.35	78%	1,419	28%	73%	23%	15%
Ireland	0.45	89%	1,584	31%	72%	23%	6%
Italy	0.49	84%	1,773	21%	74%	23%	8%

Japan	0.55	73%	1,714	33%	74%	18%	33%
Netherlands	0.28	78%	1,378	23%	61%	38%	16%
New Zealand	0.51	84%	1,729	22%	73%	20%	20%
Norway	0.06	65%	1,403	23%	63%	16%	2%
Portugal	0.57	91%	1,719	33%	74%	29%	8%
Spain	0.43	80%	1,653	23%	71%	28%	11%
Sweden	0.21	77%	1,602	19%	62%	18%	3%
Switzerland	0.70	69%	1,640	60%	81%	41%	NA
United Kingdom	0.55	85%	1,646	42%	71%	17%	25%

Source: OECD Statistical Databases and International Institute for Democracy and Electoral Assistance (IDEA).
Note: U.S. rankings are in parentheses.

tance as a share of GDP. The high-CI countries are also those with the largest share of household income accruing to the richest 1 percent of households. It's fair to say that in the highly commercialized economies, market values trump social values: the poor, both those at home and abroad, are more or less forgotten. I would surmise that in such societies, individuals are so overwhelmed by market values (bargaining, self-interest, competition) that they lose touch with other values (compassion, trust, honesty).

Whatever the cause, the United States is privately rich but socially poor. It caters to the pursuit of wealth but pays scant attention to those left behind. And though American culture emphasizes individualism and the pursuit of individual wealth perhaps more than any other society, that focus does not lead to greater happiness.

Of course such worries about hypercommercialism are not new. Karl Marx famously critiqued the "commodifaction" of social life from the perspective of the left. Yet trenchant criticism of excessive consumerism has also come from the religious and moral right. The famous German free-market thinker Wilhelm Röpke launched a famous and powerful critique against soulless advertising and mass consumerism in his book *A Humane Economy* in the middle of the twentieth century. Röpke observed that advertising "separates our era from all earlier ones as little else does, so much so that we might well call our century the age of advertising."[10]

Our great sociologists and economists also remind us that it's not only mass society that has succumbed to mass commercialization, but also the rich. Early modern capitalism was built not on the goal of luxurious consumption by the rich, but rather on the virtue of prudent consumption and high saving by the entrepreneur. The German sociologist Max Weber described the highest ethic of early capitalism to be "the earning of more and more money, combined with the strict avoidance of all spontaneous enjoyment of life," as befitting the Protestant values of the time.[11] The British economist John Maynard Keynes made a similar observation about the moral underpinnings of British capitalism in the late nineteenth century. The point, he wrote, was that late-nineteenth-century society tolerated the rich because they lived properly and correctly, by accumulating vast wealth but not consuming it. As Keynes put it:

> Herein lay, in fact, the main justification of the capitalist system. If the rich had spent their new wealth on their own enjoyments, the world would long ago have found such a régime intolerable. But like bees they saved and accumulated, not less to the advantage of the whole community because they themselves held narrower ends in prospect. . . . The capitalist classes were allowed to call the best part of the cake theirs and were theoretically free to consume it, on the tacit underlying condition that they consumed very little of it in practice. The duty of "saving" became nine-tenths of virtue and the growth of the cake the object of true religion.[12]

As another example, America's greatest late-nineteenth-century capitalist, steel man Andrew Carnegie, similarly distinguished between the worthy calling of making money and the proper use of the wealth once made. In his famous and enormously influential "The Gospel of Wealth," Carnegie defined what he called the "duty of the man of wealth":

> To set an example of modest, unostentatious living, shunning display or extravagance; to provide moderately for the legitimate wants of those dependent on him; and, after doing so, to consider all surplus revenues which come to him simply as trust funds, which he is called upon to administer, and strictly bound as a matter of duty to administer in the manner which, in his judgment, is best calculated to produce the most beneficial results for the community—the man of wealth thus becoming the mere trustee and agent for his poor brethren,

bringing to their service his superior wisdom, experience, and ability to administer, doing for them better than they would or could do for themselves.[13]

In this way, wrote Carnegie, the wealth of the capitalists would be deployed for the benefit of the entire community. Carnegie established several major philanthropic institutions in the United States and Europe, such as the Carnegie Endowment, the Carnegie Institute of Technology (now Carnegie Mellon University), and numerous Carnegie libraries around the United States. He in turn inspired John D. Rockefeller to establish the Rockefeller Foundation, perhaps the most successful and influential philanthropic effort in modern history, as it contributed to fundamental advances in the fight against poverty, hunger, and disease, and to countless breakthroughs in the sciences and public administration. Carnegie's social gospel lives on today in the philanthropic efforts of Bill Gates, Warren Buffett, George Soros, Ted Turner, Bill Gross, and other wealthy Americans who are giving away vast sums in the pursuit of poverty eradication, public education, disease control, and strengthening of democratic institutions. Gates and Buffett have also actively encouraged dozens of their fellow billionaires to commit to donating at least half of their wealth in philanthropic efforts.

What does not live on, however, is the original moral underpinning of capitalism. Today's great wealth holders, with the notable exception of the few leading corporate philanthropists, are much better known for their profligacy than their asceticism. Birthday parties, weddings, anniversaries are celebrated with high profile, multimillion-dollar bashes that are designed for the paparazzi and public titillation in service of their self-gratification. And the public duly obliges by keeping their eyes firmly fixed on the round-the-clock cable coverage. Hypercommercialism has reached the highest levels of the society, and has helped blind the super-rich to the dire needs of the rest of society.

Advertising in the Facebook Age

The TV age is quickly becoming the broadband age, when information is carried into our lives through a dizzying array of Internet-linked devices. A great debate has begun: what will the Internet and always-on connectivity mean for our society?

When the Internet was first invented and the World Wide Web became a new vehicle for mass communication and diffusion of information, many pioneers of the new technology believed that it would be profoundly democratizing and anticommercial in its effects. Access would be free or nearly so, and everybody's voice could contribute equally to the new global debate and discussion. The old monopolies of information would quickly be dissipated, and a new global cooperation would ensue.

Those hopes, alas, are quickly fading. The Internet has apparently fragmented, rather than unified, the public square. Many observers argue convincingly that the logic of largely self-contained groups organized on the Internet around shared beliefs is leading to further polarization and increasingly aggressive surliness in the public debate.

As for commercialization, the Internet offers advertisers and marketers the most powerful tool yet for directing their messaging to target groups. By monitoring our online behavior—the websites we visit, the purchases we make, the individuals we "friend" on social networks—advertisers have new tools to spread messages and to use social relations to track customer behavior, create fads, and foment peer pressure. Major websites such as Google and Facebook have been only too ready to turn the virtual communities they assemble over to the marketing firms. Remarkably, Google topped $25 billion in advertising revenue in 2010, and Facebook hit $1.86 billion. The not-so-hidden persuaders have been invited even more personally into our lives and vulnerabilities through the wonders of the new social networks.[14]

Each day we are discovering new risks to privacy and to Web-empowered marketing, which is not surprising given the fact that some businesses will cross any line in the quest for profit. The latest development is a host of companies that create detailed dossiers on Web users, including their names, demographic information, addresses, financial information, buying patterns, social networks, political affiliations, and much more. This information is collected by way of small computer codes, "cookies" or "Web bugs," that the firms secretly insert into personal computers when certain websites are visited or enabled, thereby allowing the firms to monitor the Internet use of the individuals and, in a Web-based network with co-operating firms, to piece together highly detailed and intrusive data sets about millions of individuals. These data sets are then sold commercially or to political campaigns and parties. According to a report in *The Wall Street Journal,* one of these companies, RapLeaf, had "indexed more than 600 million unique email addresses . . . and was adding more at a rate of 35 million per month."[15]

The evidence regarding the Internet and our psyches is even harsher. For a public already spinning from relentless TV, DVDs, movies on demand, MP3 players, and ever-smarter phones, the Internet seems to be rewiring not only our social networks but our neural networks as well. The latest concern of neuroscientists is that Internet browsing may undermine our long-term concentration in favor of our short-term responsiveness to stimuli. We don't read on the Internet so much as we scan the screen. Surfing is different from reading, both emotionally and cognitively. We can retrieve facts much faster, but we retain them for less time.

Psychologists and sociologists will no doubt increase their focus on our sensory overload in general. Studies of information transmission in our digital age show the remarkable increase in overall information flows per person but don't yet reveal the consequences to our mental well-being and still less for our society. A remarkable study by the Global Information Industry Center documents the startling increases in information flows and the changes in composition as well.[16] In 2009, the average American consumed "information" for around 11.4 hours per day, up from 7.4 hours per day in 1980 and no doubt still less in earlier years. These information flows come in a remarkable range of delivery systems: television (including network, satellite, cable, DVD, mobile, and other), print (books, magazines, and newspapers), radio, telephones (fixed and mobile), movies, recorded music, and computers (including games, handheld devices, Internet, e-mail, and offline programs).

The study measured the flow of information in three ways: by hours spent receiving the information, by number of words transmitted, and by number of gigabytes of information transmitted. The last puts a premium on video and computer games. The information per American for 2009, in total and as shares of the respective categories, is shown in Table 8.2. Notice that TV still dominates in terms of hours spent (4.91 per day) and words received (44,850 per day). TV is second in terms of gigabytes behind video games. I say "still" because of the evidence that TV use is now apparently declining among younger people in favor of other forms of information flows such as computers, mobile phones, and e-readers. Electronic screens are ubiquitous and in round-the-clock use, but now in a widening array of devices.

Table 8.2: The Daily Flow of Information, 2009

	Hours per Day	Percentage of Total	Words Consumed	Percentage of Total
Television	4.91	41.6	44,850	44.8
Radio	2.22	18.8	10,600	10.6
Telephone	0.73	6.2	5,240	5.2
Print	0.6	5.1	8,610	8.6
Computer	1.93	16.4	26,970	27.0
Computer games	0.93	7.9	2,440	2.4
Movies	0.03	0.2	200	0.2
Recorded Music	0.45	3.8	1,110	1.1

Source: Data from Global Information Industry Center (2009).

An Epidemic of Ignorance

Print media continues its long-term decline. In 1960, print delivered an estimated 26 percent of words transmitted. By 2008, that had declined to 9 percent. While TV absorbed 42 percent of the daily hours the average American spends receiving information, print media accounted for a meager 5 percent. Reading for fun is a disappearing practice among the young, and purchases of books went into a steep decline a decade ago. As Americans stop reading, ignorance of basic facts, especially scientific facts about such politically charged issues as climate change, has soared. Reading proficiency is also plummeting.[17]

It would be a profound irony if the new "information age" in fact coincides with the collapse of the public's basic knowledge regarding key issues that we confront both as individuals and as citizens. It's far too early to tell whether the Internet and other connected devices will end up leaving society dumber or better informed. Will video games and online streaming of entertainment end up crowding out more meaningful reading and gathering of information? These risks seem real, at least according to the flood of recent books such as *The Dumbest Generation, Idiot America, The Age of American Unreason,* and *Just How Stupid Are We?*

Recent polling data and academic studies do suggest that Americans lack basic shared factual knowledge. As one author recently put it, "The insulated mindset of individuals who know precious little history and civics and never read a book or visit a museum is fast becoming a common, shame-free condition."[18] If American high school test scores continue to rank poorly relative to other countries, so, too, will our economic prosperity, sense of economic security, and place in the world. Even more ominously, our capacity as citizens will collapse if we lack the shared knowledge to take on challenges such as balancing the federal budget and responding to human-induced climate change.

The Pew Research Center occasionally surveys the basic knowl-

edge of the American public in its News IQ Quiz.[19] At the end of
2010, only 15 percent could identify the prime minister of the
United Kingdom and only 38 percent could choose the incoming
U.S. House speaker from a list of four names. Slightly under half (46
percent) knew that the Republicans would control the lower house
of Congress but not the Senate. And 39 percent correctly picked
out defense as the largest budget item in a list that included Social
Security, interest on the debt, and Medicare. None of these gaps in
knowledge is a cardinal sin. As Pew put it, "the public knows basic
facts about politics, economics, but struggles with specifics." But
when the country must grapple with complex choices about taxes,
spending, military outlays, and the rest, the lack of basic knowledge
becomes dangerous. A poorly informed public is much more easily
swayed by propaganda and much less able to resist the dark maneu-
vers of the special-interest groups that pull the strings in Washington.

Reclaiming Our Mental Balance

In sum, America has become a media-saturated society, the first in
history. Our days are filled with on-screen work; then we spend hours
at home each day glued to TV sets, DVD players, video games, Internet chat rooms, and Facebook pages, with the flood of electronic
media trumping every other activity and form of social interaction.
We are a technology-rich, advertising-fed, knowledge-poor society.
The media networks and social networking outlets are owned and
operated by enormous business conglomerates that are ever more
closely aligned with the political system. The economic self-interest
of these corporate giants, and the owners behind them, ensures a relentless stream of corporate messages, personalized advertisements,
and deliberate scientific misinformation on subjects such as climate
change.

The logic of profit maximization, combined with unprecedented breakthroughs in information and communications technology, has led to an economy of distraction the likes of which the world has never before seen. The end result is a society of consumer addictions, personal anxieties, growing loneliness in the midst of electronic social networks, and financial distress. This is true of the super-rich as well as the rest of society.

Despite great American affluence, our decisions as consumers of goods, services, and bytes are not delivering the well-being and peace of mind we crave. Americans urgently need to regain our footing. The starting point is that we must recognize the snares that the economy has set for our own psyches. We must begin by reclaiming our balance as individuals, consumers, citizens, and members of society. Let us begin on that task in the next chapter.

PART II

The Path to Prosperity

CHAPTER 9.

The Mindful Society

This chapter and the ones that follow propose some workable steps toward a new American economy, a healthier society, and a more ethical basis for the study and practice of economics itself. These steps start from a simple premise: that the problems of America begin at home, with the choices we are making as individuals. Through clearer thinking, we can become more effective both as individuals and as citizens, reclaiming power from the corporations. The American economy itself continues to be productive and technologically dynamic. The problem is not the breakdown of productivity but the way we are living with that productivity. The relentless drumbeat of consumerism into every corner of our lives has led to extreme shortsightedness, consumer addictions, and the shriveling of compassion. When we are distracted, we allow the lobbyists to run away with power that rightfully belongs to the citizenry. As individuals, we need to regain the balance of our own lives between work and leisure, saving and consumption, self-interest and compassion, individualism and citizenship. As a society, we need to establish the right relationship of markets, politics, and civil society to address the complex challenges of the twenty-first century.

The future belongs not to the Tea Party but to America's youth, who are the most progressive and diverse part of American society today. The change will start mainly with the so-called Millennial Generation, those between the ages of eighteen and twenty-nine in 2010, who are socially connected, Internet-savvy, and searching for a new mode of social involvement and political engagement. Obama was to be their man, but unless he dramatically alters course, he seems more likely to be a transitional figure than a transformative one.

We need deeper changes than those on offer today, changes that restore our personal balance and the foundations of our trust in society. We need a *mindful society,* in which we once again take seriously our own well-being, our relations with others, and the operation of our politics.

The Middle Path

Two of the greatest ethicists in human history, Buddha in the East and Aristotle in the West, hit upon a remarkably similar prescription for the long-term happiness of humanity. "The Middle Path," said Buddha in the fifth century B.C., would keep humanity balanced between the false allures of asceticism on the one side and pleasure seeking on the other. Two centuries later and half a world away, Aristotle gave his fellow Greeks a similar message, that "moderation in all things" was the key to *eudemonia,* or human fulfillment. Aristotle, like Buddha, sought a path between two more extreme views of his day: the Stoics on one side and the Epicureans on the other.

The essential teaching of both Buddha and Aristotle is that the path of moderation is the key to fulfillment but is hard won and must be pursued through lifelong diligence, training, and reflection. There is nothing simple about moderation: the snares and distractions that lead us to extremes are everywhere. It is easy to become addicted to hyperconsumerism, the search for sensory pleasures, and the indulgence of self-interest, leading to a brief high but long-term unhappiness. It is easy to adopt a self-defeating philosophy of disregard for others. The escape path of asceticism or isolation from society is no more satisfying. The solution is a middle path, built on the hard work of self-knowledge. Neither Buddha nor Aristotle had illusions about the ease of this middle course. As Aristotle said, "I count him braver who overcomes his desires than him who conquers his enemies; for the hardest victory is over self."[1]

Ancient ethics, therefore, begins with a sense of fragility—of our psyches and our search for happiness. Each of us is thrust into a world of temptation, desire, and illusion, and we must find a lifelong path in the midst of these allures and traps. All of these insights were already necessary two millennia before TV and Mr. Bernays's powerful methods of propaganda. How much more vital these messages are today, when much of the economy is organized precisely to set those traps.

The middle path of Buddha and Aristotle is currently challenged by the crude libertarianism of the free-market Right, which holds that the freedom of the individual is the only valid aim of ethics and government. In this crude view, individuals know what is best for themselves and should be left alone, untaxed by the state and unbothered by ethical responsibilities toward others, as long as they don't cause direct harm to others. These ideas are expressed by the Tea Party movement and by many of America's richest citizens, who would absolve themselves of any ethical responsibility toward the rest of society.

There are many errors in libertarian philosophy, but the biggest of all is its starting point: that individuals can truly find happiness by being left alone, unburdened by ethical or political responsibilities to others. Buddha and Aristotle knew better. Without accepting social and political responsibilities, the individual cannot actually find fulfillment. Happiness arises not only through the individual's relationship with his wealth, as some economists simplistically assume, but through his relations with others. A society of compassion, mutual help, and collective decision making is not good just for the poor, who may receive help, but also for the rich, who may give it.

Politics provides an integral part of each individual's sense of purpose. Remove the role of government, and the individual loses his bearings. There can be no lasting happiness in anarchy. Take away an individual's moral responsibility, and he or she descends into loneliness and disorientation. Compassion, cooperation, and altruism are essential to human well-being. Being a responsible member of political society—by asking not what your country can do for you but what you can do for your country—should therefore not be viewed as a coerced concession of the individual toward society, but as an essential way in which each individual finds personal fulfillment. Our well-being depends fundamentally on our recognizing and nurturing our basic duality: as individuals, with distinctive tastes and aspirations, and as members of a society, with responsibilities to and values shared with others.

America still has time to rescue itself, so great are its resources—human, technological, and natural. It has been running down its wealth, but the wealth remains very high, enough to sustain us with a very high quality of life as we prepare for the future, if we take care to look ahead collectively. For that, however, we will need to escape from the compulsions of the present. First, we will need to break free from the relentless and mindless propagandizing of the media, where the main message is that we should concentrate on shopping and our quest for higher personal income.

We will need, in short, to achieve a new *mindfulness* regarding our needs as individuals and as a society, to find a more solid path to well-being. Mindfulness, taught Buddha, is one of the eight steps on the way to self-awakening. It means an alertness and quiet contemplation of our circumstances, putting aside greed and distress. Through sustained effort, mindfulness leads to insight and to an escape from our useless cravings.

That mindfulness should start with each of us making the effort to regain control of our personal judgments as individuals who must balance consumption and saving, work and leisure, individualism and membership in society. Our mindfulness should then extend to a more considered understanding of our social relationships and responsibilities: as workers, citizens, and members of the community. Mindfulness, I would suggest, is crucial in eight dimensions of our lives:

- *Mindfulness of self:* personal moderation to escape mass consumerism
- *Mindfulness of work:* the balancing of work and leisure
- *Mindfulness of knowledge:* the cultivation of education
- *Mindfulness of others:* the exercise of compassion and cooperation
- *Mindfulness of nature:* the conservation of the world's ecosystems
- *Mindfulness of the future:* the responsibility to save for the future
- *Mindfulness of politics:* the cultivation of public deliberation and shared values for collective action through political institutions
- *Mindfulness of the world:* the acceptance of diversity as a path to peace

Beyond the Craving for Wealth

Mindfulness of self means that we once again take time to understand the sources of our own happiness. Americans today routinely assume that higher take-home pay and consumption of goods are the keys to happiness and therefore that tax cuts are the quintessence of well-being. Yet experience and reflection tell us something very different. The greatest benefits of higher income accrue to the poorest households, to enable them to meet their unmet basic needs. For the middle class and especially for the rich, many factors other than income are far more important for personal happiness. Good governance, more trust in the community, a happier married life, more time for friends and colleagues, and meaningful and secure work all rank as far more important than another few percent of personal income. Yet many of these sources of long-term happiness can be achieved only through *collective action*, including politics, not through individual decision making in the marketplace. Even more telling, many of the uses of personal income today—for television viewing, fast foods, cigarettes, gambling, long commutes, and the like—are behaviors that often bring "buyer's remorse" (a regret about the level of consumption and a desire to cut back) rather than true satisfaction.

There is also a huge difference between having more income (or wealth) and relentlessly craving more income. More income—if properly deployed—can be a source of personal happiness and security, but devoting one's energies in a narrow-minded way to gaining it can be a source of endless frustration and unhappiness. The difference could not be more important. Having more income gives a mild, and mostly temporary, boost to satisfaction, holding other things constant. Aggressively orienting one's life toward becoming rich, however, leads to prolonged and measurable unhappiness. Individuals with a high "materialist" orientation, for whom earning and spending money are a central aim of life, are systematically far less happy and secure than nonmaterialists.

The good news is that only a modest level of income is needed to meet basic needs. Once a society achieves that level of income across the society, there is the opportunity to refocus many of the society's energies toward sources of well-being that can't be reached by the market alone. Consider life expectancy, a key measure of well-being. By the time a society reaches a per capita income of around $3,000, life expectancy is generally 70 years or higher (compared with 78.3 years in the United States in 2009). Many countries much poorer than the United States either exceed or are very close to the U.S. life expectancy. Chile, for example, with a GDP per capita of $9,400 in 2009, roughly one-fifth of America's at $46,400, has a life expectancy of 78.7 years, slightly higher than in the United States. Costa

Rica, Greece, South Korea, and Portugal are considerably poorer than the United States in per capita GDP, but have life expectancies that are higher.[2]

Similarly, though the United States is one of the world's richest economies by per capita income, it ranks only around seventeenth in reported life satisfaction. It is superseded not only by the likely candidates of Finland, Norway, and Sweden, which all rank above the United States (as we saw in chapter 2) but also by less likely candidates such as Costa Rica and the Dominican Republic. Indeed, one might surmise that it is health and longevity rather than income that give the biggest boost to reported life satisfaction. Since good health and longevity can be achieved at per capita income levels well below those of the United States, so too can life satisfaction. One marketing expert put it this way, with only slight exaggeration:

Basic survival goods are cheap, whereas narcissistic self-stimulation and social-display products are expensive. Living doesn't cost much, but showing off does.[3]

For affluent societies, therefore, our personal happiness depends not so much on our income as on our *attitude toward income and how we use it*, both as individuals and collectively. If our material desires are modest and realistic and our consumption behavior is attentive to our deeper needs, our happiness is raised. Yet, as we saw in the preceding chapter, we are only partly aware of our own cravings and desires. With patience and training, individuals can overcome their blind cravings and addictions and achieve long-term satisfaction. The challenge of beating these addictions, however, is greater than in the past. Not only must we control our inherent cravings, we must also resist the round-the-clock coaxing by advertisers and hucksters whose job is to promote still more temptations and desires.

There are three general approaches to restoring mindfulness of self in our confused and noisy times. The first can be called cognitive: we need to study the sources of our own happiness and that of others. When we do, we learn that income plays a much less important role than we might imagine. We learn to enrich our lives far more by the quality of our personal and work relations and our generosity to others. Giving up some income through taxation in order to achieve shared social objectives, for example, makes ample sense when the limited role of personal wealth in happiness is kept in perspective. Through cognitive training, we can also cultivate the sense of a lifelong plan, one that depends on moderation in our consumer habits and consistency in saving for the future. Financial advisers and planning tools can help us balance consumption and saving over the life cycle, to ensure enough to support our children through school and ourselves into retirement years.

Research psychologists are also offering interesting cognitive guidance for those with adequate incomes but not adequate personal well-being. A recent "how-to-spend-it" guide by the Harvard psychologist Daniel Gilbert and his colleagues suggests eight specific principles to derive more happiness from income.[4] First, buy experiences instead of things, since experiences (vacations, trips to the museum, concerts, dining out) offer long memories to savor. Second, and crucially, use our incomes to help others instead of ourselves, because as hypersocial animals, "almost anything we do to improve our connections with others tends to improve our happiness as well."[5] Third, buy many small pleasures instead of a few big ones, in essence slowing down to smell the roses. Fourth, buy less overpriced insurance (such as product warranties), because we adjust much better to adverse shocks than we suppose. Fifth, pay now and consume later, rather than buying now on the credit card and paying later. The anticipation of a future purchase will give us anticipatory joy, which the authors call a source of "free" happiness. Impatient purchases, on the other hand, give us fleeting benefits and long-term debt. Sixth, be attentive to the details of a purchase, since they may disproportionately affect the happiness of the experience. Seventh, beware of too much comparison shopping, since it can focus our attention on unimportant distinctions. Eighth, listen to others about what can bring happiness. They can add new and useful perspectives.

The second approach might be called reflective or meditative. We are swept along today by the pseudo-urgency contrived by PR and advertising. The advertisements scream at us to buy; the presidential press conferences scream at us to invade. The mechanisms are the same: propaganda is deployed to overcome our real interests by appeals to emotion, notably to fear or sensory pleasure. Buddhists have long developed and deployed a special tool for rebalancing needs and daily sensations: meditation. This kind of mind training aims to unplug the mind from the daily sensory overload to regain a balance with longer-term needs. A related step today should be to unplug from the TV, the mobile phone, and the Facebook page. Systematically unplugging to gain quiet time and composure is a necessary step toward breaking free of many of today's most addictive compulsions.

The third approach is practice. As Aristotle rightly emphasized, we foster virtue by practicing virtue. Virtuous qualities are self-reinforcing, just as are harmful addictions. Acts of compassion awaken our desire to be even more compassionate. The cultivated practice of increased household saving, more leisure time, increased compassionate giving, and other acts of moderation build the courage, stamina, and pleasure of virtuous behavior.

The Importance of Meaningful Work

Nearly every study of happiness underscores the importance of meaningful work to personal well-being. Unemployment is the single largest factor in the public's unhappiness and political restiveness. Yet America's work environment has deteriorated notably over the past quarter century. Unemployment is high and stagnant; fear of job security is pervasive; corporate malfeasance is shockingly high; and the mismatch of jobs and skills is becoming a national crisis and scandal. We need a new mindfulness of work to recover our bearings.

There are vast improvements possible in the quality of working life for average workers. American workers have little job security, no guaranteed vacation time, little flexibility regarding working hours, meager union protection, and no representation on the corporate boards regarding compensation, employment, work sharing, training, and other issues. Libertarians claim that any further worker representation in company decision making would destroy U.S. competitiveness. Yet throughout northern Europe, workers participate in corporate deliberations and often decision making, without a loss of productivity and with more creative solutions on job flexibility and vacation time.

Many European governments have also pioneered and demonstrated the efficacy of "active labor market policies," which use government funding to match workers to jobs and to improve targeted job training for skills that are in demand. The U.S. labor market is increasingly mismatched. High-skilled workers find good jobs, while poorly skilled workers settle for poverty-level pay or fall out of the labor force altogether. The unemployment rate of college graduates is around 4 percent, but for workers with a high school education or less, the rate is three times that.[6] Yet the United States is pushing more and more poorly trained young workers into the labor market and doing little to help them stay in school.

Knowledge in an Age of Complexity

Mindfulness of knowledge is an approach to life and science exemplified by the Dalai Lama. He has written and said on numerous occasions that his own belief system, Tibetan Buddhism, must always keep an open door to science and that all Buddhist doctrines are open to revision based on new scientific evidence. He has taken this pledge much further by sponsoring and attending many sessions of Buddhist monks and Western scientists, and these meetings are leading to new insights regarding the interface of neuroscience and human happiness. That kind of openness to science is urgently needed in America today.

Most Americans have little idea about the scientific underpinnings of their lives and of public debates. When they type on a computer and transmit an e-mail, they don't realize that this seemingly straightforward action embodies some of the greatest scientific and technological discoveries of the twentieth century, including quantum mechanics, solid-state physics, optical physics, and computer science. Nor do they realize that the same laws of nature that underpin their e-mails underpin the science of climate change (e.g., the laws of quantum mechanics and optical physics that determine that carbon dioxide absorbs infrared radiation and thereby warms the planet). Nor do they realize that the basic physics of greenhouse gases, that carbon dioxide absorbs heat energy, predates the beginning of quantum mechanics by three-quarters of a century.[7]

The fact is that technology is so effective and well packaged in our phones, computers, seed varieties, and elsewhere that Americans can remain scientifically illiterate, and sometimes even averse to science, while at the same time benefiting from the very advances in science and technology that they blithely deny. Perhaps if we had to understand our technologies in order to use them, we'd have a remarkable spurt in scientific knowledge! Short of that, we must convince our fellow citizens that knowledge of science, and expert knowledge more generally, is vital to our well-being and even survival. Fortunately, Americans overwhelmingly appreciate science even when they don't cultivate their own knowledge of it. Eighty-four percent of Americans in a recent Pew survey "see science as having a mostly positive effect on society."[8]

The mindfulness of knowledge, therefore, properly begins with the recognition of the complexity of our economy and the need for scientific and technical expertise to help manage it. With 7 billion people trying to gain or to maintain a foothold of prosperity on a crowded planet already under unprecedented ecological stress, only advanced technologies—such as high-yield food production, renewable energy sources, sophisticated recycling of industrial materials, and efficiency of resource use—can hope to cope. Perhaps with several billion fewer people on the planet, we could contemplate a reversion to simpler lives. Such hopes today, however appealing they are to some people, are an anachronism. We will have to work hard and fast, and with the best technological tools, to achieve a planet that is prosperous, fair, and sustainable.

One well-meaning variant of antiscience is the illusion that we should revert to simpler ways: all-organic farming, local foods, and preindustrial knowledge. Yet these are illusions as great as denial of climate change. Preindustrial knowledge could support only around one in ten of the planet's residents today. At this point in human history, we have no choice but to try to live effectively with advanced technologies and to understand them, govern them democratically, and try to ensure that they serve broad human purposes.

Mindfulness of knowledge assuredly does not mean leaving all matters to the experts. Experts do agree on many things, but they have no special talent to make critical choices for all of us when it comes to social values, risks, and priorities. They have their own biases and special interests, and certainly their own blind spots as well. Mindfulness of knowledge therefore requires not only respect for expertise but also respect for democratic governance. We need to identify new ways for the public to share in complex problem solving, advised by experts but with the citizenry given a central role in shaping its own future.

The federal government has done a notably poor job in recent years of encouraging an informed debate about complex policy options. The health care debate during 2009–2010, for example, was held largely behind closed doors. Aside from a few designated experts who participated in the backroom policy deliberations, America's large and talented public health community mostly watched from the sidelines, as did the general public. Even for me, a professor in a major school of public health, the twists and turns of the deliberations were mostly baffling. So many powerful interests were at play that honest opinion was never spoken.

Reviving Compassion

The most difficult challenge in America today is mindfulness of others. The social safety net is frayed. The poor are suffering while the politicians discuss cutting the social safety net even further. Mindfulness of others is typically far stronger within an in-group than across racial or ethnic divides. Religious fundamentalists, for example, are more likely to harbor racist sentiments than are adherents to mainline religious denominations. Sociologists have long surmised that the greater racism among white evangelical Protestants reflects the stronger in-group bonds within fundamentalist religious families and communities.[9] The problem has been exacerbated by the residential stratification of the society. As we have noted, the nation has increasingly sorted its communities according to race, class, and even political ideology. Any kind of realistic understanding of the lives of "different" others has suffered accordingly.

I have already discussed the American "poverty trap." The result is a system of handouts, in which the poor are not helped enough to overcome poverty but just barely enough to survive in poverty. Thus, a society that disdains handouts ends up living by them rather than promoting true solutions with lasting value.

Instead of these endless meager handouts and ancillary high social costs (such as crime and punishment), a society truly mindful of others would address the needs of the poor in a way that attempts to end the poverty trap rather than simply to react to it. Yet in the short term that would require more public funding so that poor children of this generation could enjoy the benefits of a healthful diet, quality preschool and public school, and assured access to higher education enjoyed by the children of more affluent households. They would then be much more likely to grow up with higher skills and incomes, able to impart those same benefits to their own children. The vicious circle of intergenerational poverty could thereby be ended or at least greatly attenuated. The increased funding would prove to be temporary, mainly for this generation of poor children. Their children would not need the same degree of help. The long-term costs of ending poverty would almost surely be far lower than the status quo of simply "managing" poverty.

Mindfulness of others goes far beyond the question of alleviating poverty. Americans, we have seen, have retreated from the public square to the private space, often to watch TV for hours each day in individual bedrooms, not even as a family. We have become a country of strangers. And that estrangement is accompanied by falling trust. We are, in the words of the sociologist Bob Putnam, "hunkering down," especially in the major cities, marked by ethnic groups that don't know and don't trust one another.[10] Markets cannot overcome the distrust. Indeed, markets have facilitated the sorting. We need new social norms and more participatory political processes—such as greater democratic decision making within local communities—to get strangers talking and working together once again.

Addressing the Ecological Overshoot

Throughout human history, ethicists and gurus have appealed to humanity to respect nature as the irreplaceable font of life and indeed to understand human destiny as part of the web of life. When the vast majority of humanity lived as farmers, the vital role of nature was obvious. The harvesting of rainwater, the cleaning of irrigation canals, and the replenishment of soil nutrients all meant the difference between life and death. Natural climatic variations, such as prolonged droughts, often spelled the downfall of vast civilizations. Cities and entire regions had to be abandoned as life-giving waters dried up.

Our age is fundamentally different in two regards. First, today's global society is much further removed from nature than in the past. More than half of humanity now lives in cities, cut off from the daily realities of nature. This is especially true of the world's rich and powerful elites. Second, and even more dangerous, the human impacts on nature are for the first time in human history so great that they threaten the planet's core biophysical functioning. We have reached, or will soon reach, dangerous thresholds of human activity that fundamentally threaten life on the planet.

Mindfulness of nature, therefore, is not a tree hugger's plea but a practical imperative for twenty-first-century survival. Our peril is unprecedented, and human knowledge, values, and social institutions are far behind the curve. The global economy has suddenly become so large—$70 trillion a year and doubling in size roughly every twenty years—that the earth's air, water, land, and climate are all under threat. Our global response to date has been so obtuse, so absurd, so shortsighted that it almost seems that humanity has a death wish. This ignorance and shortsightedness can lead us to disaster. Of course, more than a death wish has been at play; the greed of powerful vested interests has been far more consequential than public confusion and shortsightedness.

The American performance in the face of ecological dangers is especially sobering. Americans impose the highest per capita impact on the planet yet show the least regard for their actions. The UN climate change treaty was signed and ratified by the United States in 1992, but the U.S. Senate has refused to take even one small step since then in limiting America's impact on climate. Many American senators are notoriously and aggressively ignorant or dismissive about the science, such as Oklahoma senator James Inhofe, who described human-induced climate change as the "greatest hoax ever perpetrated on the American people."[11] Politicians may be knowledgeable but still deeply cynical, playing for campaign contributions rather than the well-being of their grandchildren. They are ready to close their eyes to the looming disaster rather than earn their pay by explaining the tough realities and difficult policy choices to their constituents and to the Big Oil and Coal interests that fund their campaigns.

Unfortunately, the ecological threats continue to multiply, yet America is passive and resistant to action. Market forces, alas, will never solve these threats but only exacerbate them, until society, acting collectively at last, mindfully commits to creating a protective cordon around the threatened planet.

Responsibility Toward the Future

We can't address any of these problems if we can't think systematically about the future. And the future extends beyond the next election. The time horizon of public deliberation in America has shrunk to an unimaginably brief scale. When we need to build infrastructure, we aim for "shovel-ready" projects. Yet infrastructure worth building cannot be shovel-ready, a fact that Obama finally acknowledged in late 2010, after championing such projects in the 2009 stimulus package. Similarly, when we go to war, we aim for a short, brief "surge" to do the job. Repeatedly, and predictably, we fall woefully short of our objectives by choosing such short-term measures.

Mindfulness of the future therefore requires a special act of will: to take moral and practical ownership of the long-term consequences of our actions and to trace those consequences as carefully as possible into the far future. One great philosopher, Hans Jonas, has argued that we need a whole new ethic for the future, since never before has a human generation held in its hands the prosperity or ruin of the generations to come.[12] We profess our commitment to "sustainability," that is, to ensuring that the future will be able to meet its needs with the knowledge, capital, and environment that we bequeath it. Yet we really don't know what sustainability entails as we continue to plunder the planet for resources and simply hope for the best.

Taking moral responsibility for the future, accepting the reality that our actions today will determine the fates of generations yet to live, is daunting enough. Taking practical responsibility is equally difficult. We are causing enormous disruptions to the planet, but we lack the ability to trace the implications of those disruptions with precision or high scientific confidence. "Futurology" was once mocked as pseudoscience. Yet now we must make it operational, at least within the boundaries of our understanding and capacity.

The sad truth about Washington today is that we lack serious institutions charged with carrying out systematic planning for the future. The Office of Management and Budget prepares federal budget proposals one year at a time. The U.S. Treasury has little capacity or mandate to undertake long-term economic strategy. There is no coordinating agency for public investments by the federal government, nor is there a planning agency, as in many other countries. Each department or agency manages the specific investment projects under its particular jurisdiction. Issues such as energy, climate, water, demographic change, and so forth are either neglected or chopped up into the work of several different parts of the government.

The United States has several important agencies that undertake high-quality analysis of global trends. The National Intelligence Council has prepared important studies about the global challenges that will face the United States to the year 2025, most notably *Global Trends 2025: A Transformed World,* in 2008.[13] The findings were stark, suggesting that

- Climate change is likely to exacerbate resource scarcities.
- Demand is likely to outstrip easily available supplies (of strategic resources, including energy, food, and water) over the next decade or so.
- Lack of access to stable supplies of water is reaching critical proportions.

- The above trends suggest major discontinuities, shocks, and surprises.

What is most alarming, though, is that the government made such dire forecasts without recognizing the need for substantive policy responses. The alarm bells were sounded, but nobody responded and nobody seems to care.

This is an increasingly common pattern. Careful work is carried out by countless agencies and scientific academies, including the Institute of Medicine, the National Academy of Sciences, and the National Academy of Engineering, as well as leading research universities and think tanks. Yet the studies are ignored as soon as they are issued. Expertise is ignored, and the agenda in Washington remains dominated by what is convenient for politicians and the interest groups that support them. Difficult issues, such as climate change, water scarcity, and the transition of energy from fossil fuels, are kicked down the road to later years.

A new mindfulness of the future would take seriously the responsibility to link expert forecasts with appropriate policy actions. The government would be charged with regular reporting on the main future national challenges, with a time horizon of ten to twenty years. Such reports, by the National Intelligence Council or other agencies, would then be discussed and debated by the president and Congress. The White House would be required to issue a policy paper in response, and Congress would be charged with taking up that policy paper. A cycle of deliberation and policy design would ensue, and the future would be viewed with the moral and political seriousness that it requires.

Politics as Moral Responsibility

Mindfulness of politics is needed to provide an antidote to the dead end of corporatocracy. Americans must regain a proper understanding of the complementary and balanced roles of government and the marketplace. Though we support the crucial role of private businesses in the market economy, we must also insist that powerful corporations stop their relentless lobbying and propagandizing so that society can address serious problems on the basis of evidence, ethics, and long-term plans.

Our politics will work again when we overcome three crises. The first is ideological, the mistaken belief that free markets alone can solve our economic problems. Only markets and government operating as complementary pillars of the economy can produce the prosperity and fairness that we seek.

The second is institutional, involving the political role of the large corporations. We must maintain a judicious view. Our major corporations are invaluable to society as highly sophisticated organizations that manage large-scale, technologically advanced operations all over the world. Yet they have become a threat to society by using their lobbying power to dictate the terms of legislation and regulations. The license to operate as a company does not include a license to pollute our politics.

The third is moral, concerning the nature of modern democracy itself. In America today, there is little systematic public deliberation, and the public's views are rarely taken seriously in the political process. One key policy decision after another is adopted behind the backs of the public, often in direct contradiction to public opinion. We need to return to a spirit of true deliberation at all levels of society, one that reconceives politics as honest group problem solving, grounded in mutual respect and shared values.

Toward a Global Ethic

The eighth step toward economic recovery is mindfulness of the world, and most importantly the recognition that today's world is deeply interconnected economically and socially, albeit with considerable discord and confusion. No significant economic trend in any part of the world leaves the rest of the world untouched. The 2008 Wall Street crisis quickly percolated to all parts of the world economy. AIDS and the H1N1 flu virus similarly spread quickly around the world. An El Niño fluctuation in the Pacific climate causes weather disturbances worldwide, and these in turn trigger sharp movements in global food prices, such as the surge in grain prices in 2010.

Just as we've created a national economy riddled with advertising and propaganda that threaten our well-being, we've created a globalized economy that lacks the necessary cooperation to keep it stable and peaceful. The combination of unprecedented economic interconnectedness on the one hand, and the deep distrust across national and regional borders on the other, may be the defining paradox of the world economy today. Many of our major global problems—climate change, global population growth, mass migration, regional conflicts, and financial regulation—will require a much higher level of political cooperation among the world's major powers than we have so far achieved. Without sufficient trust across national borders, the growing global competition over increasingly scarce resources could easily turn into great power confrontations. Without trust, there is little chance for the coordinated global actions needed to fight poverty, hunger, and disease. Without trust, governments will be at the mercy of footloose global corporations that move their money to tax havens around the planet and pressure governments to lower tax rates, labor standards, environmental controls, and financial regulations. Mindfulness of the world therefore really amounts to a new readiness to adopt global norms of good behavior that aim to protect poor countries as well as the rich, weak countries as well as the powerful.

The great theologian Hans Küng has undertaken a profound effort during the past quarter century to identify a *global economic ethic* based on the world's leading religions. Küng found that diverse religious traditions share fundamental ethical standards regarding economic life and behavior, which can enable the world to identify and embrace a truly global economic ethic. According to Küng, the common thread of conviction is the Principle of Humanity: "Being human must be the ethical yardstick for all economic action."[14] The economy should fulfill the basic needs of human beings "so that they can live in dignity." From this basic humanistic principle, Küng identified several ethical themes with universal standing: the importance of respect and tolerance for others; the right to life and its development; sustainable treatment of the natural environment; the rule of law; distributive justice and solidarity; the essential values of truthfulness, honesty, and reliability; and the core value of mutual esteem.

Küng's findings, and their recent embrace by many other ethicists, are heartening. They show us the way to harness global diversity yet find common touchstones across what to some appear to be impenetrable divides. They give us the confidence to envision economics not only in technical terms but also as part of a global human framework guided by humane principles. The global market economy must remain guided by humane purposes and not be regarded as an end in itself.

Most important, the Principle of Humanity bids us to respect one another through a renewed and heightened appreciation of our common fate as human beings and our common hope for dignity, solidarity, and sustainability. Küng's studies of the world's religious traditions reaffirm the key point that what unites humanity is vastly more important than whatever might divide us. They also remind me of the eloquence of President John F. Kennedy in his remarkable search for peace in the year after the Cuban missile crisis, the final year of his life. Kennedy reminded us that

> Across the gulfs and barriers that now divide us, we must remember that there are no permanent enemies. Hostility today

is a fact, but it is not a ruling law. The supreme reality of our time is our indivisibility as children of God and our common vulnerability on this planet.[15]

How, then, to find the path to peace? Kennedy was ever pragmatic and idealistic at the same time:

So, let us not be blind to our differences—but let us also direct attention to our common interests and to means by which those differences can be resolved. And if we cannot end now our differences, at least we can help make the world safe for diversity. For, in the final analysis, our most basic common link is that we all inhabit this small planet. We all breathe the same air. We all cherish our children's future. And we are all mortal.[16]

Those words, and the powerful vision behind them, led to the signing of the Limited Nuclear Test Ban Treaty in the summer of 1963, which helped to pull the world from the nuclear abyss. Today's sources of tension—terrorism, instability, extreme poverty, climate change, hunger, and shifting global power—may be different from before, but the path to peace through mindfulness of the world, built on common interests and mutual respect, remains the same as in Kennedy's time.

Personal and Civic Virtue as an Approach to Life

The mindful society is not a specific plan but rather an approach to life and the economy. It calls on each of us to strive to be virtuous, both in our personal behavior (regarding saving, thrift, and control of our self-destructive cravings) and in our social behavior as citizens and members of powerful organizations, whether universities or businesses. Our current hyperconsumerism on a personal level and corporatocracy on a social level have carried us into a danger zone. We have become like the rats that press a lever for instant pleasure, courting exhaustion and ultimately starvation. We have created a nation of remarkable wealth and productivity, yet one that leaves its impoverished citizens in degrading life conditions and almost completely ignores the suffering of the world's poorest people. We have created a kind of mass addiction to consumerism, relentless advertising, insidious lobbying, and national politics gutted of serious public deliberation.

The mindful society, with its eight areas of mindfulness—toward self, work, knowledge, others, nature, the future, politics, and the world—aims to help us refashion our personal priorities as well as our social institutions, so that the economy can once again serve the ultimate purpose of human happiness. By itself, mindfulness will not end our self-destructive consumer addictions or the political bind of corporatocracy. But it will open the way to a reenergized, virtuous citizenry, one that is ready to rebuild American democracy and put it back into the hands of the people.

CHAPTER 10.

Prosperity Regained

The aim of this chapter and the next is to chart a path from here to 2020, one that restores hope, direction, and decency to American society. We are on the wrong track, Americans shout in unison. Then let us steer back to the right track and show clearly how we can restore prosperity and purpose. The starting point should be clearer goals for society and pragmatic ways to achieve them.

Setting Goals

In Table 10.1, I suggest a set of economic goals and timelines. The first goal addresses the current jobs crisis. Today's 9 percent unemployment rate should be 5 percent by mid-decade and sustained at that lower level until 2020. There will be many policies to help get us there, involving labor market reforms, greater leisure time, and a long-term boost to worker skills. We'll look at those alternatives in a moment.

The second goal, which is closely related, is to address the education crisis. By 2020, at least 50 percent of those aged twenty-five to twenty-nine should hold a bachelor's degree or higher, up from 31 percent in 2009.[1] That is the sine qua non for competing suc-

Table 10.1: Goals and Targets, 2011–2020

Goal 1. Raise Employment and the Quality of Work Life

- Reduce unemployment to 5 percent by 2015.
- Improve governance of CEO compensation.
- Guarantee paid maternity and paternity leave in all firms of a hundred employees or above.

Goal 2. Improve the Quality of and Access to Education

- Raise the share of twenty-five- to twenty-nine-year-olds with a bachelor's degree to 50 percent by 2020.
- Raise the U.S. ranking in global test scores to within the top five in all categories: reading, science, and mathematics.

Goal 3. Reduce Poverty

- Cut the national poverty rate to 7 percent by 2020, half of the 2010 rate.
- Reduce the share of America's children growing up in poverty to below 10 percent by 2020.

Goal 4. Avoid Environmental Catastrophe

- Reduce America's greenhouse gas emissions from 2005 to 2020 by at least 17 percent.
- Ensure that low-carbon energy supplies account for at least 30 percent of U.S. power generation by 2020 and 40 percent by 2030.
- Have 5 million electric vehicles on the road by 2020.

Goal 5. Balance the Federal Budget

- Reduce the budget deficit to below 2 percent of GDP by 2015.
- Eliminate the budget deficit by 2020.
- Stabilize government health care outlays at 10 percent of GDP.

Goal 6. Improve Governance

- Provide public financing for all federal elections.
- Limit corporate financing of campaigns and lobbyists.
- End the revolving door.
- Consider constitutional amendments on term length and limits.

Goal 7. National Security

- End the military occupations of Iraq and Afghanistan.
- Rebalance the outlays on defense, diplomacy, and development.
- Create by 2012 a national security strategy in line with the National Intelligence Council's *Global Trends 2025*.

Goal 8. Raise America's Happiness and Life Satisfaction

- Establish national metrics for life satisfaction.
- Raise life expectancy to at least eighty years.
- Move from twenty-second to top five in least corrupt countries (Transparency International Corruption Perceptions Index).

cessfully in the twenty-first-century global economy. To get there, today's students will have to perform better in the key subjects of math, science, and reading. Here, too, we should set goals, based on global benchmarks. America needs to end its long slide in school performance. It should certainly be able to score within the top ten countries in those three subjects by the year 2015 and the top five by the year 2020.

Third, we need an honest approach to poverty, not one that blames the poor and leaves them to their fate. We know that the single most important key to ending the cycle of poverty is to enable today's children growing up in poverty to reach their full human potential. That in turn requires that America as a society invest in the human capital—meaning the health, nutrition, cognitive skill, and education—of every child in the nation, whether born to wealth or poverty. By 2015, every child in the country should be enrolled in comprehensive early childhood development programs, ensuring the access of poor and working-class parents to quality child care, nutritional monitoring, safe day care, and quality preschool. As I describe below, no investment in our children will be more important for the long-term health of the nation.

Poverty rates stagnated for three decades and then began to increase after 2008. One-fifth of today's children are growing up in poverty. By 2020, let us make that no more than 10 percent. Overall, more than 14 percent of Americans were living below the poverty line in 2010. By 2020, let's cut that rate in half. There will be no single key to success: education, training, high employment, and health care must all play their role.

Fourth, none of these gains will last long if we continue to hurl headlong into an environmental and natural resource catastrophe. America has cause to overhaul its infrastructure in any event: the roads, bridges, levees, water and sewerage systems, and power grid are antiquated and dilapidated. But we have further reason to reinvest in the core infrastructure: it needs to be overhauled decisively to introduce smart and sustainable energy use and transport for the twenty-first century, to achieve three interlocking goals: efficiency, reduced dependence on imported oil, and the transition to a low-carbon economy. Obama has set an emissions target for 2020: a cut of 17 percent relative to 2005. I will add another goal: a revamped power grid and transport infrastructure to ensure at least 5 million electric vehicles on the road by the end of the decade, on the way to a "tipping point" at which electric vehicles become a commercially viable proposition without special government support because of the services that they deliver.[2]

Fifth, we must get the soaring public debt under control. The budget deficit in 2010 was around 10 percent of GDP. Part of that was cyclical, caused by unusually low tax collections and unusually high unemployment insurance and other transfers due to the weak economy. Yet even with some recovery, the medium-term budget deficit is stuck at around 6 percent of GDP, enough to cause a devastating accumulation of debt and the potential for a budget crisis within a few years. Taxes will need to rise, especially on the top income earners, who have enjoyed an unprecedented bonanza in the past thirty years.

Sixth, we need to make government function effectively once again. Not only is our government in the hands of corporate lobbies, but its basic administrative machinery has collapsed. Policy making is relentlessly short term; there is little planning; and America's vast expertise is not properly tapped. Without effective public administration, even a well-financed government is doomed to failure.

Seventh, a key to success will be much smarter foreign policy, especially a shift from "hard" power (military) approaches to "soft" power (diplomatic and assistance) strategies. We are squandering trillions of dollars in useless wars, breaking the budget and the national morale in the process. By ending these futile wars and redirecting our energies to the core reasons for conflict—widespread insecurity, extreme poverty, a scramble for resources, and rising environmental stresses—we will enhance our security at a tiny fraction of today's military outlays. By 2015, we should be able to slash the military budget by at least half, from 5 percent of GDP to between 2 and 3 percent of GDP, and redirect a part of those savings to better investments in global stability.

Eighth and finally, these goals should be seen as society's ultimate objective: greater life satisfaction, both today and in future generations. For that we need better measurements of what underpins life satisfaction, going beyond mere market income to include leisure, good health, a safe environment, and fairness and trust within society. With better guideposts and indicators of happiness, we should be able to answer seriously, not as a matter of hype, the famous question that Reagan posed in his election campaign against Jimmy Carter in 1980: "Are you better off today than you were four years ago?"

New Approaches to Medium-Term Economic Policy

To achieve these core objectives, we will need to adopt a new approach to economic policy. We will need a mixed economy approach, relying on the two pillars of government and markets; we will need a commitment not only to efficiency but also to fairness and sustainability; we will need a longer-term vision based on investments and structural change; and we will need to act holistically, with policy innovations introduced simultaneously across several sectors of the society. Here is a brief sketch of some of the most important policy initiatives.

A New Labor Market Framework

America's jobs crisis reflects mainly a failure in the labor market itself, not a failure of the macroeconomy. By that I mean that lasting solutions to jobs will be found not by turning the dials of Federal Reserve credits or boosting aggregate demand through budget "stimulus" but rather by improving the skills of the workforce, the quality of working life, and the proper functioning of the labor market. Several countries in Europe, including the Scandinavian economies, Germany, and the Netherlands, have achieved great success through a range of "active labor market policies" targeted at building skills, creating flexible and satisfying work conditions, and matching workers with appropriate jobs. It is time the United States turned to an active labor market policy of its own.

America's job challenge begins with the skills deficit. Consider the December 2010 unemployment rate: 9.4 percent of the labor force, with a total of 17.5 percent of the labor force either unemployed or on involuntary part-time work. Yet the unemployment rate varies considerably by age and education levels. Among those sixteen to twenty-four, it was a staggering 19.3 percent, while for those twenty-five years and older, the overall unemployment rate was less than half that, 8.3 percent.

As I've repeatedly noted, we now have a starkly divided labor force for those with a college education and those without. With construction jobs lost following the housing bubble, and with lower-skilled manufacturing jobs long gone to China, Mexico, and other emerging economies, lower-skilled workers face very low wages, weak job attachment, and diminished chances of landing a stable job. We saw earlier that median earnings for workers without a high school diploma are a meager $20,000 per year and for those with a high school diploma $27,400. College graduates average $47,800 and holders of advanced degrees $63,200. The education/earnings gradient is steeper than ever, as the bottom has fallen out of the labor market for low-skilled workers.

The crisis is the worst for youth, especially minority youth, aged sixteen to nineteen in the labor force. The key *long-term* jobs strategy must therefore be educational attainment and skill formation. In general, this should entail the goal of universal high school completion, a 90 percent or higher continuation rate to college or vocational school, and a 50 percent or higher continuation rate to a bachelor's degree. By 2020, at least half of nineteen- to twenty-three-year-olds should be on their way to a bachelor's degree. We can agree with a recent congressional advisory panel that "America's global competitiveness depends on the ability of our high school graduates to earn at least a bachelor's degree."[3] For students who have already dropped out, the goal should be a targeted effort to bring such youth up to at least a high school equivalency diploma and then on to a community college or vocational school. A tight labor market will not suffice: those kids lack the skills they will need to function for the next forty years in the labor market, not just the next business cycle.

Bolstering the skills of the U.S. labor force is the core long-term solution, but the jobs crisis is pressing in the short term. What can be done about the 9 percent unemployment rate? Business recovery will make a modest dent, perhaps lowering the rate to 7–8 percent, or 10–12 million workers, with almost 10 million more suffering from hidden unemployment (having withdrawn from the labor force or working very few hours per month).[4] For those workers, the solutions depend on circumstances. Millions of young people currently unemployed should not be in the labor force at all. They should be finishing high school, vocational school, community college, or a bachelor's degree. Their problem is lack of financing for education and the pressing need to keep food on the table right now. A short-run measure, therefore, would be to increase public subsidies for a return to school of at least 1 million to 2 million of today's unemployed young people under age twenty-five, cutting the unemployment rate by around 1 percentage point as a result. The budgetary cost would be on the order of $15,000 per student per year, or $15 billion to $30 billion in total. Remembering that the gross domestic product is $15 trillion per annum, we see that the added outlays would be on the order of 0.1 to 0.2 percent of GDP.

Another part of the short-term solution, which can actually blend with the longer-term benefits, would be increased job sharing with shorter working hours. Today's full-time workers in America spend around 1,700 hours per year at work, roughly 200 hours or five weeks more per year than most of their European counterparts. If work hours were diminished by 5 percent, for example, the same total work hours could be parceled among 5 percent more workers. This is not merely a short-term remedy, though it could serve as that; it is also part of a long-term reform to help Americans rebalance work and leisure.

The sharing of work through reduced work hours and more employment has been under way, highly successfully, in Germany. The German government rearranged various social benefits (e.g., unemployment compensation) to promote a downward adjustment of work hours rather than number of workers during the latest downturn. The German unemployment rate was held down by around 1 percentage point or more through job sharing. This approach has not been explored in the United States, where adjustments are left wholly to firms and the brunt of the downturn has been felt not in work hours but in number of workers.

European countries' active labor market policies also include much greater outlays than in the United States on job retraining and career services to match workers and jobs. Given the amount of flux in the world economy and technology, old jobs are not coming back. Middle-aged workers are often bereft of the information communications technology (ICT) skills they need for the new economy, and job training is needed to restore their employability. Yet such efforts are costly. Many European countries spend on the order of 1.0 percent of GDP on active labor market policies programs, compared to just 0.2 percent of GDP in the United States. All these measures—youth subsidies to return to school, retraining of older workers, and job matching services—would require another 0.5 percent of GDP per year.[5]

Macroeconomic measures to boost aggregate demand, including more fiscal stimulus and quantitative easing by the Fed, should be put aside. They are no solution for America's job crisis and threaten to destabilize the financial markets and undermine the country's long-term budget solvency. Yet increased public spending on infrastructure, properly financed, will have a kind of "stimulus" effect, not through aggregate demand per se but through the increased employment of relatively low-skilled construction workers. The challenge vis-à-vis infrastructure, described below, is to recognize that the necessary projects are not shovel-ready; they will come on line in the course of a decade, not a year.

Breaking the Poverty/Education Trap

I've repeatedly emphasized a dismal reality of America's education system: the failure of low-income and even middle-income kids to find a successful path to a bachelor's degree.[6] Many poor kids drop out of high school. Others finish high school but can't surmount the financial barriers to begin college. Many others start college but can't finish, dropping out because of rising debts and the need to work. All along the path from preschool to the bachelor's degree, a stark income gradient prevails: poor kids are left behind in a society in which individual households and local communities, rather than the society as a whole, bear the brunt of educational costs.

As a result of the local financing of education, the variation in spending per pupil between richer and poorer communities is vast. When public school districts within a state are arrayed according to outlays per student, the per student outlays of districts at the 95th percentile of spending are often twice the outlays per student at the 5th percentile of spending and a full 50 percent higher than the median outlays. In my home state of New York, for example, the median school district spends $16,000 per student, while the district at the 95th percentile spending level provides $29,000 per student.[7] Poor children in many cases will need even greater than average outlays to help overcome the severe liabilities of growing up in poor neighborhoods, late starts in learning, and fewer opportunities to learn at home from parents with low educational attainments (and often single-head households).

A major federal function in education should be to help supplement the financing per student in lower-income districts and then to spend the money in effective ways, including on innovative educational programs. Currently, federal financing of primary education accounts for roughly 8 percent of total financing of primary and secondary education, $50 billion of $584 billion in the 2006–2007 school year.[8] There are roughly 10 million school-aged kids living in poverty. Suppose as a very rough illustration that their education is supplemented—through vouchers, support for charter schools, extracurricular activities, and other means—on the order of $5,000 per pupil per year to improve their school, home, and neighborhood conditions. That would require a total budget of roughly $50 billion per year, doubling the current federal outlays for primary and secondary schools and adding roughly 0.3 percent of GDP to the budget. This is only the roughest of guesses of what is needed, but it does offer a sense of the scale of additional education funding that might be sought at the primary and secondary level.

Various estimates have been made for the incremental financing of higher education needed to raise the share of young people completing a bachelor's degree. Currently, around 30 to 35 percent of all young people complete a bachelor's degree. With an annual age cohort of around 4 million per year, that means roughly 1.2 million to 1.5 million bachelor's degrees per year. Suppose we aim for an additional 1 million degrees per year, enough to ensure that 50 to 60 percent of each cohort achieves a bachelor's degree. McKinsey has recently estimated that at the current cost of higher education per student, federal funding of tuition would need to rise by roughly $50 billion per year, or 0.3 percent of GDP, above the current outlay of $300 billion per year.[9] In the initial years, part of this funding should be used to help 1 million to 2 million of today's unemployed youths under twenty-five to return to school for a bachelor's degree.

Even with more overall education funding, of perhaps 0.5 to 1.0 percent of GDP per year, the exact pathways to educational improvement remain fraught with uncertainty and will require experimentation, innovation, and lots of learning from best practices. One current fad is to put the lion's share of the blame on poor teachers and then to attack teachers' unions as coddling bad teachers. This is yet another example of a naive yet alluring "magic bullet," when the problems are more complex and require several types of interventions. Attacking teachers' unions is simple and inexpensive, but something doesn't quite fit. The evidence is overwhelming that many kids on their way to dropping out before a high school diploma are already off track by fourth grade. Their problems in that case are not particular teachers but the overall circumstances of their lives. As a recent report summarizes:

> Most future dropouts begin to disengage from school during early adolescence, and during the middle grades achievement gaps often begin to grow. By the time students enter high school, they have one foot out the door and are not prepared to succeed in a rigorous college- and career-readiness high school curriculum. We should start with the feeder middle grade schools to low graduation rate high schools and ensure all students not only stay on track to graduation during the middle grades, but also are engaged in meaningful learning activities that leave them well prepared for high school.[10]

The reason for the long, slow fuse on high school dropouts seems to be the following:

> Dropping out is a process that begins long before a student enters high school. Research shows that a student's decision to drop out stems from loss of interest and motivation in middle school, often triggered by academic difficulties and resulting grade retention. Research also shows that a major cause of retention is failure to master content needed to progress on time, which in many cases, is the result of not being able to read proficiently as early as the 4th grade.[11]

The hard charge against teachers' unions seems misplaced for other reasons as well. Teachers' unions are not major hindrances in high-income suburbs, only in low-income schools. The unions have become a convenient scapegoat in urban areas because they divert attention from the real ills of urban poverty. Moreover, busting the unions seems on the surface to promise lower costs and higher quality. This is just one more magic bullet that distracts us from the hard, consistent work that we need to do to raise the quality of education for all children, and especially poor children.

Yes, we certainly need innovation in educational delivery and in ways to promote and ensure teacher competence. The best charter schools are providing new and innovative models (though charter schools overall have a mixed track record).[12] It seems clear, though, that innovation will be best achieved through a high level of trust among school administrators, teachers, and the community, a kind of trust that can be achieved whether the teachers are in unionized public schools or nonunionized charter schools. Teachers' unions will participate in this renovation and upgrading of education when they are partners of reform, not its victims.

Investing in Early Childhood

Even before first grade, however, we must also attend to the needs of the youngest and most vulnerable members of society, children ages zero to six. America is failing millions of young children every step of the way. Trying to make up for those failures starting after age six is far more expensive and less successful than starting at birth. As the Nobel laureate James Heckman and many of his colleagues have shown, the highest returns to human capital come from investing early, at the start of life.[13] Yet instead of investing, we are leaving a large proportion of our kids to suffer a lifetime of adversity caused by growing up in poverty.

Our kids are the most vulnerable and poverty-ridden group today.

It wasn't always like this. A half century ago, the elderly were the social group with the highest rate of poverty, with 35.2 percent of those above sixty-five living below the poverty line in 1959. Then came the expansion of Social Security and the introduction of Medicare. The poverty rate of the elderly plummeted to 25.3 percent in 1969, 15.2 percent in 1979, 11.4 percent in 1989, and 9.7 percent in 2008. The pattern for children, however, has been a different story. In 1959, the poverty rate for children under eighteen was 27.3 percent. The rate fell to 14 percent in 1969 but then began a long-term climb to 16.4 percent in 1979, 19.6 percent in 1989, and 19.0 percent in 2008. One in five of America's children now grows up in poverty.[14]

Most of us don't appreciate the horrendous costs of early childhood poverty; they are beyond our intuition, unless we become far more mindful of the poor. The biggest scientific finding of recent years in human development is the vital role of the earliest years of life, from pregnancy through age six, the period known as early childhood development (ECD). The early childhood years are the foundation for all that follows. When mothers are healthy and properly nourished during pregnancy, when childbirth is safe, and when the young child is properly nourished, provided with quality health care, raised in a safe and nurturing environment, and afforded the chance to learn and socialize in preschool, the child is likely to reap lifetime benefits of better health, higher school attainment, and higher labor-market earnings. When, on the other hand, the child is born underweight; raised in a dangerous and stressful environment; subjected to environmental hazards of pollution, noise, and other threats; and precluded by poverty from preschool and quality child care, the consequences can be disastrous, not just in childhood but for decades onward. Early childhood undernourishment, for example, can lead to chronic poor health in adulthood and greatly reduced productivity at work.

Another key finding is that our failure to invest in our children at the crucial stage, ages zero to six, can be very hard to compensate for later on. If a skyscraper stands on shaky foundations, extra efforts on the higher floors are never going to make the building secure! This means that many of our educational efforts in the United States, for example in reforming high schools, are coming far too late in the day. We might be able to help some kids along through compensatory actions and should surely try to do so, but we will be much more successful if we start at the start, ensuring healthy early childhood development for all kids.

In a brilliant essay, Gösta Esping-Andersen, the leading expert on Sweden's social welfare state, asks why social mobility is now so much higher in Sweden than in the United States.[15] He notes that in all high-income countries, the parents' socioeconomic status shapes a child's educational and earnings prospects, but much less so in Sweden than elsewhere and much more so in the United States. In Sweden, even a child growing up in relative poverty has almost the same education and earnings prospects as a child growing up at the top of the income curve. Esping-Andersen suggests convincingly that Sweden's distinction lies not in its support for public education, which is roughly matched by other countries, but in its public support for *families and their children from the earliest age*, even before formal schooling.

All of Sweden's families have access to affordable high-quality day care, which is publicly provided. This enables mothers to work without leaving their children behind in an unsafe environment. Female heads of household, a group marked by a high rate of poverty in the United States, are not poor in Sweden. Remarkably, their poverty rate in Sweden, according to Esping-Andersen, is only 4 percent, compared with the United States, where the Census Bureau recorded a 30 percent poverty rate in 2009.[16] Similarly, all of Sweden's children are afforded high-quality preschooling.

The main point, according to Esping-Andersen, is that it is the provision of public services, notably the universal access to affordable day care, even more than income support to families, that is key to the elimination of poverty among families with children.

Sweden's public services, of uniformly high quality, ensure a decent start for all children.

Sweden's public financing for child care, preschool, and pre-primary school amounts to 1 percent of GDP, compared with just 0.4 percent of GDP in the United States.[17] The needs in the United States, of course, are even greater than in Sweden, given the vastly higher proportion of children growing in poverty. Yet in the United States, at least half of those needs are likely to be met by middle-class and rich households out of their own incomes, rather than through comprehensive public coverage. Let's pencil in an additional 0.5 percent of GDP as of 2015 as a very rough estimate of what will be needed to ensure comprehensive early childhood development programs in the United States. Once again, the precise budgeting will require extensive learning by doing and the step-by-step scaling up of successful models.

Real Health Care Reform

Low- and middle-income Americans have suffered from stagnant wages and been pressed down by international competition and rising health care costs. The relentless rise of health care costs in the past couple of decades occasioned the nearly sixteen-month saga of health care reform at the start of the Obama administration. Yet though the reform accomplished two important goals—expanding coverage to the poor and protecting coverage of those with preexisting health conditions—there is very little in the legislation that will slow the increase in health care costs for a given amount of real health care delivery. In fact, health care costs are likely to rise, not fall, in the coming years as the new measures are implemented. What happened is clear enough. The private health care insurance industry, the pharmaceutical industry, and the American Medical Association blocked the deeper reforms that could have brought cost inflation under control. As one leader in the industry has put it, "health care will not reform itself," since the vested interests are too powerful.[18]

Several careful studies have shown how the private-sector interest groups in the health care sector hike up their costs and prices, knowing that they will be reimbursed by the government (in the case of Medicare and Medicaid) or by private purchasers of health care insurance, who have no real alternative. According to one study, the excess costs of U.S. health care in 2003 amounted to an estimated $1,645 per person, or roughly 4 percent of GDP.[19] The study found that excessively high costs permeate the entire health care system, including hospital care, outpatient care, drugs, and health care administration. Doctors' salaries in the United States are far higher than in other countries; so, too, are drug prices. Privately owned outpatient clinics have high costs and excess capacity. And the costs of health care administration and health insurance (such as the handling of claims) are estimated to be around six times as much as the median in the OECD (high-income) countries![20]

The Scandinavian countries run their health care systems at roughly half the cost of the United States and with much better results in life expectancy and reduced child mortality. They do so by emphasizing a "systems approach" to health. Health care is publicly financed but privately provided. One systemic difference with the United States is Scandinavia's much greater attention to primary care, which heads off expensive and chronic conditions that arise and intensify when they are ignored until too late. Primary care doctors are the "connectors" between patients and specialists. Management of the overall health care system is much more transparent. Billing and administration are not bureaucratic nightmares involving private insurance companies. And doctors work more seamlessly together on complex cases, avoiding a massive duplication of administration and of expensive medical tests.

As Obama himself noted during the health care reform debate, there are examples of such successes in the United States, including Kaiser Permanente and the Cleveland Clinic. He even visited the latter to make the point. Yet the reform legislation gave barely a nod in that direction. The lobbyists had won long before the visit by promising to support the legislation (or at least not fight against it) as long as the basic structures of the overpriced health care system were not touched.

A Pathway to Energy Security

The greatest infrastructure challenge of the coming decades is to wean America from its dependence on fossil fuels, both to reduce greenhouse gas emissions and to cut the country's dependency on rapidly depleting and highly unstable energy supplies. This is a complex challenge with four goals: national security, energy security (plentiful, low-cost energy), environmental security, and industrial competitiveness. There is currently no national plan to date on how to achieve even one of these goals, much less all four simultaneously. Comprehensive strategies will involve several types of energy (solar, wind, nuclear, fossil fuels with carbon sequestration), several new types of energy use (hydrogen fuel cells, battery-powered vehicles), and new types of urban design.

There are bottlenecks in every direction. In the original creation of much of the nation's infrastructure, federal and state governments used eminent domain to acquire the land and other resources needed to provide the public goods. That has become considerably harder over time. The right of individual landowners and communities to stall projects has stopped abuses but also made it much harder to modernize the infrastructure. Environmentalists are blocking not only coal-fired power plants but low-carbon energy technologies as well. In recent years, environmentalists have fought wind power off Cape Cod, solar power in the Mojave Desert, high-voltage transmission lines to bring renewable energy to New York City, underground sequestration of carbon dioxide at several proposed sites, and nuclear power plant licensing throughout the country.

What will actually be built is now anybody's guess. Projects can take decades to reach approvals and years or decades more till the first groundbreaking. Until recently the problem was known as NIMBY, Not in My Back Yard. Yet now things are even worse. We've arrived at the BANANA economy: Build Absolutely Nothing Anytime Near Anything.

The glaring gap is the lack of a national strategy. There are dozens of bits and pieces of public policy strewn throughout energy legislation, the 2009 stimulus act, transport legislation, and specific tax policies for alternative energy sources and electric vehicles. They do not add up to a coherent strategy. The Obama administration has announced the goal of a 17 percent reduction of greenhouse gas emissions by 2020 compared with 2005, yet it did not announce any policy to achieve it or even a scenario of how it might be accomplished. Without that, the goals are numbers plucked from thin air, disconnected to the investments in new electricity grids, vehicles, and power plants that could actually get us there.

The transition to a low-carbon energy economy will not be free. Low-carbon energy is more expensive and often less convenient than conventional fossil fuels. Coal can, of course, be burned throughout the day and night, while solar power is available during daylight hours and the wind blows intermittently. Our electricity is currently provided by roughly 50 percent coal, 20 percent nuclear energy, 20 percent natural gas, and the rest mainly by hydropower.[21] To move to an energy system that is mainly low-carbon, whether nuclear or renewable energy or coal combined with the capture of CO_2 emissions, will probably require an extra $50 or so per ton of CO_2 emissions avoided by shifting to cleaner energy. Back-of-the-envelope calculations suggest that the total cost of moving to a low-carbon economy would therefore be around $200 billion per year by 2050, compared with a $30 trillion GDP by midcentury, or roughly 0.6 percent of GDP in outlays. Of course, if the low-carbon energy technologies prove to be much less expensive than now or the conventional fossil fuel energy sources rise significantly in price, the incremental costs of shifting to a low-carbon economy could be much less than 0.6 percent of GDP.

My colleagues and I have been designing a gradual transition path to get from here to there, one that would not disrupt fossil fuel–based energy systems in the short term but would enable a dramatic transformation to a low-carbon energy system by 2050.[22] The idea is to levy a small tax on existing fossil fuels and use it to give a sizable subsidy to low-carbon energy (e.g., wind and solar power or carbon capture and storage at existing coal plants). Since the existing fossil fuel–based energy system is so large and the new low-carbon energy sector is so small, even a very small tax on fossil fuel could pay for a quite generous subsidy today, enough to encourage the entry of new low-carbon energy sources to the market. By maintaining suitable subsidies over time, the size of the low-carbon sector would grow. The fossil fuel tax would rise gradually over time, and the subsidy paid to low-carbon energy producers would decline gradually over time, in a manner that maintains an overall net incentive (equal to the sum of the tax and the subsidy) to keep moving toward a low-carbon energy system.

Consumers would never experience a sudden jolt in energy prices, while low-carbon energy producers would receive a predictable and generous subsidy to support the long-term transition to the new system. The system would be self-financing, since the revenues from fossil fuel taxes would cover the subsidies provided to the alternatives. Over the course of several decades, technological learning cycles (for example, of electric vehicles and solar power) would reduce the costs of low-carbon energy systems compared with today's fossil fuel–based technologies. It's also possible that the market prices of coal and oil might become so high because of rising scarcity that low-carbon renewable energy systems such as wind and solar power would become the market-based low-cost alternatives even without public subsidies to help get them started.

Ending Military Waste

The biggest single item in the budget is the military, which claims at least 5 percent of GDP, around one-fourth of total federal outlays, and the preponderance of U.S. foreign policy attention. The magnitude of these outlays is enormous and their rationale is highly questionable. Military spending will be around $738 billion in fiscal year 2012, not including another $250 billion or so for homeland security, intelligence gathering, veterans' benefits, and other military-related outlays. The total budget directly or indirectly attributable to the military is thus a staggering $1 trillion or so per year.

Around $150 billion per year relates directly to the Iraq and Afghanistan wars, both of dubious if any value to American security. Another large part relates to the maintenance of thousands of nuclear warheads without any obvious purpose, since a tiny fraction of this number would ensure the deterrence of any attack. A staggering $200 billion involves missile defense, other procurement programs, and research and development.[23] In many cases, the generals themselves have declared that they do not need the proposed weapons systems, but powerful lobbies and supportive members of Congress keep the systems in place.

Ending the wars in Iraq and Afghanistan, closing many of the hundreds of military bases around the world established since World War II, and canceling some of the high-cost and dubious weapons systems would allow massive savings of $300 billion or more from the bloated Pentagon budget. Of course, that is picking a fight with America's leading industry and perhaps still most powerful lobby (in close competition with oil, coal, banking, and health care). The military contractors have the advantage of employing workers in virtually every congressional district in the country. Jobs rather than defense has for decades been the watchword of the military-industrial complex, a network so powerful that even the end of the Cold War barely dented the military budget as a share of national income.

Our Ultimate Economic Goals

It is easy to lose sight of the ultimate purpose of economic policy: the life satisfaction of the population. That ultimate goal should be unassailable for a country founded precisely to defend the inalienable right to the pursuit of happiness. Yet not only do we miss myriad opportunities to promote happiness through our collective undertakings, we even miss the opportunities to measure happiness so that we can gauge how we are doing as a nation. Our fixation on GDP/GNP crowds out our attention to more important indicators. As Robert F. Kennedy, Jr., put it:

> For too long we seem to have surrendered personal excellence and community value in the mere accumulation of material things. Our gross national product now is over 800 billion dollars a year, but that gross national product, if we judge the United States of America by that, that gross national product counts air pollution, and cigarette advertising, and ambulances to clear our highways of carnage. It counts special locks for our doors and the jails for people who break them. It counts the destruction of the redwoods and the loss of our natural wonder in chaotic squall. It counts Napalm, and it counts nuclear warheads, and armored cars for the police to fight the riots in our city. It counts Whitman's rifles and Speck's knifes and the television programs which glorify violence in order to sell toys to our children. Yet, the gross national product does not allow for the health of our children, the quality of their education, or the joy of their play; it does not include the beauty of our poetry or the strength of our marriages, the intelligence of our pub-

lic debate or the integrity of our public officials. It measures neither our wit nor our courage, neither our wisdom nor our learning, neither our compassion nor our devotion to our country; it measures everything in short except that which makes life worthwhile. And it can tell us everything about America except why we are proud that we are Americans.[24]

There have been growing efforts to expand the range of indicators to measure better what's important for our well-being. The World Values Survey and Gallup International have each pioneered various measures of subjective well-being, which psychologists and economists have found to be stable, slowly evolving, and useful for social diagnostics. The Human Development Index (HDI) is another well-known attempt to combine economic indicators with social indicators (literacy, school enrollment, and life expectancy) to give a more rounded picture of well-being. The American Human Development Project has recently extended the HDI to American states, counties, and congressional districts, an enormously helpful contribution to assessing the diversity of America's economic and social conditions.[25]

No country has taken the challenge of measuring, and raising, happiness more seriously than the Himalayan Buddhist Kingdom of Bhutan. Back in 1972, the country's fourth monarch, Jigme Dorji Wangchuk, called for the country to orient its policies to promote the gross national happiness rather than the gross national product. This challenge has not been taken lightly or figuratively. The government of Bhutan established the Gross National Happiness Commission to oversee a series of metrics that would quantify and track the changes in national happiness.[26] GNH is measured in nine domains:

- Psychological well-being
- Time use
- Community vitality
- Culture

- Health
- Education
- Environmental diversity
- Living standard
- Governance

Each of these is measured by a series of quantitative indicators. What is notable is the combination of relatively standard economic measurements such as household income and education with measures of cultural integrity (e.g., the use of dialects, engagement in traditional sports and community festivals), ecology (e.g., forest cover), health status (e.g., body mass index, number of healthy days per month), community well-being (e.g., social trust, kinship density), time allocation, and general mental health (e.g., indicators of psychological distress).

The worldwide movement to measure happiness and the quality of life is now expanding very rapidly. The OECD launched a Global Project on Measuring the Progress of Societies in 2004, and the European Commission is moving forward on its own set of integrated indicators. There have been countless recent attempts to correct GNP to account for its many anomalies (subtracting various "bads" such as pollution, congestion, and resource depletion from the standard GNP accounts), starting with the Measure of Economic Welfare (MEW) pioneered by William Nordhaus and James Tobin. The Genuine Progress Indicator (GPI) is a similar initiative to correct GNP for several factors such as inequality, congestion, and pollution. In 2005, the *Economist* Intelligence Unit demonstrated that "quality-of-life" across countries is reasonably well explained statistically by a combination of measurable economic, political, health, job security, and community indicators. Many scholars have confirmed similar results in recent academic studies.[27] Recently the French government convened a commission headed by Joseph Stiglitz and Amartya Sen to propose a new set of indicators, and in 2010 the U.K. government announced that it would directly monitor subjective well-being in annual surveys.[28]

It is time for the United States to take seriously the measurement and monitoring over time of Americans' well-being. Two key facts—that self-reported happiness has been stuck or even declining as income has grown and that the United States is falling behind many other countries in happiness and its underlying determinants—make this new effort especially urgent. Table 10.2 illustrates the kind of well-being measures that would be collected each year in addition to the standard national income accounts. Gallup International, for example, uses opinion surveys to assess the average "life satisfaction" in 178 countries by asking "All things considered, how satisfied are you with your life as a whole these days?" The OECD has created an index of child well-being that aggregates over six dimensions: material conditions, housing, education, health, risk behaviors, and quality of school life. Other indicators might include variables such as life expectancy, student test scores, and the poverty rate, all shown in the table. Clearly, the United States has its work cut out for it to raise its standard of average well-being compared with what other high-income countries are achieving.

Table 10.2: Indicators of National Well-Being (Rankings, with 1 = "Best")

Country	Gallup International Life Satisfaction (178 Countries Ranked)	OECD Child Well-Being Ranking (21 Countries Ranked)	Life Expectancy at Birth (192 Countries Ranked)	OECD PISA Rankings (65 Countries Ranked)	OECD Poverty Rate (16 Countries Ranked)
United States	14	17	6	17	16
Denmark	1	5	5	24	1
Finland	2	3	4	3	5
Netherlands	4	1	4	10	6
Norway	3	6	3	12	5
Sweden	4	2	3	19	2

Source: Gallup, OECD Statistical Databases, World Health Organization.

CHAPTER 11.

Paying for Civilization

In fiscal year 2011, the federal government covered around 39 percent of its spending, roughly $1.4 trillion of $3.6 trillion, by borrowing.[1] Each year's borrowing adds to the total public debt. In 2007, the government debt held by the public amounted to around 36 percent of GDP.[2] By 2015 the debt is expected to soar to 75 percent of GDP.[3] Some economists try to tell us not to worry as we rack up the debt. They pitch tax cuts today as a demand stimulus (according to the Democrats) or a supply stimulus (according to the Republicans), without telling us about the long-term costs. I have my serious doubts about such short-sighted arguments.

As the debt rises, the burden of paying the interest on it will rise as well. Today we spend around 1.5 percent of GDP to pay the interest.[4] By 2015, it could be around 3.5 percent of GDP. By 2020, it could reach 4 percent of GDP or more. This interest servicing will crowd out other vital spending, for example for infrastructure or help for the poor. Or it will require a hugely contentious tax increase, with revenues that instead should have been used for essential public goods. Or it will cause a future financial crisis as global lenders lose confidence in the capacity and willingness of the

U.S. government to honor its debts other than by inflation (printing money to pay them off). It's better, therefore, to try to stabilize the debt relative to GDP and then begin a process of gradual reduction in the debt-to-GDP ratio.

This chapter, then, is about our government paying its bills on time through adequate tax collections, rather than borrowing from the future. As the great Supreme Court Justice Oliver Wendell Holmes, Jr., wrote, "I like to pay taxes. With them I buy civilization."[5] It is a sentiment utterly unrecognizable in America today, where an ongoing thirty-year tax revolt predominates. Without adequate taxation, we can't live in a civilized country. Middle-class Americans are so sure that higher take-home pay is the key to their happiness that they've lost track of the need to pay taxes to fund society-wide undertakings and avoid an explosion of public debt. More important, middle-class Americans have repeatedly given the green light to tax cuts for the richest Americans, allowing income and wealth to concentrate among a tiny fraction of the population. The richest then invest a very small fraction of their wealth to dominate the airwaves, enrich members of Congress and their families, and preserve their privileges. Congress needs little cajoling by lobbyists; it has itself become a millionaire's club, with 261 members, almost half, of today's Congress holding at least $1 million in assets.[6]

Getting the rich to accede to Justice Holmes's wisdom is a big part of the challenge. Getting the government to plan and implement long-term policies properly and competently is another. The two changes are, of course, inseparable. There is no way to increase the scale of government if the government remains as incompetent and corrupt as it is today. This chapter takes up the challenge of how to pay for a government that does its proper job. The next chapter takes up political reform, how to take government back from the corporatocracy and put it back into the service of public well-being.

The Basic Fiscal Arithmetic

America's peacetime budget deficit is unprecedented: $1.3 trillion in 2010, equal to 9 percent of the national income. And the deficit could well remain above $1 trillion for years to come. The problem with economic reform in America is how to pay for public goods: quality education, college completion, advanced energy technologies, improved roads, safe child care, and decent health care. The quality of life is deteriorating because we refuse to pay for the public goods needed for a civilized society.

The Tea Party's answer is to leave the needed investments to the private market. This, as we've seen in earlier chapters, will not do. We are required, in one way or another, to address the budget deficit and at the same time address the challenges that we've inherited from these market failures and the powerful forces of global capitalism.

The lack of budget resources is now the fundamental constraint on effective governance and a sustainable recovery. It's fair to say that all our civilian programs other than the entitlements programs are paid for with borrowed money and borrowed time. The result, as we know, is political paralysis. As much as we'd like to do more and better things, we simply can't afford them. And the squeeze on civilian discretionary programs has tightened considerably over the years, since Ronald Reagan put the country on the course of repeated tax cuts.

There is nothing more important today than understanding the basic arithmetic of the budget and of household incomes to understand the predicament.

This is shown in Figure 11.1. Under the current tax system, the federal government will collect around 18 percent of GDP in 2015, with the breakdown shown in the chart. For this baseline calculation, I assume that the Bush-era tax cuts that were extended at the end of 2010 for two years will be extended again after 2012.[7]

Figure 11.1: Revenues and Outlays as a Percentage of GDP in 2015 Budget Projections

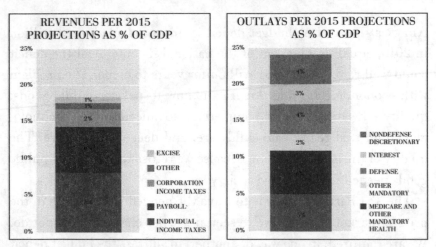

Source: Data from Office of Management and Budget Historical Tables and author's estimates.

There are three main sources of federal revenues. Roughly 8 percent or so of GDP in 2015 will come from personal income taxes, around 6.3 percent will come from payroll taxes for Social Security and Medicare, and 2.2 percent from the corporate tax. The rest, around 1.5 percent, will come from a variety of excise and other taxes.

To prepare a spending baseline for 2015, I divide the budget into six main categories. Under current law Social Security will account for around 5 percent of GDP. On current trends, health care spending (Medicare, Medicaid, and veterans' health care) will account for around 6 percent. Other mandatory spending, such as unemployment insurance, disability pay, and the Earned Income Tax Credit, will account for another 2 percent. Military outlays will absorb 4 percent, and interest payments on the publicly held government debt will amount to around 3 percent. I assume that discretionary civilian spending will amount to around 4 percent of GDP, roughly the average of 2005–2008, before the crisis and the stimulus package. In total, therefore, a reasonable baseline for 2015 puts total spending at around 24 percent of GDP.

The single most important point about this accounting is the following: The budget baseline revenue of around 18 percent of GDP will not even cover mandatory spending (13 percent) plus the military (4 percent) plus interest on the debt (3 percent). *This means that on the baseline, all civilian discretionary spending, and then some, would have to be paid for with borrowed money.*

It might be wondered how Clinton managed to balance the budget, and indeed run a small surplus, at the end of the 1990s. There were four parts to that. First, military spending fell to just 3 percent of GDP, compared with 5 percent today. That saved 2 percentage points of the budget, a good move that should be repeated. Second, revenues soared to around 20 percent of GDP on the back of a hot economy fueled by the temporary dot-com bubble and with top tax marginal rates slightly higher than today. Unfortunately we can count on tax revenues of only around 18 percent of GDP on the basis of the current tax system. Third, interest payments were only 2 percent of GDP in 2000 and will be close to 3 percent in 2015,[8] if not more. Fourth, mandatory programs accounted for only 10 percent of GDP and are likely to be around 13 percent by 2015. This sums to a shift of 6 percent of GDP toward deficit, even assuming that defense spending declines to 3 percent of GDP.

We must recall, too, that Clinton and the Republican-led Congress of that period deeply shortchanged key public expenditures—on education, infrastructure, energy, foreign assistance, poverty relief, R&D, and other areas. They squeezed spending below the levels needed to maintain U.S. competitiveness and social well-being in order to keep domestic spending at 15 percent of GDP. With our aging population, rising health care costs, and growing needs in infrastructure, education, energy, and other areas, domestic spending by 2015 will have to be far higher than 15 percent of GDP.

Deficit Cutting Beyond Illusions

Suppose that we want to close that deficit to zero or near zero (with the more precise target discussed below). We need to find budget cuts plus tax increases that sum to around 6 percent of GDP. Most Americans say that they'd like to do this through spending cuts rather than tax increases. Budget cutting certainly sounds more appealing, as long as there is tremendous waste in the budget. The public indeed imagines that the civilian budget is laden with fat. The problem is that the public's favorite targets for budget cutting arc nowhere close enough to do the job. The notion of closing the deficit through budget cuts alone is a fantasy, though a popular one. Considerably higher revenues as a share of GDP will be needed.

Consider two of the politicians' favorite targets for budget cuts: budget "earmarks" for pet projects within congressional districts (such as the famous "bridge to nowhere") and foreign aid. Earmarks are on the order of $16 billion per year.[9] One percent of GDP is $150 billion per year. Hence earmarks account for 0.1 percent of GDP. Foreign assistance is approximately $30 billion per year, or 0.2 percent of GDP.[10] Combining the two categories, their complete elimination—warranted or not—would save just 0.3 percent of GDP, compared with a target of 5 to 6 percent in deficit cuts. So we're at far less than a tenth of the solution, even with a draconian and unwise total elimination of foreign aid (which the public believes should be a larger fraction of the budget than now).[11]

The mandatory programs represent additional potential targets for cutting waste, and at first glance much larger and meatier ones. Much of the public believes that the mandatory programs are one giant transfer machine, in which the deserving middle class is taxed in order to transfer income to the undeserving poor, especially to minorities who live on the public dole. In the 1980s, Reagan riffed repeatedly about "welfare queens" who allegedly stole from the public purse by collecting illegally on multiple welfare accounts. That image has stuck in the public mind. Let's therefore take a closer look at the mandatory programs to see what might plausibly be cut.

As shown in Figure 11.2, the mandatory programs consist of universal programs such as Social Security and Medicare (for all elderly), social insurance programs such as unemployment com-

Figure 11.2: Mandatory Spending as a Percentage of GDP for 2015

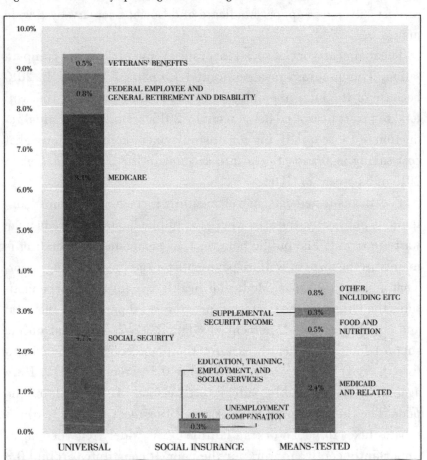

Source: Data from Office of Management and Budget Historical Tables.

pensation, and means-tested transfers for the poor such as food stamps.[12] The universal programs make up two-thirds of the mandatory spending, roughly 10 percent of GDP. There is relatively little political controversy over the outlays on those programs. The public strongly supports Social Security, Medicare, federal employee retirement and disability, and veterans' benefits.[13] Any cuts in those programs would inevitably be very gradual and stretched out over decades. There are few if any short-term savings in this category, and with the aging of the population, we can expect an increase in such outlays by around 1 percent of GDP by 2020. Even Tea Party activists strongly support Medicare and Social Security by a wide margin.

The main category of social insurance is unemployment compensation. This program reached around 1.3 percent of GDP in 2010 because of the high unemployment rate in that year, but this will tend to revert to around 0.4 percent by 2015, assuming a gradual reduction of those qualifying for unemployment compensation. That cost saving is already taken into account in the baseline deficit in 2015 of 6 percent of GDP.

The means-tested category of spending is certainly the most contentious politically, the area where the public believes there is huge waste to trim.[14] The public believes that means-tested spending is mainly in the form of welfare payments for the (undeserving) poor. That is simply not true. Medicaid (health care for the poor) constitutes the largest of means-tested programs, 60 percent of the total and equal to around 2 percent of GDP. There is no broad public support for ending health care for the poor. Food stamps constitute the next largest program, roughly 0.5 percent of GDP. Here again, there is no public outcry to take food off the table of the poor. The third program is the Earned Income Tax Credit, which rebates taxes to poor working families. It is widely regarded as an important incentive to work for the poor. It constitutes around 0.3 percent of GDP.

Finally comes the welfare program that has been most contentious for decades: aid to poor families with dependent children. Welfare, formerly known as Aid to Families with Dependent Children, is now known as Temporary Assistance for Needy Families, or TANF. *This program makes up only 3.5 percent of the means-tested programs and just 0.1 percent of GDP.*[15] America cut back on "welfare" from the 1970s onward. Family income support fell from 0.4 percent of GDP in 1970 to under 0.2 percent in 2010.[16] Welfare still looms large in the public's imagination, but it plays little role in the budget and the deficit. It's been a long time since America was generous to its poor families with children!

The upshot is that we could eliminate foreign aid, earmarks, and welfare payments in the TANF program entirely, and the combined effect would be to save just 0.5 percent of GDP out of a structural deficit of 5 to 6 percent of GDP. The hot-button items of the budget are a distraction from real budget balancing. Unless we are willing to slash Social Security, Medicare, Medicaid, veterans' benefits, or food stamps to the bone, we have to look elsewhere to close the deficit.

What about waste, fraud, and abuse in civilian discretionary programs? Once again, there is much less than meets the eye. Civilian discretionary spending constitutes everything the government does aside from retirement, health care, social insurance, income support, and the military, yet the total is only around 4 percent of GDP. That modest level of spending is spread out over many areas, including general science, space science (NASA), health science, agriculture, commerce, transportation (including highways), environment (including water resources), energy, regional development, education, training, housing, the justice system (including the judiciary and penal system), public administration, international diplomacy, and international development assistance. Each of these areas of spending constitutes less than 1 percent of GDP. There are no areas of obvious massive waste. A few billion dollars of savings can surely be achieved by ending wasteful agriculture subsidies, but that would barely dent the overall budget deficit. Total spending on public administration—the much-derided "federal bureaucracy"—amounted to just $20 billion, or 0.13 percent of GDP, in fiscal year 2010.[17] When it comes to saving vast budgetary resources through cuts in waste, there is simply not vast waste to cut in civilian outlays.

Here is another way to show the falsity of the idea of vast waste hidden in the civilian budget. Obama established the National Commission on Fiscal Responsibility and Reform with a mandate to find

a path to budget balance. The commission was charged with identi-
fying specific areas of budget cutting, yet it couldn't find large waste
to trim. Here is the list that the commission proposed and the estimated dollar savings for the year 2015, when GDP is expected to be
$18.6 trillion:[18]

- Reduce congressional and White House budgets, $800 million.
- Impose a three-year wage freeze on federal workers, $20 billion.
- Reduce the size of the federal workforce, $13 billion.
- Reduce federal travel, printing, and vehicle budgets, $1 billion.
- Sell excess federal real estate, $100 million.
- Eliminate all earmarks, $16 billion.
- Reform Medicare sustainable growth, $3 billion.
- Repeal support for long-term affordable care (the CLASS Act),
  $11 billion.
- Reduce Medicare fraud, $1 billion.
- Reform Medicare cost sharing, $10 billion.
- Restrict Medicare supplemental insurance, $4 billion.
- Extend Medicaid rebates to "dual eligibles," $7 billion.
- Reduce excess payments to hospitals for medical education,
  $6 billion.
- Cut Medicare payments for bad debts, $3 billion.
- Accelerate savings for home health care providers, $2 billion.
- Medicaid savings, $6.3 billion.
- Medical malpractice reform, $2 billion.
- Reform health benefits for federal employees, $2 billion.
- Reduce agriculture spending, $1 billion.
- Eliminate in-school subsidies in student loan programs, $5
  billion.
- Other specified saving, $1 billion.

This is a long list, to be sure, but it is not an impressive one in
terms of budget savings as a percent of GDP. It sums to a mere $115
billion, or roughly 0.6 percent of GDP in 2015. And that's an opti-

mistic assessment. Many of the supposed savings would not really materialize. Others may be ill advised, such as cutting support for long-term health care. The commission also called for other large savings by way of limiting cost-of-living adjustments and other gimmicks, rather than through specified cuts.

This is all pretty thin gruel. The supposition that there is massive waste to be cut in the civilian budget is simply a myth. To recapitulate: ending all earmarks and foreign aid and achieving all of the specific cuts on civilian programs proposed by the deficit commission, even if such choices were meritorious, would amount to less than 1 percent of GDP.

True health care reform, the kind that not only expands coverage but actually reduces America's bloated costs, could probably save as much as 1 percent of GDP per year in net budgetary outlays (lower spending and higher taxes) in reforms carried out over several years. This budget saving would reflect a combination of lower direct outlays for government-provided health care (such as Medicare) and a cutback on the deductibility of private health insurance, especially of high-cost plans purchased by high-income individuals.

This leaves one more part of the budget: the military. Here the prospects for budget savings are even brighter. The Iraq and Afghanistan occupations currently bloat the military budget by around 1 percent of GDP. Another 1.5 percent of GDP could certainly be cut back on procurement of unneeded nuclear weapons and other weapons, and a scaling back of international military bases. The military budget could be trimmed to around 2.5 percent of GDP by 2015, which is 1.5 percent of GDP less than in the baseline that I just outlined.

In total, cutting military outlays to 2.5 percent of GDP would reduce the baseline deficit to 4.5 percent of GDP in 2015. Another 0.5 percent of GDP could be saved in areas identified by the deficit commission and another 1 percent on true health care reform. In total, we might trim around 3 percent of GDP from the baseline deficit in these categories, leaving a 2015 deficit of some 3 percent of GDP.

Yet that is not the end of the story. We have not yet factored in the need to *augment* certain spending programs even as we cut others. According to the discussion in the preceding chapter, we need to *increase* outlays on certain public goods. The list from the preceding chapter is as follows, together with my rough estimate of the *additional* spending that is needed as a percentage of GDP:

- Job training, job matching, and other active labor market policies, 0.5 percent
- Primary and secondary schools, 0.3 percent
- Higher education, 0.4 percent
- Child care and early childhood development, 0.5 percent
- Modernization of infrastructure, 1 percent
- Research and development, 0.3 percent
- Diplomacy and foreign assistance, 0.5 percent

This suggests that the current spending needs to be *augmented* by around 3.5 percent of GDP in order to meet the vital challenges of jobs, schooling, early childhood development, infrastructure, and international affairs. Let's be conservative and round down to 3 percent of GDP in the added outlays needed to address the country's structural challenges in education, infrastructure, science, and other areas.

The upshot is the following: We start with a baseline structural budget deficit of 6 percent of GDP. We can identify justified savings of perhaps 3 percent of GDP from that in spending, mainly by cuts in the military and reductions in health care costs. But we must add back another 3 percent of GDP in spending to increase the supply of public goods. The chronic financing gap for mid-decade (2015) is therefore on the order of 6 percent of GDP, taking into account the *plausible cuts in existing programs plus the plausible need to expand other programs.*

In this scenario, total federal spending would settle at around 24 percent of GDP in 2015, compared with revenues of around 18 percent. No doubt those are rough numbers in need of refinement. Still, they point us to the essential conclusion: that the United States will need substantially more revenues to close the budget deficit, especially recognizing the need to increase federal spending in certain critical areas.

I have been relatively conservative in the added spending that is needed. These projections do not make room for any significant transfer of income to relieve poverty, offer new housing assistance, or cover a jump in interest rates on the public debt. They assume that defense outlays as a share of GDP can be reduced by half of the current level, from 5 percent to 2.5 percent, an approach that will certainly be resisted by the Pentagon and many key interest groups. If these assumptions are too optimistic, the budget deficit in 2015 is likely to be much larger than estimated, with the need for even more stringent measures to raise revenues or cut spending.

Let me add a final note on the work of the Obama deficit commission. The deficit commission assumed that total spending and revenues could settle at 21 percent of GDP. It did so because it utterly neglected the need for existing, much less new, civilian spending in key areas such as infrastructure, education, training, and R&D. It is relatively easy to balance the budget if one presumes that new kinds of public spending are not needed. Yet that is no way to pay for civilization.

Budget Lessons from Abroad

All of this discussion prompts a crucial question: how do Canada, Denmark, Norway, Sweden, and other countries manage to educate their young, fight poverty, modernize their infrastructure, enjoy a life expectancy well above America's, and still maintain a budget that is more in balance than America's? After all, in 2010, the United States had the second-largest budget deficit as a share of GDP among the high-income countries, ahead of only Ireland (see Figure 11.3). The

Figure 11.3: Budget Deficit in OECD Nations as Percentage of GDP, 2010

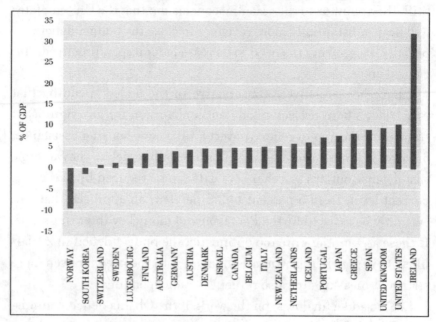

Source: Data from OECD.

social democratic economies of northern Europe, where government plays a much larger role in the economy, had deficits under 3 percent of GDP in Denmark, Finland, and Sweden, with a surplus of 10 percent of GDP in Norway, achieved mainly by saving a considerable fraction of its oil and gas revenues for the benefit of later generations.

The answer, of course, is that the other countries tax their citizens more heavily in order to supply more public goods, including, in the case of Scandinavia, universal access to health care, higher education, and child care and support for families with young children. The comparison in tax collections is shown in Figure 11.4. The United States has the second lowest tax revenues as a share of GDP among all of the countries shown, just slightly larger than Australia. We see that the countries in deepest budget crisis in 2010 were not those with among the lowest nor the highest government spending, but those with the lowest tax revenues: Greece, Ireland, Portugal, Spain, the United Kingdom, and the United States. All these coun-

Figure 11.4: Tax Revenues as a Percentage of GDP for OECD Nations, 2009

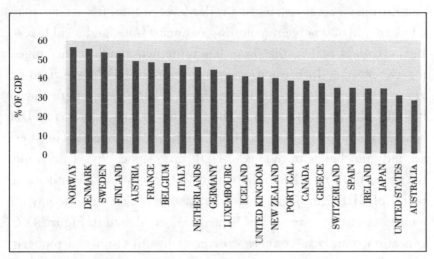

Source: Data from OECD Statistics Database.

tries are running enormous budget deficits. They seek to provide public services and income transfers but are not willing to pay for them through public revenues.

To understand America's budget predicament, it is useful to examine the changes in tax revenues as a share of GDP that have taken place in the United States and other high-income countries

Figure 11.5: Change in Tax-to-GDP Ratio Between 1965 and 2009 for OECD

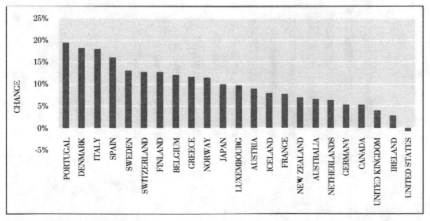

Source: Data from OECD Statistics Database.

since the early 1960s. Half a century ago, both the United States and European countries had a similar level of total taxes relative to GDP, roughly 30 percent (counting national, state, and local taxes). In the United States, that level has remained roughly unchanged for five decades. In Europe, taxes as a share of GDP have risen by around 10 percentage points on average. These changes are shown in Figure 11.5, which measures the rise in revenues relative to GDP, comparing 1965 and 2009. In the United States, there has been essentially no change in the tax-to-GDP ratio since 1965. In Europe, the tax-to-GDP ratio has risen in all countries, by 5 to 20 percentage points of GDP. Europe has used that rise in tax revenues to pay for a more extensive range of public services, as shown in Figure 11.6: education, family allowances, universal health care, and modernized infrastructure. It has also used the higher revenues in general to keep the budget deficit under control.

The divergence between the United States and Europe reflects a divergence both of fiscal means and of fiscal ends. Though Europe generally has higher tax rates on all kinds of income, the biggest difference with the United States is that European countries all have a value-added tax (VAT) as a cornerstone of the budget. In Europe,

Figure 11.6: Gross Public Social Spending as a Percentage of GDP, 2010

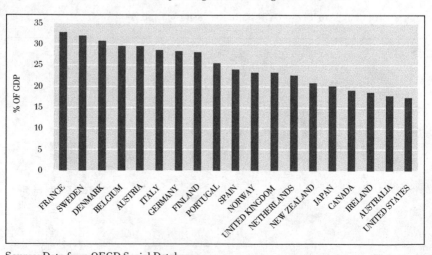

Source: Data from OECD Social Database.

the VAT routinely collects around 10 percent of GDP. In the United States, by contrast, the federal budget collects less than 1 percent of GDP in excise taxes akin to the VAT. This is the main difference in the fiscal means.

The main difference in the fiscal ends is a divergence in the vision of government in the United States and Europe. In the United States, the anti-government politics that became the dominant political thrust of the last thirty years blocked an increase in total tax collections as a share of GDP. The United States therefore cut back on public investments in education, science, energy, and infrastructure, and squeezed outlays for the poor, just when they were most urgently needed.

Anti-tax ideologues in the United States claim that Europe pays a heavy price because of its higher taxes. This is hard to swallow, however, given that northern Europe is ahead of the United States on most indicators of material well-being: educational performance, subjective well-being, poverty rates, life expectancy, and so forth. Yes, it's true that GDP per person is still higher in the United States than in most of Europe (though not higher than in Norway, for example), but that really doesn't prove much about taxes or even about social well-being. U.S. GDP per person may be higher, but the average living standard of the median citizen is not: much of America's higher GDP reflects higher health care costs, longer work hours and less leisure time, longer commutes, more military spending, and a high proportion of income at the very top of the income curve.

More important, the higher GDP per person predates any differences in tax systems, stretching back to the late nineteenth century. In 1913, for example, America was 52 percent richer than Western Europe, and in 1998, it was also 52 percent richer than Europe.[19] America's long-standing advantage in GDP per person has been in its geography rather than its economic system. America has vastly more land and natural resources per person than Europe does. This has been the source of its enduring advantage (just as Norway's high oil and gas earnings account for its higher GDP per person than in the United States). Americans have bigger houses, bigger farms, and bigger cars, not to mention more natural capital per person in the form of oil, gas, and coal. These have been the sources of America's higher income per person stretching back to the nineteenth century.

The real point for us is that despite America's vast natural resource advantages, it has actually ended up with a *lower* average quality of life in many ways than in northern Europe. Yes, America's GDP per capita is higher, but it is not bringing widespread benefits for the society. To ensure that the benefits reach more of society, the United States will have to invest more in public outlays for education, infrastructure, and the other priorities that I've identified.

Budget Choices in a Federal System

Americans will surely need to pay higher taxes to balance the budget and "pay for civilization." Yet another thought arises: why not allow tax and spend decisions to be made at the state and local level? Areas that would like to provide more public goods could do so, and areas that are averse to public goods could organize their states and cities as they see fit. To some extent, of course, this already happens. The federal government accounts for about 65 percent of total revenues, while state and local governments account for 35 percent.[20] There is a huge variation in taxes per citizen across the states. My own state of New York has an income tax that rises to a top rate of 9 percent, and New York City adds another 2.9 percent. The state sales tax rate is 4 percent, plus another 4.875 percent in the city. New Hampshire, by contrast, has neither an income tax nor a sales tax.[21]

Economists use the concept of "fiscal federalism" to denote the situation in the United States, Canada, China, India, and elsewhere, in which governments at the national, state (or provincial), and local level have their own tax collections and separate provision of public goods. The system may include collection of revenue at one level of government and its transfer to another, such as when the federal government collects revenues and then returns them to the states as block grants to administer various programs. The question then arises as to the appropriate levels for collecting revenues and providing public goods and services. Why not, for example, simply leave the decisions to the most local level and thereby allow maximum freedom of choice? There are three reasons.

First, certain public goods are best provided at a higher level of government. National defense, clearly, should depend on the federal government, not the fifty states. Some are clearly the responsibility of governments at all levels, such as planning and implementing the national highway system or a national power grid. In these cases, indeed, the situation is even more complex because the goods and services involve the private sector alongside multiple levels of government.

Second, there is a collective action problem that makes tax collection more convenient at the higher level of government, that is, at the federal level rather than the state and local level. The fifty states are in competition with one another for businesses and wealthy citizens. By keeping its tax rates just a bit lower than the others', each state can attract business and revenues. Yet the result is a race to the bottom, as described for the global economy in tax competition between nations. Each of the fifty states shaves the tax rate to entice business to come over the state border, until all of the states together are starved for cash. The race to the bottom among the states can be obviated in part by a unified federal tax collection that is then returned to the states so that they can implement programs that are tailored to each state's needs.

Third, the differential provision of public goods in different jurisdictions leads to mobility of households as they sort themselves in response to the changing tax and spending conditions of the state and local governments. In part this is exactly what is desired. Economists have long studied a conceptual model in which sorting allows each household to choose just the spot where it would like to live: the place that delivers just the right combination of parks, good schools, public concerts, and other amenities, balanced by high or low tax collections as needed to supply that level of public goods. The result is a "Tiebout equilibrium," named after the economist Charles Tiebout, who first proposed it.[22]

In some cases this sorting can work well, but there are obvious reasons why it can create enormous trouble. If one jurisdiction decides to provide more generous help for the poor, it ends up being flooded by low-income residents in just the same way that businesses and wealthy individuals flee from high-tax jurisdictions. Once again, there is a race to the bottom when it comes to supporting the poor, which is a public function that should be shared across the society, not a small part of it. Similarly, the sorting will tend to lead to segregation by income, as rich households move to affluent jurisdictions in search of good schools and other public amenities. Land prices and property taxes increase, squeezing poorer families out of the more affluent communities. The society divides between rich communities and poor communities, with reduced spillovers and contacts between the various parts of society. This can leave the poor trapped in poverty, resulting in a massive loss of well-being not only for the poor but also for the rich, who end up absorbing the indirect costs of poverty (in terms of lower worker productivity, higher crime rates, larger transfer programs, more political instability, and so forth). The point is that when there are spillovers in human capital, the sorting of the population across local jurisdictions can be disadvantageous for the entire society, rich and poor alike. The solution is an adequate provision of public goods across the entire society by the federal government, as a backstop to local financing and local provision of services.

The upshot of these considerations is that local governments are often the most effective providers of public goods such as schooling, public health, and local infrastructure (roads, water and sewerage, and other systems), since these programs are best tailored to local needs. At the same time, the federal government should supplement local financing by collecting federal taxes and transferring them to state and local governments for local implementation. The famous *subsidiarity principle* should in general determine the level of government best suited for implementation. The subsidiarity principle holds that the public good should be provided by the lowest level of government that is competent to provide it, for example, schools at the local level, major roads at the state level, national highways and national defense at the federal level. Americans, quite rightly, strongly endorse subsidiarity. A robust 70 percent of Americans endorse the view that "the federal government should run only those things that cannot be run at the local level."[23]

Here's the bottom line. Currently the United States collects around 18 percent of GDP in tax revenues at the federal level and another 12 percent of GDP at the state and local levels. Washington currently returns around 4 percent of GDP in tax revenues to the states to implement health, education, and infrastructure programs at the state and local levels.[24] To close the budget deficit and implement needed new spending programs, the United States will have to raise overall tax revenues by several additional percentage points of GDP. I am suggesting that, to the maximum extent feasible, the new spending programs—for education, early childhood development, infrastructure, and so forth—should be implemented at the state and local levels using increased taxes collected by Washington but then returned to the individual states for program design and implementation.

Time for the Rich to Pay Their Due

With a chronic budget deficit of around 6 percent of GDP, tax revenues will have to rise. It is high time that super-rich taxpayers picked up much of this cost. The top 1 percent of American households now collects around 21 percent of household income, which amounts to around 15 percent of GDP. These households pay roughly 31 percent of their income in federal taxes, so that their net-of-federal-tax income is around 10 percent of GDP. In 1970, the top 1 percent collected around 9 percent of household income, or 6 percent of GDP, and paid roughly 47 percent of that in federal taxes, for a net-of-federal-tax income of around 3.3 percent of GDP. The post-tax income of the richest 1 percent of the population has therefore increased by more than 6 percentage points of GDP since 1970.[25] Most of the population has been squeezed, while the rich have enjoyed a bonanza. It's time once again for those at the top to contribute more to solving the nation's problems.

The first step of the solution would be to end the Bush tax cuts for households above $250,000. The top tax rate would rise from 35 to 39.6 percent. This would collect an additional 0.5 percent of GDP. That's a necessary start but by far not sufficient to close the budget deficit. To collect even more revenue, the top rate could be lifted above 39.6 percent, as it is in many European countries.

Even without raising the top rate above 39.6 percent, however, another 0.5 percent of GDP or so could be collected by closing a series of tax loopholes that now benefit the rich. For example, capital gains are currently taxed far below regular income, and the deficit commission called for capital gains taxes to be raised to the level of regular income (albeit with a drop in the tax rate of regular income). Mortgage interest is tax-deductible even for mansions and second homes. This deduction could be restricted to a single residence, with a cap on the size of the tax-deductible mortgage. Expensive health care insurance purchased by the rich is now fully tax-deductible and should be subject to a ceiling on the tax deductibility. Hedge fund managers, some of the world's richest people, are actually taxed at only 15 percent of their income through a loophole that is least justified of all. Congress and the president should gather the courage to tell their billionaire contributors that they too will have to pay income taxes at normal rates.

Another part of the solution might be to tax some of the massive accumulated wealth of the rich. The top 1 percent of wealth holders owns around 35 percent of the nation's total wealth, which is roughly equal to the wealth of the bottom 90 percent of the population.[26]

According to the latest wealth data of the Federal Reserve Board in the Flow of Funds, the total net worth of households is around $56.8 trillion.[27] The wealth of the top 1 percent is therefore around $20.6 trillion. With roughly 113 million households, the average wealth of the richest 1 percent is roughly $18.2 million per household. Suppose that we levy a tax on the net worth *above* $5 million per household, so that the average tax base would be roughly $13.2 million per household ($18.2 million minus $5 million), for a total tax base of $14.9 trillion. A tax of merely 1 percent on net worth above $5 million per household would therefore collect around $150 billion, or 1 percent of GDP.

The combination of higher income taxation and wealth taxation would thereby raise at least 2 percentage points of GDP from the very top earners. But even if they had to pay another 2 percent of GDP, there would certainly be no need to shed tears for the rich. Their net-of-tax income would remain around 10 percent of GDP, a share of national income two-thirds higher than the 6 percent of GDP in 1980.

There are still other approaches to raising taxes on top earners and those engaged in tax evasion. The corporate income tax is now a sieve, with so many loopholes and ways to shelter income in foreign tax havens that the tax collection has declined from around 3.5 percent of GDP in the 1960s to around 1.5 percent of GDP now. By tightening the rules on foreign income and other loopholes, it should be possible to raise another 1 percentage point of GDP. Such a tax would be borne largely by the top wealth holders, who are the predominant shareholders. Of course, the current global political dynamic is to cut corporate taxes rather than to raise them, as part of a race to the bottom being played by the leading economies, even though virtually all economies would benefit by collecting higher corporate tax payments. International coordination in corporate tax policies among the major economies (such as the G20) could therefore be a boon for all countries by enabling each country to hold the line against tax cuts made in competition with other governments.

Curbing tax evasion is another route to added revenues. In a very detailed study of 2001 tax returns, the IRS concluded that there was a "tax gap" of roughly $345 billion (implying a noncompliance rate of 16 percent of taxes owed).[28] Around $55 billion of that nonpayment was clawed back by the IRS through enforcement processes, leaving a net underpayment of taxes of roughly $290 billion, equal to almost 3 percent of GDP in taxes not paid. The single greatest cause is the underreporting of personal income from business activities, especially from nonfarm proprietorships and various kinds of partnership income. Tightening tax compliance through a variety of means could likely reduce the underreporting by perhaps 0.5 to 1 percent of GDP (a not inconsiderable $75 billion to $150 billion per year).

Yet another way to raise revenues would be higher taxes on oil, gas, and coal, both to collect more revenues and to help shift energy demand to low-carbon sources for both climate and national security reasons. A rough calculation shows that a price of about $25 per ton of CO_2 emitted, equivalent to roughly 2.5 cents per kilowatt-hour of electricity and 25 cents per gallon of gasoline, would collect around 1 percent of GDP in revenues per year. As I explained earlier, the fossil fuel tax could be phased in over several years, even decades, in line with the gradual transition to a low-carbon economy.

The United States is absolutely ripe for a rise in gasoline taxes. The nominal gasoline excise tax rate has been fixed at 18.4 cents per gallon since 1994.[29] Inflation alone has reduced the real value of that tax per gallon by around 30 percent. As with other federal tax rates, the U.S. excise tax rate on gasoline is extremely low by international comparison. We might conservatively assume that by 2015 an extra 0.5 percent of GDP could be collected by some combination of a higher gasoline excise tax and modest carbon levies on other fossil fuels (such as on coal at the utilities).

Other possibilities include a tax on bank balance sheets (proposed by Obama but not enacted) and a tax on financial transactions. Even a tiny levy on each stock trade or foreign exchange transaction could raise tens of billions of dollars, much of which currently shows up in the gargantuan bonuses on Wall Street. New York State, for example, levies a transfer tax on the sale of stock shares of a mere $0.01 to $0.05 per share, depending on the share price. This small tax collects around $15 billion per year.[30] Under the pressure of the Wall Street lobby, however, the New York State government has, since 1981, been rebating the revenues right back to the brokerage firms.

A final option, one that will likely be adopted sometime in the coming decade, is to introduce a value-added tax. The United States is the last of the high-income countries to introduce such a tax, and the absence of the VAT is the main reason why U.S. tax collections as a share of GDP are much lower than in Europe. The VAT is relatively easy to collect, creates low distortions, and raises considerable revenues. The main problem is that it is mildly regressive, meaning that it tends to collect a higher proportion of incomes of low- and middle-income households than of rich households. Even that might be acceptable and fair, however, if the tax proceeds are used overwhelmingly for the poor. Then the overall combined effect of increased taxes and spending would still be progressive on balance, that is, helping the poorest disproportionately to their income.

The upshot is the following: Perhaps 4 percent of extra GDP could be collected as of 2015 mainly by taxing the rich (2 percent), tightening corporate taxation (1 percent), strengthening tax enforcement (0.5 to 1 percent), taxing financial transactions, and taxing carbon emissions (0.5 percent). Introducing a VAT would raise even more revenues and could be phased in over several years. The point is that there are lots of options, and most of them could be concentrated near the top of the income distribution, where they belong.

How far should we go in raising tax revenues? To balance the budget entirely, we would have to raise 6 percent of GDP, identified earlier as the financing gap. To stabilize the ratio of debt to GDP, we can afford to aim a little bit lower. Suppose that we aim to stabilize the debt-to-GDP ratio at around 60 percent of GDP, a policy that would at least keep the U.S. budget out of long-term trouble. If the GDP is itself growing by around 3 percent per year, a year-in, year-out budget deficit of 1.8 percent of GDP is consistent with a stable debt-to-GDP ratio. In other words, closing 4 of the 6 percentage points of GDP of the structural deficit would be enough to stabilize the debt-to-GDP ratio at 60 percent.

My point is not to settle the precise issues on spending and taxes, as these should be left to a far more detailed analysis by budget experts and to vigorous public deliberation and decision making. My point here is to insist that the rich should pay their way, and that they can easily afford to do so. All of the angst of canceling vital government programs to close the deficit is a charade put on by the rich for the rich. With a fair tax structure and a just contribution of the rich to the rest of society, we can afford a truly civilized America.

Let me clarify a point about this argument. Opponents of tax increases on the rich claim that the rich already pay more than their fair share. They claim that as much as half of the working population pays no federal taxes at all and that the richest 1 percent already pays 40 percent of the federal income taxes, compared with just 21 percent of pretax household income they receive. More taxation of the rich, according to these numbers, looks punitive.

These claims are not correct, however. First, almost all workers pay federal taxes, in the form of payroll taxes for Social Security and Medicare if not as federal income taxes. It is simply not correct to claim that the poor and working class escape from federal taxation. Second, the issue is not really the share of taxes paid by the rich but the level of taxation relative to income. Suppose that taxes were eliminated for everybody except the top 1 percent of households, whose taxes are reduced to just $1 per year. In this extreme (and deliberately silly) example, the rich would pay all the taxes, but we would not call their tax burden high.

To assess the burden of taxation, we should compare the taxes levied relative to income. In this regard, the income tax rates paid by the richest 1 percent have declined markedly from 1980 till now, falling from around 34.5 percent of income in 1980 to around

23.3 percent of income in 2008.[31] Yes, the poorer households also received tax cuts (the average tax rate on the bottom 50 percent declined from 6.1 percent in 1980 to 2.6 percent in 2008), but against meager and stagnant incomes; the rich, on the other hand, received tax cuts against soaring incomes and ended up with a historically unprecedented share of the nation's post-tax income.

Let me close this discussion by repeating a point that I made at the start of the book. I am not in the slightest against the accumulation of wealth, even vast wealth. I am not recommending a "class war." There is no case for equalizing incomes through massive redistribution, and there would be a lot of grief and economic chaos if we tried. My point isn't to bleed the rich but to call upon them to pay a decent and responsible share of the national needs. If poverty were eliminated, if all who wanted to go to college could afford to do so, if the poor lived as long as the rich, we could worry less about the responsibilities of the rich to the rest of society. We are not far away from those hallowed goals—if we invest in them. That's the rub. We need the rich today to do their modest part to enable all of society to share in prosperity. By passing that hurdle, we would reduce the need for long-term transfers from rich to poor in the future.

The Return to Civic Responsibility

For thirty years, tax increases have been vilified and rejected at the polls. That might continue, but if so, America's days as global leader and prosperous economy are numbered. For thirty years, almost all proposals for initiatives to upgrade the infrastructure and improve education for the poor have been crippled by inadequate budgets. Let me suggest three reasons why a new political majority might mobilize around a program of reduced deficits and increased public investment.

First, and most important, a new fiscal framework is needed to lift the United States out of its current economic crisis and its dangerously large budget deficit. Second, political support for higher taxation on the rich is stronger than it appears. Recent opinion surveys suggest a readiness of the broad public to support a rise in the tax burden on high-income households. Third, the United States may be set for a fundamental realignment of the "governing majority" on fiscal issues as a younger and more progressive generation comes to the fore of politics and as minorities (especially African Americans and Hispanics) constitute a growing proportion of the voting population.

A new governing majority will depend on two breakthroughs. The first is that voters, not big money, once again determine election outcomes. We need to break out of the money-politics-media trap. The second is that government be able to translate increased revenues into effective public services and infrastructure. We need, in short, a return to civic virtue, in which Americans recommit to contributing to the common benefit and to cooperating for mutual gain. Yet we won't even get started if the public's confidence in Washington remains so dreadfully low. Reform of government is a vital component of any successful economic reform. The challenge of government reform is the topic of the next chapter.

CHAPTER 12.

The Seven Habits of
Highly Effective Government

We have seen that winning campaigns and holding power require money and lots of it. Turning money into power and power back into money are Washington's two main industries. The big corporations and the politicians play the leading roles. The corporations finance the campaigns and then lobby for corporate deregulation and the contracting out of core government functions. The politicians squeeze money from the corporations in return for political services.

In 2010, the conservative members of the Supreme Court "discovered" a new constitutional right of corporations to plow their shareholders' money into political campaigns without legal limits, special internal controls, validation by shareholders, or any obligation of disclosure, in a decision called *Citizens United v. Federal Election Commission*. In his dissent, Justice John Paul Stevens harshly criticized the conservative majority for ignoring common sense as well as a hundred years of settled law:

Although they make enormous contributions to our society, corporations are not actually members of it . . . The financial resources, legal structure, and instrumental orientation of corporations raise legitimate concerns about their role in the electoral process.[1]

The role of big money in politics has completely sidelined competent public administration. Government has been outsourced to private contractors, the ones who pay the campaign bills for Congress and the White House, which sign the checks for the contracts. As a result of deregulation and outsourcing of federal functions, we live through one abject failure after the next.

The list of recent government failures is long and growing. The intelligence agencies failed to anticipate 9/11. The Bush administration launched a war over Iraqi weapons of mass destruction that did not exist. The Iraq and Afghanistan occupations were totally botched, brought down by ignorance, lack of planning, and corruption of U.S. contractors. Hurricane Katrina shattered our confidence in our emergency response system. The banking crisis shattered our confidence in financial regulation. The banking bailout destroyed any remaining sense of fairness between Wall Street and Main Street. And now we face budget deficits unprecedented since World War II, but continue to grant massive tax breaks to the richest Americans.

Can government do better? Of course it can, as it does in many other parts of the world. But to do better, Americans need to be crystal clear about what is going wrong so consistently. I propose that the federal government adopt Seven Habits of Highly Effective Government:

- Set clear goals and benchmarks.
- Mobilize expertise.
- Make multiyear plans.
- Be mindful of the far future.
- End the corporatocracy.

- Restore public management.
- Decentralize.

Set Clear Goals and Benchmarks
There is a lot to be said for stating our goals clearly. John F. Kennedy, one of America's most inspiring leaders, explained it this way:

> By defining our goal more clearly, by making it seem more manageable and less remote, we can help all peoples to see it, to draw hope from it, and to move irresistibly toward it.[2]

Great leaders set great goals. When Kennedy called for America to send a man to the moon and back within the 1960s, he gave a remarkable explanation for why he called on America to make such an arduous and challenging effort:

> [W]e choose to go to the moon in this decade and do the other things, not because they are easy, but because they are hard, because that goal will serve to organize and measure the best of our energies and skills.[3]

America should define its long-term economic goals similarly. There is, of course, no single moon shot, no variable such as gross domestic product or the unemployment rate, that can encapsulate all of our economic aspirations, but we can effectively define the major goals of a mindful economy as I did in chapter 10, with specific targets for the year 2020. In a mindful society, such goals will be widely known, and progress toward the goals will be systematically reviewed each year in the State of the Union address and the annual budget proposal. Specific objectives are frightening to make and even harder to achieve. Yet, as Kennedy said, the aspiration to accomplish great goals helps us organize the best of our energies and skills.

One part of setting bold but achievable goals is to benchmark America's performance with other countries. There are many such benchmarking exercises, but they are paid little attention by Washington and the public. If the political leadership and the American public begin to pay more attention to these benchmarks, they will better understand the case for reform.

Mobilize Expertise

The problems facing America have become much more complex over time, and the political class lacks the capacity to deal with them. The problems are global, interconnected across many areas of politics and policy, and often highly technical. The climate change challenge, for example, involves agriculture (both as a source of greenhouse gas emissions and as a highly vulnerable sector), electricity generation and distribution, federal and private land use, transportation, urban design, nuclear power, disaster risk management, climate modeling, international financing, public health, and global negotiations. Could one imagine a problem less easily handled by a layman Congress operating on a two-year election cycle?

The government's departments are organized along the traditional lines that reflect the era when issues hit the American political radar screen, not the crosscutting challenges that we face today. The departments of Labor and Commerce date from 1913, during the Progressive Era. The Department of Energy dates from 1977, following the first oil crisis. It was almost dismantled by the Reagan administration on free-market principles. We have no departments for sustainable development, climate change, international economic development, or national infrastructure. The White House offices in these areas provide no substitutes for a department. Obama's former "climate change czar" Carol Browner had a staff of fewer than a dozen professionals, almost all of whom were focused on congressional liaison rather than the technical substance of the climate change and energy agenda.

Congress is notoriously ill equipped to deal with these technical issues. Among the 535 members of Congress, those with advanced scientific and engineering training include three physicists, one chemist, six engineers, one microbiologist, and sixteen medical doctors, accounting for just 5 percent of the members.[4] Several decades back the Office of Technology Assessment (OTA) helped Congress navigate through the technology thicket. The OTA lasted from 1972 to 1995 and was then closed by a Republican-dominated Congress imbued with free-market fervor and the belief that science doesn't matter (or, perhaps more accurately, that it is threatening to powerful interests).

America's scientific and technological experts in academia and industry would be honored to contribute their knowledge toward national problem solving, but they are too rarely asked. Expertise can be harnessed through special commissions and research programs led by leading scientific bodies (such as the National Academy of Sciences, the National Science Foundation, the National Institutes of Health, and the national laboratories). Both Congress and the administration need stronger and more systematic scientific advice. Congress should reestablish the Office of Technology Assessment, and the President's Council of Advisors on Science and Technology (PCAST) should be considerably strengthened and tasked with preparing major public studies on key policy issues.

Make Multiyear Plans

The lack of clear goals, inherent complexity of issues, and mix of scientific confusion and disinformation would probably be enough to stop most coherent action in its tracks. Yet there are even greater obstacles at play in the executive branch. Even when it tries, the federal government suffers a chronic inability to develop and implement sophisticated plans.

The problem, as noted earlier, starts with the two-year national election cycle, by far the most frequent of any major economy. The president also makes an extraordinary number of political appointments at the top of each department. This has the ostensible advantage of bringing in fresh ideas with a change of political mandate. However, in practice, it leads to amateurism, a revolving door between senior officials and private business, and an incredibly time-consuming process to fill the administration's top jobs. After one year in office, according to the Partnership for Public Service, the Obama administration had filled only around 60 percent of the top five hundred jobs.[5] This has meant that throughout the administration, senior teams were not even in place as the 2010 elections approached.

All these problems of short-termism are compounded by an antiplanning mentality. More than two years into the Obama presidency, we've yet to see a coherent plan on almost any front. Health care reform was pushed through Congress without a plan. There is still no energy and climate plan. There is no plan to eliminate the budget deficit. Nobody in his right mind should advocate rigid central planning (in which the government tries to fix wages, prices, and outputs across the economy), but nobody should believe that complex challenges of science and technology, higher education, modernization of infrastructure, climate change mitigation, and the restoration of budget balance can be addressed without a careful, multiyear planning process within government.

The closest we now come to multiyear planning is the Office of Management and Budget, but OMB is focused largely on year-to-year budgets. Upgrading OMB or another agency to prepare multiyear plans for public-sector action will sound absolutely heretical to most Americans, but the truth is that most successful governments have such an agency or department, and make use of it especially to address the kinds of public investment challenges that America has been neglecting during the past thirty years.

One key—perhaps *the* key—to effective planning is to embrace complexity. The economy is a complex system, linking millions of public and private enterprises and billions of consumers around the world. With a complex system, there is rarely a single solution to a problem. "Magic bullets," or single-minded solutions, are the favorite prescriptions of superficial analysts. Beware! Whether we are dealing with balancing the budget, improving education, reducing unemployment, or addressing immigration, the solutions are likely to be messy and complex, change over time, and involve multiple levels of government, from the international to the local. Plans are vital, but they must include several interlinked policies, be adaptive over time, and be open to a wide range of participants from business, government agencies, and civil-society institutions. The point is that the solutions won't come through the easy nostrums of our day, whether tax cuts, stimulus spending, immigration crackdowns, or getting tough on teachers' unions. The only thing in common with these kinds of "plans" is that they are based on oversimplicity in a complex economy and society.

Be Mindful of the Far Future

We cannot, of course, peer into the distant future, but we can still train ourselves and orient our political system to be mindful of the far future, a time horizon, for example, of at least two generations ahead. The U.S. government pioneered such thinking with the establishment of national parks in the Yellowstone National Park Act of 1872, signed by President Ulysses S. Grant; the American Antiquities Act of 1906, signed by President Theodore Roosevelt; and the National Park Service Organic Act of 1916, signed by President Woodrow Wilson. The new National Park Service was directed "to conserve the scenery and the natural and historic objects and the wild life therein and to provide for the enjoyment of the same in such manner and by such means as will leave them unimpaired for the enjoyment of future generations."[6] In a world rife with environmental degradation, such future-oriented stewardship has become a matter of survival.

The president should devote part of every State of the Union speech to describing the implications of our actions today—in science and technology, environmental threats, demography and aging, saving and investment—for an average American in the year 2050.

This alone would open the eyes of the citizenry to our stewardship for the future. After all, today's newborns will be a mere forty years old at midcentury. We need not presume to shape the distant future; we need only respect the prospects of those newly born today.

End the Corporatocracy

As long as practical politics revolves around raising large sums for media campaigns, America's corporatocracy will remain in place and the downward economic slide will continue. During the past decade, the curtain has been pulled away from the Wizards of Washington who manipulate campaign financing, lobbying outlays, and revolving doors, and the public now understands the flow of corporate money much better than in the past. Politicians would be foolhardy to believe otherwise. Rather than despair, I therefore ask instead what might be done. How can the broken system be fixed? For that, we need to identify practical steps that could extricate the federal government from the clutches of the lobbies.

- **Provide public campaign financing.** No longer should we let Obama or any other supposedly reform-minded presidential candidate walk away from public campaign finance, as Obama did in 2008. The Democrats and Republicans are equally tarnished by private campaign finance, and neither party should be trusted. Federal campaign financing should be extended to congressional elections.
- **Provide free media time.** Broadcast TV should be required to set aside a fixed amount of time for free media according to explicit allocation rules.
- **Ban campaign contributions from lobbying firms.** Lobbying firms are a cancer on the political process. Employees of registered lobbying firms should be banned from making campaign contributions to candidates or political parties.
- **Stop the revolving door.** Senior federal employees should be barred from employment in registered lobbying firms for a

minimum of at least three years from their departure from federal service. They should also be prohibited from accepting employment in any company that lobbied their agency during their tenure in public office.

- **Take away the trough.** Corporations currently view campaign financing as a corporate investment, to obtain tax cuts for the wealthy, deregulation, no-bid government contracts, earmarks, and other perquisites of power. By directly opposing such abuses of the federal budget, corporations will have less reason to try to buy politicians through campaign financing.

When Obama became president, many of us hoped he would chase the moneylenders out of the Capitol. The financial crisis had exposed the tawdry side of Wall Street and politics and the intertwined tentacles connecting the two. Yet before the first stock market bell of his presidency had rung, Obama had installed a pro-banking team at the White House, led by Larry Summers. For the first two years of his administration, he sided mostly with the bankers, providing bailouts but asking for and getting too little in return regarding restraints on salaries, bonuses, and other abusive behaviors of the past. The bankers, not surprisingly, continued to feign surprise and hurt when anybody suggested their complicity in the crisis or the need to restrain their gargantuan pay. Whether Obama will ever take on Wall Street and the other corporate interest groups remains an open question, though hopes have grown somewhat dim.

Defeating the corporatocracy is, of course, easier said than done. American politics is a deeply entrenched, mutually supportive duopoly of parties, while the public is distracted and swayed by propaganda. Even if we know the means needed to break the power/money nexus, getting them adopted will require active political struggle. My guess is that it will be the rise of a credible third party, focused heavily on removing money from politics, that will sooner or later break the duopoly. It's not as if the problem is so complex that it is hidden from view. It is widely known, but the public does not know where to turn. Any political movement that offers a way forward will tap a very deep vein of disappointment, anger, and political mobilization. A new political party can be combined with other forms of political agitation—consumer boycotts, protests, media campaigns, and social networking efforts—to put the most egregious leaders of the corporatocracy on notice. As I discuss in the next chapter, my belief is that the young generation of Millennials, today's young people aged eighteen to twenty-nine, will have both the motive and the means to take on this challenge.

Restore Public Management

The constant "reinvention" of government has amounted mostly to poorly supervised handouts for private contractors, such as Halliburton and Blackwater in the war zones and the "Beltway bandits" who swarm around the U.S. development aid programs. The extent of contracting vastly exceeds agencies' ability to oversee the contractors' work. The contracting process, frequently no-compete arrangements, encourages corruption on an unprecedented scale. Tens of billions of dollars have gone astray in recent years while the "war lobby" encourages Congress to prolong the senseless occupations of Iraq and Afghanistan. The proper approach is to rebuild public management, not to turn it over to voracious private firms.

A starting point for proper public management would be a significant increase in trained professional managers within the departments, recruited on the basis of salaries competitive with those in the private sector. Political appointments would be reduced in number and converted to senior civil service appointments. Renewed efforts would be made to monitor, evaluate, and audit all outsourced programs. The enormous, corrupt, and wasteful no-compete contracts of the Pentagon would be brought to an end.

Decentralize

America is an enormous and diverse country that can be managed only with considerable local variation in its policies. For a long time, the political Left has routinely looked to Washington to impose its will on the entire country, on social issues such as sexual mores, income redistribution, education policy, health care, and other issues. These efforts have mostly backfired. Rather than finding compromises on these contentious issues that allow for local variations in policies, pressures for Washington-imposed uniformity have often led to an anti-Washington backlash with no results at all. It is time for those in favor of a more activist government to accept the doctrine of *subsidiarity*. This doctrine, as I noted earlier, holds that policy problems should be addressed at the most local level of government that is capable of providing a solution. Education, health, roads, water treatment, and the like can generally be addressed locally. Most tax collection, on the other hand, should be national, to reduce the serious problem of tax competition between states and localities.

There is another compelling reason for decentralization of social services. The most powerful tool for breaking extreme poverty is a holistic community-based development strategy that combines vocational training and job placement, early childhood development, educational upgrading, and local infrastructure. Each part of the antipoverty effort supports all of the others. This kind of ground-up development effort must in practice be led by the communities themselves but backed with financing from the federal and state governments.

Options for Fundamental Change

My recommendations in this chapter can be called ameliorative: they aim to use moderate means to turn around a moderately broken situation. We have to ask, however, whether this will be enough. The despair and cynicism in America are deep. There is a widespread feeling that nothing will change. Perhaps only a more dramatic break with today's political institutions can work.

One obvious starting point would be a third party, to break the corrupted duopoly of the Democrats and Republicans. The obstacles to such an effort are real but not quite as insurmountable as is often believed. In recent years we have had several important third-party candidates for president, including John Anderson in 1980, Ross Perot in 1992 and 1996, and Ralph Nader in 2000 and 2004. Each achieved ballot access across most of the United States, and each generated a significant following and made a significant contribution to the political debate.

My view is that a broad-based national party that stood for effective governance, the end of the corporatocracy, and investments in America's future could command the vital center of politics, a kind of radical centrism.[7] Perhaps an ARC—Alliance for the Radical Center—Party could test the waters in 2012. The party would be centrist because America's centrist values, which balance individualism and social responsibility, offer a basis for a new prosperity. It would be radical in that it would signal a decisive break with the recent past. The costs of launching a third party would be small, and the potential benefits could be enormous if it accomplished nothing more than awakening public awareness and putting pressure on the two corrupted major parties to clean up their acts.

A more fundamental set of constitutional reforms would usefully shift America's majoritarian constitutional system toward more parliamentarism, perhaps aiming toward a French-style mixed presidential-parliamentary system. Constitutional change is inherently slow and hazardous, the ultimate Pandora's box of politics. We can't yet know whether fundamental constitutional change will be needed to rescue American democracy. But if it is, we should aim for the benefits of parliamentary systems: a coherent government that combines the executive and legislative branches under a prime minister; a longer-term perspective of four to six years rather than our current two-year cycle; and more proportional representation, to give more weight and voting power to the poor and minorities so that their concerns, too, will be addressed—and redressed.

Saving Government Before It's Too Late

The bad old joke complains about the lousy restaurant where the food is terrible—and the portions are too small. Arguing for a larger role of government feels about the same. Yes, the federal government is incompetent and corrupt—but we need more, not less, of it. On the one hand, we need a more active role of government to address fundamental collective challenges such as infrastructure, clean energy, public education, health care, and poverty. On the other hand, the government is so dysfunctional that our tendency is to want to cut rather than expand its role. This chapter, I hope, has suggested some ways to overcome this impasse. We need more government, but also a much more competent and honest government. Economic reform and political reform must go hand in hand. Without the one there cannot be the other.

The best hope is to take big money out of big politics and to reform the public administration so that it can handle social problems of greater complexity and a longer time horizon. At a technical level, there are clear steps that can be adopted to achieve such aims. Many of these suggestions are already the law of the land in other, better-managed countries. Yet our public management problems did not emerge by accident; they reflect, in most cases, the influences of vested interests, which have all too often steered government processes toward narrow private advantage.

Who will provide the political base for cleaning up the U.S. government? All Americans should look toward the group with the biggest stake: young Americans. From the campuses to the workforce, today's Millennials, aged eighteen to twenty-nine in 2010, are already showing a distinctive generational character. They are more open, more diverse, more wired, more networked, better educated, and more committed to making government work than the generations before them. One is tempted to call the current crisis the unintended and unwelcomed bequest of the baby boomers—my generation—to America's young. America, I predict, will change more due to its youth than to their parents. How that can happen is the story of the next and final chapter.

CHAPTER 13.

The Millennial Renewal

Economic crises open the door to deep political change. The future is up for grabs. Yet the dangers also multiply. There are, after all, many more possible wrong turns than right ones. The most common outcome is that the government continues to lose competence, direction, and financial capacity. The hardest change to pull off is constructive change in the middle of a crisis. As Alexis de Tocqueville observed about the French Revolution, "The most dangerous moment for a bad government is when it begins to reform."[1]

America's deepening crisis has not yet led to any significant reforms or change in the manner of governance. If anything, the vested interests have held their ground. The Obama administration has been a government of continuity rather than change, as Wall Street, the lobbyists, and the military have remained at the center of American power and policy. This stasis has discredited government still further. American white, middle-aged conservatives are enraged at their loss of wealth and security and have lashed out at the government for adding to their debts but not to their relief. The Tea Party movement has resulted and has dominated the media coverage. The poor, meanwhile, have hunkered down, withdrawing from hope and activism as they scramble to survive and make ends meet. The young have been biding their time, trying to stay afloat in the face of high unemployment and little income.

This holding pattern cannot continue. It is like a cartoon character that runs off a cliff, looks down, yet remains suspended in midair. We know something is about to happen, but what?

There are three main tendencies at play and of course huge imponderables. The first tendency is inertia. The vested interests still have the money and the power but have lost their legitimacy and the public trust. Big banks, big insurance companies, and big arms manufacturers are close to Congress and the White House and have successfully resisted any serious intrusions into their prerogatives. The second tendency is backlash. The Tea Party is a concoction of the anger of middle-aged, middle-class white Americans who sense that their cohort is slipping from economic security and social dominance. They are furious, of course, and are easily manipulated by the status quo interests. That's an old story. Time is against them.

The third tendency, the one with the long-term play, is generational change. Opinion surveys show that something truly new is in the works. The Millennials are different from their predecessors. If the boomers are the children of TV, the Millennials are the children of the Internet. The boomers sat for hours each day transfixed by the tube; the Millennials multitask for hours each day, networking with Facebook friends, catching snippets of news, watching videos, and surfing the Net. In the meantime, they are facing unique and difficult job prospects. But there is more. The Millennials are ethnically diverse, socially liberal, better educated (though struggling to meet tuition to complete four years of college), and more trusting of government. Obama was their hope and has been their first political disappointment.

The imponderables are enormous. The U.S. crisis has a complex global context. The emerging economies are not waiting for the United States to sort itself out. Global competition is intensifying. Our major firms are footloose. If they don't make profits in the United States, they look abroad to much faster-growing markets.

Nor is the ecological crisis waiting for the United States to act. Climate change, complete with intense storms, famines, floods, and other disasters, continues to intensify. And political instability is rife, especially in the regions that are suffering from a combination of poverty, population growth, and severe environmental stress. In that category we should include Afghanistan, Yemen, Somalia, Sudan, and the countries of the Sahel. The U.S. military is involved in all of them, but with no benefit, since the underlying causes of the crises have no military solution.

Nobody can predict political outcomes in circumstances like these. Life is full of surprises, both positive and disastrous. The years 1989–1991 fit into the spectacularly positive column. A social disaster, the Bolshevik Revolution and Soviet communism, which had been born in the chaos of World War I seventy-five years earlier, quietly gave way to peaceful political change. A great leader, Mikhail Gorbachev, presided over the change of order, and one of the greatest triumphs of modern politics resulted: a mostly peaceful dismantling of an empire. Ironically, very few Americans have an appreciation of what actually transpired, and, as is so often the case, claim credit when the credit is due to others.

Yet equally disastrous accidents happen as well. Any sane, responsible citizen of the world should ponder the dates 1914, 1917, and 1933. The first marked the onset of World War I, not the war to end all wars as was advertised at the time, but the war to rip Europe asunder, with a wound so deep it has taken till now to heal, and the healing is still not completed. The second was the moment Russian chaos was manipulated by Vladimir Lenin to launch the ruinous experiment with Soviet socialism. The third, in the depths of the Great Depression, was the unexpected and wholly accidental rise to power of Adolf Hitler.[2] The economic crisis of 1933 meant that anything could happen, and the very worst did. The world was bled as never before and perhaps never again, since a similar total war could end the world itself.

These are morbid thoughts, but they are my darker forebodings prompted by the current political drift in the United States. Most of the time, drift leads only to more drift. Time is lost, but without calamity. Yet once in a while, political drift ends up in disaster. When the political and economic situation is as dangerous as it is today, cynicism and loss of time are far more dangerous than they look. History plays cruel tricks on the unserious. American political leaders have been in an unserious mood for years, unwilling to level with the American people.

The propositions that I've laid out in this book are politically feasible. They start with the individual: to pull back from hypercommercialism, unplug from the noisy media a bit, and learn more about and reflect on the current economic situation. A mindful economy calls on each of us with an above-average income to understand that if we are prudent, we can make do with a little less take-home pay. Much of affluent households' consumption can be trimmed without disaster and quite probably with some gain in equanimity and satisfaction. The affluent probably incur as much buyer's remorse as they do lasting pleasure from their luxury purchases.

It is, in my view, the Millennials, aged eighteen to twenty-nine in the year 2010, who more than any other group will shape the future of America in the next twenty-five years. They embody the future with all its complexity and transformation. Though 80 percent of Americans over the age of sixty-five are white non-Hispanic, only 61 percent of the Millennials are white non-Hispanic. (The data here and that follow are from a recent Pew Research Center study.)[3] Around 19 percent are Hispanic, another 13 percent are African American, and 6 percent are of other ethnicities, including Asian and Native American. Still younger cohorts, those between ages zero and fourteen, are even more racially diverse, with only 55 percent white non-Hispanic, 23 percent Hispanic, and 15 percent African American.[4]

The Millennials are politically progressive, believing in a larger role for the government. Sixty-seven percent support a "bigger government providing more services," compared with only 31 percent of those over sixty-five. This is the result not only of their ethnic profile but of their age, optimism, and generational outlook. White non-Hispanic Millennials, as well as Hispanic and African American Millennials, are more progressive than their older counterparts. They will also resist the deficit-increasing implications of further tax cuts on the rich. It is today's generation, after all, that will be paying the bills left behind by the boomers.

The Millennials, of course, have a longer time horizon than other adults in the society, so it is not surprising that they are activists regarding long-term investments such as clean energy and infrastructure. Far more than older adults, they recognize the science of climate change, and far more than the older cohorts, they support action. They will be the main beneficiaries of a modernized infrastructure or the main victims of continued decay. Of course, in a truly mindful economy, the parents of Millennials (like me) will care deeply about the world we are bequeathing to our children and their children.

The greatest challenge in American society has always been the reality of diversity. It divided the country from the start, led to a bloody civil war, created an apartheid society for a hundred years afterward, and unleashed the most dramatic social change from below of the twentieth century during the civil rights era. The shock waves of the civil rights era have reverberated ever since. It is therefore of historic importance that Millennials show every sign of greater tolerance than their predecessors. This seems to be true regarding every hot-button issue of religion, sex, and race. The Millennials are less religious and less often affiliated with a specific denomination; they are less evangelical in outlook; and they are less likely to attend weekly services. They overwhelmingly accept homosexuality (63 percent say that homosexuality "should be accepted by society," as opposed to 35 percent of those over sixty-five). They believe by a narrow majority that abortion should be legal in all or most cases (52 percent compared with 37 percent of those over sixty-five). Their favorable attitudes toward interracial relations and intermarriage befit a generation that was born and raised well after the achievements of the civil rights era.

The Millennials, as a result, are less likely to be divided or even torn asunder by the culture wars of the boomer generation. They will live naturally with diversity. They will accept a more activist government. They will be more attuned to environmental needs. All this points in the direction of the mindful economy, if the healing strengths of the Millennial generation's tolerance and optimism are mobilized for collective political action.

What, then, are the real barriers to political change? Of course, the current vested interests will continue to fight fiercely for power and privilege. Wealth can certainly defend itself aggressively, through media power, financial largesse through lobbying and campaign financing, and more nefarious means. We had a taste of that power in 2008, when the banks not only won their bailouts but also got the White House and Congress to turn a blind eye to the continuation of outlandish bonuses even in the midst of the storm.

Alternatively, the anger of the Tea Party could presage a much more explosive environment of street unrest, but it is hard to envision the middle-aged and elderly Tea Partiers at the barricades! Or the economy could deteriorate to the point of creating a downward spiral of rising budget deficits, a deepening political crisis, and yet further deficits. That's the path that leads to hyperinflations and defaults on government debt. Such disasters are more frequent than we in the United States tend to realize. Thank goodness, we've never experienced such an upheaval, at least since the Revolutionary War and Civil War. I've helped to clean up hyperinflation in many other countries, however. Fortunately we're not close to that now, but another five to ten years of drift could certainly bring us closer to the fiscal cliff. One recalls the dark joke in the waning days of the Soviet collapse: "Comrades, we were at the edge of the cliff, and we've just taken a giant step forward!" A few more tax cuts for the rich, and we'll be in a position to say the same.

Real change will not come easily because there is so little consensus on the way forward. America may well continue to choose very badly, for example by cutting taxes further despite the gaping deficits or continuing to reject decisive action on climate change because of the poor economic conditions. Politics, alas, is filled with "positive feedbacks," meaning in essence that one damn thing leads to another, with each disaster causing the next. In recent years, the outsourcing of government services to incompetent and corrupt contractors has led to repeated failures, leading to more criticism of government and then, ironically, to still more outsourcing! The collapse of government becomes, in essence, a self-fulfilling prophecy.

All this means that it's extremely difficult to get on the right track. Yet it's certainly possible. The actual solutions are within reach and require only moderate changes of course. And the pace of change accelerates these days because the spread of ideas is so much faster than in the past. What seems outlandish and impossible one moment becomes mainstream and inevitable the next.

Eyes on the Prize

When short-term navigating is so difficult, the key is to keep one's eyes on the long-term prize. We spend an inordinate amount of time worrying about the latest wiggle in consumer confidence, industrial production, or new orders. Great fortunes are made and lost depending on who can guess better, even when little can really be done about the economy's short-term meanderings. A far better use of our time would be to maintain long-term focus on the issues that will have mattered decisively when we look back after a quarter century. I believe that four issues will prove to be decisive for America and its place in the world: education, environment, geopolitics, and diversity.

The first decisive issue will be education. The path to national prosperity, life satisfaction, and sustainability in the twenty-first century will depend heavily on education, and especially on a large proportion of today's young Americans being able to complete higher education, albeit a higher education that has been fashioned to fit the needs of our times. The labor-market data tell the brutal truth: low-skilled workers are either scraping by in near poverty or failing to find work altogether. There is almost no chance today of securing a well-remunerated career without a college degree or its equivalent in vocational training. Low-skilled jobs are being filled by recent immigrants prepared to accept wages a cut above those of their home countries, replaced by outsourcing, or eliminated by reengineering the jobs away entirely using advanced information technology. Young people know these facts and are prepared to go deeply into debt to achieve a higher degree. Yet steeply rising tuition and onerous borrowing terms have led to epidemics of dropouts or limited enrollment in the first place.

One of the bright spots in education is the potential, still in its early days, for information technology to transform the educational process, making it more effective and accessible to all. More and more curricula can be found online; more and more distance learning can link disparate parts of the world together. Each Tuesday morning at Columbia University I have the joy of participating in a "global classroom" with twenty campuses around the world linked via Internet-based videoconferencing into a global discussion of sustainable development. As the discussion bounces from Beijing to Ibadan, Nigeria, to Antananarivo, Madagascar, to New York City, the thrill of global problem solving comes to life for hundreds of young people around the world. If anyone is equipped to carry this technological potential forward, it is today's Millennials and their younger brothers and sisters!

The second decisive issue will be environment. Today the issues of climate change, water scarcity, resource depletion, and biodiversity seem like special problems that can be relegated to the Sunday talk shows and newspaper science sections. Within a generation, and probably much sooner, these will loom as the largest challenges facing the planet. The world is headed over the cliff, exceeding or soon to exceed the safe global boundaries on countless ecological fronts: greenhouse gas emissions, pollution from nitrogen-based and phosphorus-based fertilizers, water scarcity, habitat destruction, and much more.[5] The United States will experience water stress in the Midwest, drought in the Southwest, extreme weather events in many parts of the country but most seriously the hurricane-impacted Gulf Coast, hypoxic zones in the estuaries, and profound coastal erosion and threats from rising sea levels. The vulnerability of the poorer countries is likely to be far worse, with at least some experiencing violent conflict as a result of encroaching droughts, floods, and other climate-induced calamities.[6]

Once again, social networking and the promise of new IT technologies will make a profound difference. Mobile telephony and wireless broadband are already making possible new breakthroughs in environmental surveillance (soil mapping, drought monitoring, discovery of deforestation and illegal fishing, crop estimation, tracking of population movements and disease transmission, and much more) and disaster response. The IT revolution created the new globalization; it can lead to the "new sustainability" as well. Once again, Millennials will take the lead in these breakthrough prospects.

The third decisive issue is geopolitics. No matter what success the United States has in recovering its dynamism and vitality in the years ahead, it is almost inevitable (barring global catastrophe) that America's relative economic position will decline. We are, I have stressed repeatedly, in the age of convergence, in which the emerging economies have the prospect of decades of economic growth that is more rapid than that of their high-income counterparts. The United States currently represents around 20 percent of gross world product (GWP), measured in purchasing-power-adjusted dollars. That is likely to decline by midcentury to perhaps 10 to 12 percent of GWP, with China and India both being larger in absolute size than the United States, though still with roughly half of its per capita GDP.[7]

Managing the shifting relations of leading and upcoming major powers has never been easy. The competition between the United

Kingdom and Germany in the first years of the twentieth century played a major role in Germany's launch of World War I. Similarly, the competition among Germany, Russia, the United Kingdom, and France in Europe, and between the United States and Japan in Asia, contributed to World War II. The potential dangers must therefore be understood and consistently averted. This will tax our diplomacy, patience, and capacity to cooperate to the maximum degree.

The fourth and greatest area of challenge, implicated in all of the first three, is managing diversity. This challenge seems to be humanity's hardest task of all. The great religions all preach the universal brotherhood of humanity, but they also simultaneously warn against the perfidy of the nonbeliever, the "other," the heathen. This duality—the capacity both to cooperate and to segregate—probably has its roots in the deepest recesses of our psyches. It most likely reflects, after all, the deepest evolutionary forces that have shaped our species: the urge to care for our young and our in-group and the need to defend our young and our turf from other clans.

Whatever the deeper neurochemistry, humans have a profound ability both to cooperate and nurture and to shun others and fight.[8] In our advanced technological age, with the capacity of our weapons to end human life, our ability to master our baser emotions and channel them toward constructive and cooperative outcomes will provide the basis for our survival. Like all of the challenges described in this book, this, too, will require unerring mindfulness. The Buddhist teaching of compassion—the training to treat all other sentient beings as objects of our care—is smart not only for our long-term mental well-being, but also for our ability to avoid self-destruction.

The challenge of diversity will be front and center of every policy and crisis, domestic and international, in the decades ahead. We have arrived at a global society, but with the clannish instincts inherited from the tropical savanna. Or, as E. O. Wilson put it inimitably in his foreword to my book *Common Wealth*, "We exist in a bizarre combination of Stone Age emotions, medieval beliefs, and god-like technology. That, in a nutshell, is how we have lurched into the early twenty-first century."[9]

John F. Kennedy and his counselor and speechwriter, Theodore Sorensen, were America's greatest exemplars of an exacting mental discipline and empathy in the quest for global survival in the midst of diversity and conflict. Kennedy was president at the height of the Cold War, when tensions and tactics nearly led the world to mutual annihilation in the Cuban missile crisis. In his reasoning and his coaxing of his fellow Americans, Kennedy invariably bade us to respect our competitors, in his time the Soviet people, and to consider carefully how they might perceive, and dangerously misunderstand, any provocative actions on our part.

The core of the Kennedy-Sorensen message was consistent: that our common humanity made it possible to find common cause in the midst of competition and that peace depended on our own virtue and ethical behavior. As Kennedy put it in his famous "Peace Speech" at American University in June 1963:

"When a man's ways please the Lord," the Scriptures tell us, "he maketh even his enemies to be at peace with him." And is not peace, in the last analysis, basically a matter of human rights—the right to live out our lives without fear of devastation—the right to breathe air as nature provided it—the right of future generations to a healthy existence?[10]

Kennedy's virtue in pursuing peace was evident to his Soviet counterparts, led by Communist Party Secretary Nikita Khrushchev. Upon hearing Kennedy's words, Khrushchev quickly responded with his desire to pursue peace as well. A few weeks later, the Limited Nuclear Test Ban Treaty was signed, setting the world on a far safer course. It is a great lesson in mindfulness that will inspire us for generations to come.

The Next Steps

The great role must now be played by each of us, as citizens, family members, and members of our society. For several decades now, money has trumped votes; expediency has clouded the future; and we Americans have been too distracted to defend our rights. We must now redress a society dangerously out of balance. Yet as large as these problems are, they can be overcome if we face them as a unified society, acting on shared values of freedom, justice, and regard for the future. In the Peace Speech a half century ago, Kennedy told his fellow Americans, "No problem of human destiny is beyond human beings. Man's reason and spirit have often solved the seemingly unsolvable—and we believe they can do it again."[11]

Let us move forward, then, with our reason and spirit. Let each of us commit first to be good to ourselves and our long-term happiness by disconnecting from TV and the media long enough each day to regain our bearings, to read more books, to ensure that we are well-informed citizens. Let us keep abreast of science and technology—on climate change, energy systems, transportation options, and disease control—so that we can support the shared public actions needed to help secure our futures. Let us study the federal budget to know what's real and what is gimmickry in our politics, so that the rich and powerful don't simply walk away with the whole prize. And let us not forget the poor around us, in our neighborhoods, and in our global village even if they are halfway around the world. Our own safety and peace at heart depend on our acts of compassion and our interconnection with those in need.

As a society, let's resolve to live up to the spirit of high accomplishment, fair play, and equality of opportunity that has defined America in its best days. America will not again dominate the world economy or geopolitics as it did in the immediate aftermath of World War II. That was a special historical moment; we can be glad that economic progress throughout the world is rapidly creating a more balanced global economy and society. Yet we need not hide from the heightened global competition either. If we again invest in ourselves—for good health, safe environment, knowledge, and cutting-edge skills—renewed American prosperity can still be secured. A strong and prosperous America will not only compete in the global marketplace but also cooperate more effectively in global politics. Our future lies in a healthy, productive balance of competition and cooperation in an interconnected society.

Every American can play a role. No class war is needed or intended. Yet as America's greatest businessmen, from Andrew Carnegie to Bill Gates, Warren Buffett, and George Soros, have known, those with great business skills have great responsibilities as well. Not only is there no excuse for hiding money in tax havens or lobbying to cut taxes that are urgently needed, there is a high civic responsibility to support public collective actions necessary and to augment those public actions with private philanthropy and leadership. The tens of billions of dollars given by Gates, Buffett, and Soros for global health, poverty reduction, good governance, and political freedom are proof of what can be accomplished by farsighted individuals who turn their unique business acumen to global problem solving as well as policy.

We are, in the end, stewards of the future at a time when our shared future is imperiled by economic divisions, shortsightedness, and a growing ecological crisis. We have great tasks ahead, to redeem once again the American trust in democracy and equality. We have a high responsibility to our children and other generations that will come. Let us begin anew.

ACKNOWLEDGMENTS

A work of political economy is necessarily a work of individual responsibility: only the author is responsible for the interpretations
of a nation's political and economic life. At the same time, such a
work is inevitably the result of countless discussions and debates
with colleagues, friends, and family. *The Price of Civilization* in
that sense is also a group product, the result of a social process over
several years of trying to make sense of America's ongoing political
and economic crises.

As always, my family was the first resort for sharing my half-baked
ideas and having the worst ones removed quickly from the kitchen.
And indeed it was the kitchen where Sonia, Lisa, Adam, Hannah,
Matt, Andrea, and I most frequently congregated to try to make
sense of the daily economic news and to try to piece it together into
a larger canvas. With gratitude to all for allowing me to clog up the
kitchen table for years with streams of opinion survey results, national accounts data, presidential budgets, and mountains of books,
book, books.

Aniket Shah, my special assistant at the Earth Institute, was the
constant, skilled, and relentless navigator at my side, helping me to
organize, analyze, and sift through mountains of data and studies,
and pressing me to be clearer, better focused, and more timely (!)

in making sense of it all. Without Aniket, there would be no book. We were overjoyed to be joined in the final months by Claire Bulger, newly arrived at the Earth Institute, whose keen eye and precision helped to clear up ambiguities and to ferret out errors through the final polishing of the manuscript.

As usual, I leaned heavily, and I hope not *too* heavily, on friends and colleagues to read various parts of the manuscript and to give me their insights and commentary. I am delighted to thank Meir Stampfer, John McArthur, and Foad Mardukhi for their very careful reading and detailed comments. I am indebted to my father-in-law, Walter Ehrlich, for his relentlessly penetrating observations and interpretations of public events, and for his thorough comments on parts of the manuscript. I give thanks, too, for the inspiration of Ted Sorensen, who generously shared with me his life-affirming vision of government as an instrument of peace and problem solving. With his passing this year, we have lost a voice of reason, compassion, and optimism. And as always I am deeply grateful to my colleagues Erin Trowbridge and Kyu-Young Lee for helping me to extend the public policy dialogue through social networks, blogs, and media debates.

For many years I have felt that America's harsh politics and divisive public discourse are shortchanging the public's deep longing for well-being. A wonderful trip to Bhutan last year, and my ongoing efforts with Bhutan's enlightened leadership to promote Bhutan's concept of "Gross National Happiness," have helped me to understand more clearly how societies in our era can champion the pursuit of happiness. I extend my special thanks, therefore, to Prime Minister Jigme Thinley; His Majesty Jigme Khesar Namgyel Wangchuk; Bhutan's permanent representative to the UN, Lhatu Wangchuk; and Karma Tshiteem, secretary of the Commission on Gross National Happiness.

America's political discourse is so toxic in part because of the irresponsibility of much of the media, notably the countless TV and radio shows that draw viewers through extremism utterly untethered from truth and basic civility. It's been a great privilege, therefore, to be able to discuss the topics of this book on television shows that are marked by good conversation, good humor, and a consistent sense of decency. I thank Joe Scarborough, Mika Brzezinski, Fareed Zakaria, Tom Keene, and Charlie Rose for their professionalism and sense of responsibility, and for welcoming me as a regular participant in their programs.

This book was written in the course of an overfilled schedule at the Earth Institute, the United Nations, and on-site work throughout Africa, Asia, the Middle East, and beyond. I could find the time for thought and reflection only because of the excellence and unstinting generosity of my colleagues in all facets of my work. I would like to give special thanks to my chief of staff, Joanna Rubinstein; my executive assistant, Heidi Kleedtke; Director's Office support Donald Wheat and Suzette Espeut; MDG Centre directors Amadou Niang and Belay Begashaw; Earth Institute COO Steve Cohen; and Earth Institute associate director Peter Schlosser. For a decade now, Columbia University has been the ideal home in every way for this range of work, and for that I am profoundly grateful for the leadership of President Lee Bollinger.

My editors and literary agents turned a book concept into a reality through their unstinting professionalism at every turn. Random House editor Jonathan Jao has been scintillating and cogent at every turn. His suggestions and editorial talents are reflected in every high point of the book. The low points, I fear, are the places where I didn't listen carefully enough to his sage editorial advice. As in my past books, Scott Moyers and Andrew Wylie guided me at every twist and turn, from the very first musings about the usefulness of a new book on America's political and economic predicament to the delivery of the final manuscript. In the course of three books now, they have made book writing a wondrous glide path from conception to landing, a talent that an inveterate and relentless traveler like me appreciates to the skies.

To all of you, I am grateful for your confidence in my ideas, while of course absolving you from association with those with which you take issue. To the readers, I thank you in advance for the joys of dialogue and collegiality that you have consistently shown me in the ongoing lives of *The End of Poverty, Common Wealth*, and my other books and articles.

FURTHER READINGS

One of the great joys in writing this book was the opportunity to read and savor dozens of major volumes and hundreds of academic papers on topics ranging from moral philosophy, to political economy, to modern American history, to neurophysiology. The book's hundreds of endnotes and list of references will help steer the reader through the massive amount of scholarly writing on the topics addressed in this book. Since there is so much material, I think it is also useful to offer some suggestions to readers on a more limited and focused journey through the literature.

The following describes some of the key books that I found to be most important as I pondered the complex landscape of American political economy. This is not a representative sample of books, nor a comprehensive account of heated debates, but rather a personal view of many of the high points of analysis. These are books that made a deep impression on me as I tried to sort out fact from opinion and truth from propaganda. I've grouped the books into major categories, though there are inevitable overlaps across these fields, as I hope the text makes patently clear.

Modern American Political History

The events detailed in the book really start in the 1960s, at the apogee of activist government, the era of Kennedy's New Frontier and Johnson's War on Poverty. *The Liberal Hour*, by G. Calvin Mackenzie and Robert Weisbrot, offers a wonderful narrative of that era. The end of activist government is treated in many places. One excellent book is *Chain Reaction*, by Thomas Edsall and Mary Edsall, which describes how the civil rights era, and the realignments it created, led from the Kennedy-Johnson 1960s to the Reagan 1980s. Another superb book describing how the 1970s were a political bridge between the liberal 1960s and conservative 1980s is *Pivotal Decade* by Judith Stein. Sean Wilentz thoroughly and cogently describes the Reagan years and their long legacy through 2008 in *The Age of Reagan*.

There has perhaps been no more consistent and able chronicler of America's descent into a modern Gilded Age than Kevin Phillips. Since Phillips first accurately proclaimed *The Emerging Republican Majority* in 1969, he has chronicled the rise of modern finance-based capitalism in America, and its debilitating effects on politics and society. Phillips's tomes on the new Gilded Age include *Arrogant Capital* (1994), *Wealth and Democracy* (2002), and *Bad Money* (2008).

The Economics of Happiness

After a long lapse in the serious study of economic well-being, economists have finally begun to take happiness seriously again as an area of research. Two exemplary recent texts in this new field are Richard Layard's *Happiness: Lessons from a New Science* and Carol Graham's *The Pursuit of Happiness*. They build on a veritable outpouring of hundreds of scholarly articles in academic journals. Another powerful book that challenges the assumed links between consumer goods and well-being is Avner Offer's *The Challenge of Affluence: Self-Control and Well-Being in the United States and Britain Since 1950.*

The Neuroscience and Psychology of Happiness

Of course, economists are not alone in trying to understand the links between consumerism and well-being. Indeed, they are late to the table. Psychologists and neuroscientists have been at it for decades, and in recent years have been making breakthroughs with powerful new tools such as brain scans. Fascinating recent accounts of these psychological and neuroscientific insights include Donald Pfaff's *The Neuroscience of Fair Play*, David Linden's *The Compass of Pleasure*, Deirdre Barrett's *Supernormal Stimuli*, and Daniel Gilbert's *Stumbling on Happiness.* If there is a consistent theme throughout these studies, it is that much of what delivers well-being depends on unconscious mental processes and brain pathways of which we are only dimly aware. Yet as a society and economy we've learned to tamper with those pathways, often dangerously, not only through narcotics use but also through pervasive and invasive advertising, the visual imagery of mass media, new and unhealthy methods of food preparation, and the relentless PR campaigns fed by corporate lobbying.

Wisdom of the Ages

Well before there were brain scans and public opinion surveys, there were philosophers who acutely considered the human condition and the pathways to life satisfaction. Two who have left a lasting mark on humanity for more than two millennia are the Buddha and Aristotle. Though Buddhism has primarily affected the course of civilization in South and East Asia, while Aristotelian thought has mainly affected the course of civilization in the West, the two great schools of thought share deep insights and also complement each other. One of my great joys in writing this book was the chance to savor Aristotle's classic tome *The Nicomachean Ethics,* considered by some in the West to be the greatest philosophical tract ever written. As for the Buddha's teachings, in addition to specific texts such as "The Four Noble Truths" and "The Eightfold Path," I have long found the Dalai Lama to be the most inspiring guide to Buddhist thought, and was especially moved by his *Ethics for the New Millennium* and *The Art of Happiness.*

In the modern era, from the European Enlightenment till today, philosophers have continued to speculate about the deep motivations of human action and the ultimate sources of human well-being. Adam Smith's *The Theory of Moral Sentiments* remains one of the most acute (and also entertaining) texts on the many motivations of individuals as they are influenced by social dynamics and status. Modern philosophers have emphasized not only what gives happiness but what delivers justice. Revisiting the famous debate between John Rawls's *A Theory of Justice* and Robert Nozick's *Anarchy, State, and Utopia* remains a very powerful way to reflect on the themes of individual liberty versus social justice and ethical responsibility. Philosopher Peter Singer has added a powerful utilitarian voice to the debate in recent books such as *The Life You Can Save.* One powerful attempt to bring together the lessons of the ancient sages, the wisdom of the modern philosophers, and the insights of modern psychology is Jonathan Haidt's *The Happiness Hypothesis.* This book is sure to stimulate thinking and debate and helped me to wend my way through the long history of human speculations on these crucial topics.

Economic Underpinnings

The main economic theme of the book is that the United States has lost the appropriate balance between the market and the government. Economic well-being depends on a mixed economy. Adam Smith knew as much. Readers of *The Wealth of Nations* (especially Book V) will recall that Smith favored the active role of government in law enforcement, public works, and education, among other areas. The two most influential "small government" texts of the twentieth century, Friedrich Hayek's *The Road to Serfdom* and Milton Friedman's *Capitalism and Freedom*, are much more frequently quoted than read. This is a shame. Both are well worth reading today, in part to remind readers that even arch–market liberals like Hayek and Friedman believed in government responsibility in the economy, not least to protect the environment, provide infrastructure, and ensure an educated population. On a related note, the German market economist Wilhelm Röpke, in *A Humane Economy*, brilliantly emphasized the need for moral boundaries to protect human values from the overbearing pressures of the marketplace.

There has been a flood of books in recent years about what has gone wrong in particular sectors of the American economy as the result of the retreat of government from economic regulation, stabilization, and provision of public goods. The list alone would take several pages just for the blunders in the financial and monetary sectors. William Fleckenstein and Frederick Sheehan scathingly and succinctly document Alan Greenspan's serial blunders in *Greenspan's Bubbles*. Andrew Hacker powerfully addresses the collapse of the social safety net for middle-class Americans in *The Great Risk Shift*. George Halvorson, CEO of Kaiser Permanente, ably explains the failures of the American health care system in *Health Care Will Not Reform Itself*. Two leading economists, Claudia Goldin and Lawrence Katz, meticulously document the government sector's underinvestments in education in *The Race Between Education and Technology*. The dangers of runaway public debt are thoroughly documented in *This Time Is Different*, by economists Carmen Reinhart and Kenneth Rogoff, who add a long and fascinating historical perspective to the dangers of budget profligacy.

The most stunning result of bad public policy has been the

surge of income inequality, especially the soaring incomes of the super-rich. Globalization may have initiated the rise of inequality in the 1970s, but deliberate and inequitable government actions to cut top tax rates, deregulate finance, and in general cater to corporate interests have greatly exacerbated the inequalities. Part of the story is the spread of international tax havens used to shelter the incomes of the rich, a story told with uncommon vigor and insight by Nicholas Shaxson in *Treasure Islands: Uncovering the Damage of Offshore Banking and Tax Havens*. A closely related aspect of the inequality is the surge of CEO take-home pay, made possible by the weak corporate governance of American shareholders and boards of directors. The key reference work on unjustified CEO compensation is *Pay Without Performance: The Unfulfilled Promise of Executive Compensation*, by Harvard Law School professors Lucian Bebchuk and Jesse Fried.

Comparative Political Institutions

As I emphasize throughout the book, Americans will benefit by learning more about market-government choices made by other societies, most notably the successful social democracies of Scandinavia. The greatest analyst of Scandinavian social democracy is sociologist Gøsta Esping-Andersen, whose books include *The Three Worlds of Welfare Capitalism* and *Why We Need a New Welfare State* (co-edited). It is also important for Americans to understand U.S. performance on key dimensions (economic, social, and environmental) compared with other high-income countries. The Organisation for Economic Co-operation and Development, the World Economic Forum, Transparency International, and the United Nations Development Programme each offer a multitude of online data and rankings that help countries to benchmark their performance, and which are useful reference points for Americans as they contemplate the options for change.

American Political Values

Perhaps my most pleasant surprise in writing this book lay in my reacquaintance with the common sense and decent values of the American people. We are told daily by Fox News that America is a conservative country well represented by the Tea Party movement. The evidence is otherwise. America is a moderate and pragmatic country, with a generous commitment to helping the poor even as most Americans insist that the poor should take the lead in achieving their own economic betterment.

Political scientists over the years have done an excellent job in describing this "centrist" position. A recent valuable contribution is Benjamin Page and Lawrence Jacobs's *Class War? What Americans Really Think About Economic Inequality.* A similar message can be found in Larry Bartels's *Unequal Democracy: The Political Economy of the New Gilded Age.* Bartels shows that Americans are moderate even if the politics are extreme, in part because the views of the rich carry a hugely disproportionate weight in Congress. The confusion between what Americans really believe and what we are told they believe is partly the result of deliberate corporate propaganda. There is no better guide to the relentless anti-science assault of major U.S. corporate polluters than the recent study *Merchants of Doubt,* by Naomi Oreskes and Erik Conway.

Of course, America's decent public values are also under threat, because of the loss of confidence in government and the waning of trust among the public. The leading scholar of the shriveling of public trust is the sociologist and political scientist Robert Putnam. Putnam's masterpiece, *Bowling Alone,* carefully documents and helps to explain the loss of "social capital" in the United States in recent decades.

Monitoring the actual values held by Americans, rather than the slanted claims about American values made by pundits and propagandists, has become easier to do through the mass availability of public opinion surveys. In addition to the important survey results from polling firms such as Gallup and Rasmussen, the Pew Research Center for the People & the Press offers a continuing stream of online, first-rate survey data. Another notable monitor of political views is the University of Maryland's innovative Center on Policy Attitudes.

The Complexity of Problem Solving

In my two recent previous books, *The End of Poverty* and *Common Wealth*, I emphasized that solutions to complex problems such as those facing America today need to be holistic, adaptive in design, and goal oriented. In short, we need "complex systems thinking" to move forward. There are no magic bullets and few shortcuts to success. The need for systems thinking will probably be most urgent in the near future in addressing the simultaneous challenges of energy security, environmental safety, and economic prosperity. A number of recent books show how to engage in such complex systems thinking about the sustainable development challenge, including Steven Cohen's *Sustainability Management*, Peter Calthorpe's *Urbanism in the Age of Climate Change*, Charles Weiss and William Bonvillian's *Structuring an Energy Technology Revolution*, Lester Brown's *World on the Edge*, and William Mitchell and co-authors' *Reinventing the Automobile*.

NOTES

Part I: The Great Crash

Chapter 1: Diagnosing America's Economic Crisis

1. U.S. Census Bureau, "Current Population Survey: Annual Social and Economic (ASEC) Supplement." According to the U.S. Census Bureau, there are roughly 44 million people, or 14.3 percent of Americans, who live below the poverty line. Another 60 million people live between the poverty line and two times the poverty line, a zone that may be considered the "shadow" of poverty.
2. Plato, "Apology," in *Five Dialogues*, transl. G.M.A. Grube (Indianapolis: Hackett, 2002), p. 41.

Chapter 2: Prosperity Lost

1. Gallup Poll, "In general, are you satisfied or dissatisfied with the way things are going in the United States at this time?," May 5–8, 2011.
2. Rasmussen Reports, "Right Direction or Wrong Track," March 2011.
3. Rasmussen Reports, "65% Now Hold Populist, or Mainstream, Views," January 2010.
4. Robert D. Putnam, *Bowling Alone: The Collapse and Revival of American Community* (New York: Simon & Schuster, 2002); Robert D. Putnam, "E Pluribus Unum: Diversity and Community in the Twenty-first Century: The 2006 Johan Skytte Prize Lecture," *Scandinavian Political Studies* 30, no. 2 (June 2007).
5. Richard Easterlin, "Does Economic Growth Improve the Human Lot? Some Empirical Evidence," in Paul A. David and Melvin W. Reder, eds., *Nations and Households in Economic Growth: Essays in Honor of Moses Abramovitz* (New York: Academic Press, 1974).
6. Betsey Stevenson and Justin Wolfers, "The Paradox of Declining Female Happiness," NBER Working Paper Series, No. 14969, May 2009.
7. Tom Rath and Jim Harter, *Wellbeing: The Five Essential Elements*, Appendix G: "Wellbeing Around the World" (New York: Gallup Press, 2010). Gallup asked respondents whether they were "thriving," "struggling," or

"suffering." The U.S. ranked nineteenth in the proportion of "thriving" respondents, behind Denmark, Finland, Ireland, Norway, Sweden, the Netherlands, Canada, New Zealand, Switzerland, Australia, Spain, Israel, Austria, the United Kingdom, Belgium, Mexico, Panama, the United Arab Emirates, and just ahead of France, Saudi Arabia, Puerto Rico, and Jamaica.

8. Philip Brickman and Donald Campbell, "Hedonic Relativism and Planning the Good Society," in M. H. Apley, ed., *Adaptation Level Theory: A Symposium* (New York: Academic Press, 1971), pp. 287–302.

9. Data from U.S. Bureau of Labor Statistics, "Employment Situation Summary" and "Overview of BLS Statistics on Employment."

As is well known, these unemployment rate figures mask an even larger crisis of underemployment. Millions more workers have dropped out of the labor force altogether because they were unable to find jobs and are therefore no longer counted in the headline unemployment rate (which includes only those actively seeking work). Millions more are on forced part-time work. Adding these two groups to the official unemployment rate suggests a true underemployment rate closer to 20 percent of the adult population. In addition, more than 2 million mostly young men are incarcerated in prisons, out of the labor force the hard way.

10. Ibid.

11. For current data, see: U.S. Bureau of Labor Statistics, "Employment Situation Summary." For historical data, see U.S. Census Bureau, *Income, Poverty and Health Insurance Coverage in the US: 2009.*

12. The 2011 estimate comes from Congressional Budget Office, "An Analysis of the President's Budgetary Proposals for Fiscal Year 2012," Table 1.5.

13. Alicia M. Munnell, Anthony Webb, and Francesca Golub-Soss, "The National Retirement Risk Index: After the Crash," Center for Retirement Research, October 2009, No. 9-22, p. 1.

14. Most private-sector pension plans are defined-contribution plans, meaning that the payout upon retirement depends on the cumulative return to the pension investments made on behalf of the individual during the working years. Many public employees at the state and local level, by contrast, have defined-benefit plans, meaning that the government employer must set aside enough funds to ensure the promised payout. If the returns on the pension investments falter, as they did in 2008 and after, more payments have to be made into the pension fund to ensure the adequacy of the investment pool to meet the promised retirement benefits. State and local governments are lagging significantly far behind the required contributions as of 2011.

15. See International Monetary Fund, "World Economic Outlook Database: October 2010," for China's national savings rate.

16. American Society of Civil Engineers, "2009 Report Card for America's Infrastructure," March 2009.

17. Organisation for Economic Co-operation and Development, Programme for International Student Assessment, "PISA 2009 Results."

High school performance is seriously lagging in many other ways as well. During the 1950s and 1960s, the high school graduation rate rose in the United States, but then it began to stagnate and even decline in the 1980s and 1990s. While there has been a slight increase in the past decade, the 2009 graduation rate (defined as the number of high school graduates divided by the number of incoming high school freshmen four years earlier) was still lower than in 1970! The U.S. Department of Education estimates a 78 percent graduation rate in 1970, falling to 74 percent in 1984, 73 percent in 1994, and 72 percent in 2001, before rising to 75 percent in 2008. The gaps between nonwhite Hispanics, at 81 percent, and minority groups (Hispanics, African Americans, and Native Americans), in the low 60s, are large and at best narrowing only slightly. Recent studies show that fewer than half of all high school graduates are "college ready," meaning that they have the literacy and numeracy to perform at the college level. U.S. Department of Education, National Center for Educational Statistics, June 2010, "The Condition of Education 2010," p. 214.

18. John Michael Lee and Anita Rawls, "The College Completion Agenda: 2010 Progress Report," The College Board, 2010, p. 10.

19. Ibid.

20. John Gibbons, "I Can't Get No . . . Job Satisfaction," The Conference Board, January 2010.

21. See the U.S. Department of Agriculture's Supplemental Nutrition Assistance Program website (http://www.fns.usda.gov/snap/) for more information.

22. For wealth inequality, see Office of Management and Budget, "A New Era of Responsibility," February 2009, p. 9. For income inequality, see Gerald Prante and Mark Robyn, "Fiscal Fact: Summary of Latest Federal Income Tax Data," Tax Foundation, October 6, 2010.

23. See Robert Innes and Arnab Mitra, "Is Dishonesty Contagious?," June 2009, and the references therein.

24. Goldman Sachs settlement: Patricia Hurtado and Christine Harper, "SEC Settlement with Goldman Sachs for $550 Million Approved by US Judge," Bloomberg News, July 21, 2010. Goldman Sachs 2009 income: Goldman Sachs website. Countrywide: Alex Dobuzinskis, "Mozilo Settles Countrywide Fraud Case at $67.5 million," Reuters News, October 15, 2010. Angelo Mozilo net worth: Kamelia Angelova, "Worst CEOs Ever: Angelo Mozilo," Business Insider, June 8, 2009.

Chapter 3: The Free-Market Fallacy

1. Jeffrey Sachs and Michael Bruno, *Economics of Worldwide Stagflation* (Cambridge: Harvard University Press, 1985).

2. Adam Smith, *An Inquiry into the Nature and Causes of the Wealth of Nations* (Oxford: Oxford University Press, 1993), Book 1, Chapter 2.

3. Specifically, once the market equilibrium is reached, there is no possible further adjustment of resources (for example, as mandated by the government) that could raise living standards for some part of the population without at the same time making some other part worse off. This notion of efficiency is called "Pareto efficiency."

4. Friedrich Hayek, *The Road to Serfdom* (Chicago: University of Chicago Press, 1944), p. 36.

5. Smith, *An Inquiry into the Nature and Causes of the Wealth of Nations*, Book 5, Section 1.
6. Efficiency should be measured in terms of goods and services of true value to consumers. A rise in the gross national product (GNP) is not enough to prove that efficiency is higher, since GNP may include market transactions that don't really raise well-being (such as those based on fraud, pollution, or a decline in nonmarket services such as leisure time).
7. Pew Research Center for the People & the Press, "Trends in Political Values and Core Attitudes: 1987–2009," May 21, 2009.
8. *Forbes*, "The World's Billionaires," 2011.
9. The army, police, prisons, and courts constitute the so-called night watchman functions of government. Pure libertarians champion a night watchman state, one that limits its activities to the core tasks of protecting private property, personal security, and national security.
10. Gallup Poll, "Views of Income Taxes Among Most Positive Since 1956," April 13, 2009.
11. Pew Research Center, "Trends in Political Values and Core Attitudes: 1987–2009," p. 43.
12. The main exceptions in history are when one ethnic, racial, or religious group leaves another to perish.
13. See responses to similar questions and topics in Benjamin Page and Lawrence Jacobs, *Class War: What Americans Really Think About Economic Inequality* (Chicago: University of Chicago Press, 2009).
14. Only a small proportion of poor children today will make it through college unless there is a drastic change in U.S. social and education policy. The disadvantages confronting poor children are too powerful and too many. Poor children grow up with poor neighborhoods, poor health, and poor schools, with parents of low educational attainment who cannot adequately help their children to succeed in school, and in the case of minorities, with the low expectations by the rest of society and with continuing discrimination and racism.

    The end result is a startlingly strong correlation in America between the parents' educational attainment and income and their children's educational attainment and income. Households that have made it through college and to affluence are likely to raise their children to a bachelor's degree and to affluence as well. Households in poverty and with low parental educational attainment are likely to bequeath their poverty to their children as well, despite every desperate effort to avoid that fate. According to careful studies carried out by the OECD, and shown in the figure on the next page, the United States actually has the lowest social mobility within the entire OECD, as indicated by the highest correlation of education levels of parents and children. This is a stunning fact, since it runs counter to the long-held supposition that the United States is the land of social mobility and opportunity for all.
15. Some may object to considering the marketplace a contrivance as opposed to a natural phenomenon reflecting humanity's intrinsic propensity to "truck, barter, and trade" (in Adam Smith's famous phrase). Yet when we consider that the modern marketplace is not based on bartering but on sophisticated

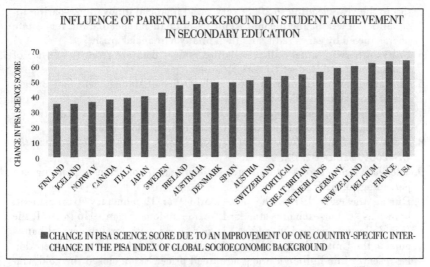

INFLUENCE OF PARENTAL BACKGROUND ON STUDENT ACHIEVEMENT
IN SECONDARY EDUCATION

■ CHANGE IN PISA SCIENCE SCORE DUE TO AN IMPROVEMENT OF ONE COUNTRY-SPECIFIC INTER-
CHANGE IN THE PISA INDEX OF GLOBAL SOCIOECONOMIC BACKGROUND

Source: Data from Organization for Economic Cooperation and Development, "Economic
Policy Reforms, Going for Growth: OECD 2010."

monetary institutions and financial markets, commercial law, corporate law,
intellectual dispute settlements, and state enforcement of contracts and protection of property, we can conclude that markets today are the product of
complex legal and institutional design as well as underlying economic motivations to trade.

Chapter 4: Washington's Retreat from Public Purpose

1. Franklin D. Roosevelt, Second Inaugural Address, January 20, 1937.
2. Ronald Reagan, First Inaugural Address, January 20, 1981.
3. Bill Clinton, radio address, January 27, 1996.
4. This great reversal of government after the 1960s is not a unique event in
   American history, according to historians. Arthur Schlesinger, Jr., among
   others, argued persuasively that America tends to experience waves of alter-
   nating public activism and retreat. In the 1870s to 1890s, for example, the
   great national industries—railways, steel making, oil, meatpacking, retailing
   by catalogue—first came into existence on a continental scale. Government
   stood in the shadows as the robber barons took the stage. The Gilded Age was
   born. Then came the reaction, first by the prairie populists who, like the Tea
   Party, railed against the depredations of Wall Street; next came the Progres-
   sives, who more systematically rolled out a series of reforms designed to rein
   in corporate abuses of the new national giants. The Progressive Era began
   to wane in the 1910s, and was swept away by the probusiness decade of the
   1920s, when America longed to return to normalcy after World War I. The
   Roaring Twenties, the prelude to the Great Depression, had strong similari-

ties to the years leading to 2008: very rapid financial innovation, soaring inequalities of wealth and income, a culture of financial speculation, real estate
booms fueled by easy credit, and then finally a financial crash.

5. Unless otherwise noted, all proceeding budget data are from the Office of
Management and Budget Historical Tables.

6. This allocation starts only in 1962 in the Office of Management and Budget
Historical Tables (Table 8.2).

7. U.S. Census Bureau, "Population Division: Historical Census Statistics on
the Foreign-Born Population of the United States: 1850–2000."

8. U.S. Census Bureau, *Income, Poverty and Health Insurance Coverage in the
US: 2009*, Tables B1, B2.

9. The chart below shows total revenues, defense and nondefense spending as a
percentage of GDP.

10. During the early 1970s, the post–World War II monetary arrangement,
known as "dollar-exchange standard," came undone. From 1946 to 1971, the
U.S. dollar was pegged to gold at $35 per ounce, with foreign central banks
outside the United States enjoying the guaranteed right to convert their dollar reserves into bullion at the guaranteed price. Nixon closed the gold win-
dow (the gold-to-dollar conversion) on August 15, 1971, as the United States
was being drained of its gold reserves. At the core of the crisis was overly
expansionary monetary policy tied to the overheated U.S. economy, which
itself was tied to the expanded costs of the Vietnam War. The United States
could not both expand the money supply and honor the redemption of dollars
into gold at a fixed price, so it gave up on the latter. The breakdown of the
dollar-exchange standard led to modern history's first peacetime era of major
national currencies unlinked to either gold or silver. The result, for several

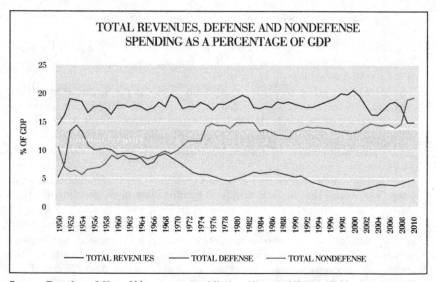

Source: Data from Office of Management and Budget Historical Tables (Tables 1.2, 3.1, and
8.4).

years, was high inflation, partly as national central banks adjusted to their newly established freedom of maneuver, and the lack of a clear monetary anchor. By the 1980s, the world's central banks had adjusted to the new era of flexible exchange rates and had brought inflation rates back down. Yet by the time this happened, conservative politicians and free-market ideologues were insisting that the burst of inflation during the 1970s was proof of the incapacity of government to manage the economy.

Many factors contributed to soaring oil prices. Partly the soaring oil prices reflected the overheated monetary conditions described. Another element of the high oil prices was the surge in oil demand relative to supply that resulted from years of rapid global economic growth. A third element was politics. The Arab nations gained control over their oil reserves in the early 1970s as supply conditions tightened and as postcolonial geopolitics unfolded. The rise of OPEC alone would have boosted oil prices in the period. Yet the Arab countries temporarily went one step further by launching a boycott of Western markets following the 1973 Arab-Israeli War. All in all, the decade was marked by high and unstable oil prices, and profound macroeconomic instability as a result.

11. Judith Stein, *Pivotal Decade: How the United States Traded Factories for Finance in the Seventies* (New Haven: Yale University Press, 2010).

12. At a key moment, Democratic senators from the Sunbelt contributed to the defeat of a prolabor bill in 1978, with Florida senator Richard Stone explaining that the prounion measures would "impede the progress of the sunbelt to attract jobs" (ibid., pp. 188–89).

13. Ibid., p. 193.

14. See Table 17.1 of the Office of Management and Budget Historical Tables.

15. See Table 3.1 of the Office of Management and Budget Historical Tables.

16. See Table 3.2 of the Office of Management and Budget Historical Tables.

17. Ibid.

18. International Energy Agency, Data Services.

19. For the change in income inequality, most recent data are for 2008. For the national poverty rate, earliest available data are for 1959. For earnings of full-time male workers, most recent data are from 2009.

20. Emmanuel Saez and Thomas Piketty, data set for "Income Inequality in the United States, 1913–1998," updated July 2010.

Chapter 5: The Divided Nation

1. I have categorized the Sunbelt and Snowbelt as follows: The Sunbelt: Alabama, Arizona, Arkansas, California, Florida, Georgia, Louisiana, Mississippi, New Mexico, North Carolina, Oklahoma, South Carolina, Texas, and Virginia. The Snowbelt: Connecticut, Illinois, Indiana, Iowa, Kansas, Maine, Massachusetts, Michigan, Minnesota, Missouri, Nebraska, New Hampshire, New Jersey, New York, North Dakota, Ohio, Pennsylvania, Rhode Island, South Dakota, Vermont, and Wisconsin.

2. Larry Dewitt, "The Decision to Exclude Agricultural and Domestic Work-

ers from the 1935 Social Security Act," U.S. Social Security Administration, 2010.

3. Lyndon Johnson knew that he was delivering the South to the Republican Party when he signed the Civil Rights Act of 1964 and the Voting Rights Act of 1965. On signing the Civil Rights Act, he supposedly turned to an aide and declared that he had delivered the South to the Republicans for a generation. It is a testament to his moral courage that he nonetheless acted so boldly.

4. Thomas Byrne Edsall and Mary D. Edsall, *Chain Reaction: The Impact of Race, Rights, and Taxes on American Politics* (New York: W. W. Norton, 1991), pp. 141–44.

5. For 1970 and 1990 Hispanic population data, see U.S. Census Bureau, "Hispanics in the US." For 2007 data, see Pew Hispanic Center, "Statistic Portraits of Hispanics in the US, 2009."

6. Zoltan Hajnal et al., "Immigration and the Political Transformation of White America: How Local Immigrant Context Shapes White Policy Views and Partisanship," University of California, San Diego Center for Comparative Immigration Studies, International Migration Conference, March 12, 2010.

Research by Hajnal et al. confirms that the rise of the Hispanic population has led to a significant conservative shift of white Americans in locales with high concentrations of Hispanics:

> [W]hite Americans who live in proximity to large numbers of Latinos tend to have more conservative views. All else equal, whites living in zip codes with larger Latino populations are less likely to want the federal government to reduce income inequality, less likely to seek increased spending on health care for the poor, less likely to want to do more to cover the uninsured, and almost significantly less likely . . . to view poverty as a serious problem. The implication of this set of findings is an important one. Latino context is now shaping core policy concerns of the American public. And it is doing so in a way that mirrors the negative reactions that have often faced the African American community in the past. In contexts where Latinos are prominent (and perhaps threatening), whites tend to be eager to reduce services and expenditures that benefit the bottom rungs of society. (pp. 21–22)

7. Congressional Budget Office, "The Impact of Unauthorized Immigrants on the Budgets of State and Local Governments," December 2007.

8. Between 1900 and 1960, every president except Californian Herbert Hoover hailed from the Snowbelt: William McKinley (Ohio), Theodore Roosevelt (New York), William Howard Taft (Ohio), Woodrow Wilson (New Jersey), Warren Harding (Ohio), Calvin Coolidge (Massachusetts), Herbert Hoover (California), Franklin D. Roosevelt (New York), Harry Truman (Missouri), Dwight D. Eisenhower (Kansas), and John F. Kennedy (Massachusetts). After 1960, the only president from outside the Sunbelt was Gerald Ford of Michigan, who took office upon Richard Nixon's resignation rather than by winning a national election. Ford went down to defeat in 1976, to Sunbelt candidate Jimmy Carter. The elected presidents between 1964 and 2004 in-

clude Lyndon B. Johnson (Texas), Jimmy Carter (Georgia), Ronald Reagan (California), George H.W. Bush (Texas), Bill Clinton (Arkansas), and George W. Bush (Texas).

9. The phenomenon at play is a result of America's two-party system, in which the winning candidate (with 50 percent plus one vote) gets 100 percent of the power. The losing side gets no representation. This is different from a proportional representation system, as in much of Europe, where the share of national seats depends on the share of national votes. In our example, a national pro-government party would get 54 percent of the seats no matter where in the country the voters live.

10. The following data are from the Pew Forum on Religion & Public Life, "US Religious Landscape Survey: Religious Affiliation, Diverse and Dynamic," February 2008.

11. For an overview of the increased sorting of American households by "education, income, race, and way of life," see Bill Bishop, *The Big Sort: Why the Clustering of Like-Minded America Is Tearing Us Apart* (New York: Houghton Mifflin, 2008); Paul Jargowsky and Todd Swanstrom, "Economic Integration: Why It Matters and How Cities Can Get More of It," Chicago: CEOs for Cities, City Vitals Series.

12. The following data are from Benjamin Page and Lawrence Jacobs, *Class War? What Americans Really Think About Economic Inequality* (Chicago: University of Chicago Press, 2009).

13. Professor Larry Bartels of Princeton University has found similar views in his own recent analysis of survey data. He identifies several characteristics of public attitudes, including strong support for equal opportunity and a belief that "some people don't get a chance to get a good education," and for the view that "rich people . . . pay less [in taxes] than they should" (53.1 percent). Larry Bartels, "Homer Gets a Tax Cut: Inequality and Public Policy in the American Mind," *Perspectives on Politics* 3, no. 1 (March 2005).

14. Pew Research Center, "Trends in Political Values and Core Attitudes: 1987–2009," May 21, 2009, pp. 72–73, 140.

15. Ibid., p. 106.

16. *USA Today*/Gallup Poll, June 11–13, 2010.

17. Jon Cohen, "Most Americans Say Regulate Greenhouse Gases," *Washington Post*, June 10, 2010.

18. Rasmussen Reports, "Support for Renewable Energy Resources Reaches Highest Level Yet," January 2011.

Chapter 6: The New Globalization

1. Adam Smith, *An Inquiry into the Nature and Causes of the Wealth of Nations* (Oxford: Oxford University Press, 1993), Book 4, Chapter 7.

2. United Nations Conference on Trade and Development (UNCTAD), "Largest Transnational Corporations," Document 5, http://www.unctad.org/templates/page.asp?intItemID=2443&lang=1.

3. For details on General Electric, see General Electric website and annual 10-K filing.

4. Foreign profits are equal to corporate earnings from abroad minus domestic earnings paid to foreign investors. Earnings from abroad include both the foreign profits of U.S. multinationals and the dividends received by U.S. residents paid by unaffiliated foreign corporations. The rising trend in the figure reflects in part the rising share of corporate profits earned by U.S. companies in their overseas operations, but may also reflect a rising tendency of U.S. companies to book their profits in overseas tax havens through artificial transfer pricing (that is, using artificial prices for cross-border transactions within the firm for the purpose of shifting reported corporate revenues to low-tax jurisdictions). Even if part of the rising share of foreign profits reflects artificial transfer pricing rather than actual changes in the location of corporate activities, the increased use of transfer pricing to avoid taxes would itself be a manifestation of the new globalization.

5. For U.S.-China trade: U.S. Census Bureau, "Foreign Trade: Trade in Goods with China." For U.S. value-added data: U.S. Department of Commerce, Bureau of Economic Analysis, "Industry Economic Accounts."

6. U.S. Bureau of Labor Statistics, "Current Employment Statistics: National."

7. U.S. Bureau of Labor Statistics, "Establishment Data: Historical Employment."

8. Ibid.

9. Shan Jingjing, "Blue Book of Cities in China," Chinese Academy of Social Science.

10. UN Population Division Home Page.

11. The current shorthand for the emerging economies is the BRIC group: Brazil, Russia, India, and China, with a combined population of around 2.7 billion. If we define an emerging market to be any fast-growing developing country that is able to attract market-based private capital for a rapid scale-up of industrial production, we would want to include dozens more countries, including Chile, Egypt, Mexico, Nigeria, South Africa, and Vietnam. The combined real GDP of the developing world grew by around 7 percent in 2010, showing the scope of rapid growth in today's developing countries.

12. H. Garretsen and Jolanda Peeters, "Capital Mobility, Agglomeration and Corporate Tax Rates: Is the Race to the Bottom for Real?," *CESifo Economic Studies* 53, no. 2 (2007), pp. 263–93.

13. See Table 2.3 of the Office of Management and Budget Historical Tables.

14. For example, see Rasmussen Reports, "Energy Update," April 2011.

Chapter 7: The Rigged Game

1. In the 2010 Swedish elections, for example, eight parties entered the Parliament and four are part of the governing coalition. The American political system, and to a lesser extent the systems of the United Kingdom, Canada, and Australia, are majoritarian; the parliamentary democracies of Western Europe tend to be consensus systems.

2. Maurice Duverger, "Factors in a Two Party and Multiparty System," in *Party Politics and Pressure Groups* (New York: Thomas Y. Crowell, 1972), pp. 23–32.
3. All data from OECD Social Expenditure Database and OECD Statistical Database.
4. Consensus is also difficult because of the vastness and diversity of America's population, with cleavages by region, race, ethnicity, and religion. America cannot be a consensus society in the same way as Denmark, Norway, or Sweden, as each of those is a country of a few million people that is ethnically and religiously homogeneous with a geographic range and diversity far smaller than those of the United States.
5. Institute for Democracy and Electoral Assistance, "Voter Turnout by Country."
6. Spending in presidential election years (2000, 2004, 2008) averages around $1.5 billion more than in nonpresidential election years, with presidential and off-year elections on the same common upward trend.
7. Robert Kaiser, *So Damn Much Money: The Triumph of Lobbying and the Corrosion of American Government* (New York: Alfred A. Knopf, 2009), pp. 343–44.
8. Gallup Poll, "Automobile, Banking Industry Images Slide Further," August 17, 2009.
9. Andrew J. Bacevich, *Washington Rules: America's Path to Permanent War* (New York: Henry Holt, 2010).
10. Dwight D. Eisenhower, "Farewell Address," January 17, 1961.
11. Peter Orszag, "One Nation, Two Deficits," *New York Times,* September 6, 2010. He writes: "It would be tough, then, to squeeze more than a half percent of G.D.P. from spending by 2015. Additional revenue—in the range of 0.5 to 1.5 percent of the economy—will therefore be necessary to reduce the deficit to sustainable levels."
12. Christina D. Romer, "What Obama Should Say About the Deficit," *New York Times,* January 15, 2011.
13. ABC News "Summary: 2009 Polling on a 'Public Option.'"
14. Congressional Budget Office, "Estimate of Direct Spending and Revenue Effects of H.R. 2," February 18, 2011.
15. Consider the following passage written by political scientist Thomas Ferguson in 1995 on the Clinton-era debate on health care, and note how well it applies to the Obama case, almost without needing to change a single word. In both 1994 and 2009, the health care industry was in the driver's seat of the legislative process:

> As this essay goes to press [in 1994], the administration is finally unveiling its long-awaited (and several times postponed) blueprint for overhauling the nation's health-care delivery system. Already, however, some of the costs of this strategy—to strike deals with as much of the existing health-care industry as possible, instead of pushing for a simple and economical "single payer" ("Canadian style") system—are plain. While the package of benefits and universal coverage the plan prom-

ises is carefully thought out and at least modestly appealing, the plan is fantastically complicated and not easy for ordinary voters to evaluate. The full costs of the network of oligopolies that the plan will create are being hidden, and savings are being claimed that are almost certainly not there. The basic design is heavily weighted in the direction of the large insurers and several other parts of the health-care industry, including teaching hospitals. A few years down the pike the financing system proposed may well create strong pressures to curtail benefits or skimp on care. (Thomas Ferguson, *Golden Rule: The Investment Theory of Party Competition and the Logic of Money-Driven Political Systems* [Chicago: University of Chicago Press, 1995], p. 327.)

Neither President Clinton nor President Obama dared to propose deep reforms to America's astoundingly overpriced private health care system. The influence of the powerful health care lobby to prevent change is the real subtext of the past thirty years of U.S. health care policy.

16. Campaign Finance Institute, "New Figures Show That Obama Raised About One-Third of His General Funds from Donors Who Gave $200 or Less," January 8, 2010.
17. Center for Responsive Politics, "Banking on Connections," June 3, 2010, p. 1.
18. Ibid, p. 3.
19. The following is based on Jesse Drucker, "Google 2.4% Rate Shows How $60 Billion Lost to Tax Loopholes," Bloomberg News, October 21, 2010.
20. See Chapter 1 of Title 26 of the Internal Revenue Code.
21. U.S. Government Accountability Office, "International Taxation: Large US Corporations and Federal Contractors with Subsidiaries in Jurisdictions Listed as Tax Havens or Financial Privacy Jurisdictions," GAO-09-157, December 2008.
22. Jane G. Gravelle, "Tax Havens: International Tax Avoidance and Evasion," Congressional Research Service Report for Congress, July 2009.
23. Nolan McCarty et al., *Polarized America: The Dance of Ideology and Unequal Riches* (Cambridge: MIT Press, 2006), p. 272.
24. Business Wire, "Business and Financial Leaders Lord Rothschild and Rupert Murdoch Invest in Genie Oil & Gas," November 15, 2010.
25. Luca Di Leo and Jeffrey Sparshott, "Corporate Profits Rise to Record Annual Rate," *Wall Street Journal*, November 24, 2010.
26. Aaron Lucchetti and Stephen Grocer, "On Street, Pay Vaults to Record Altitude," *Wall Street Journal*, February 2, 2011.

Chapter 8: The Distracted Society

1. Coen Advertising Expenditure Dataset, quoted in Douglas Galbi, "U.S. Advertising Expenditure, 1998–2007," Purple Motes blog, February 16, 2009.
2. Thorstein Veblen, *The Theory of the Leisure Class: An Economic Study of Institutions* (New York: Macmillan, 1902), pp. 68–101.
3. Edward Bernays, *Propaganda*, 1928:

The conscious and intelligent manipulation of the organized habits and opinions of the masses is an important element in democratic society. Those who manipulate this unseen mechanism of society constitute an invisible government which is the true ruling power of our country. We are governed, our minds are molded, our tastes formed, our ideas suggested, largely by men we have never heard of. . . . There are invisible rulers who control the destinies of millions. It is not generally realized to what extent the words and actions of our most influential public men are dictated by shrewd persons operating behind the scenes. Nor, what is still more important, the extent to which our thoughts and habits are modified by authorities. (pp. 9, 35)

4. U.S. Census Bureau, "No. HS-42: Selected Communications Media: 1920 to 2001."
5. Henry J. Kaiser Family Foundation, "Food for Thought: Television Food Advertising to Children in the United States," March 2007, p. 2.
6. Joe McGinniss, *The Selling of the President 1968* (New York: Trident, 1969).
7. Henry J. Kaiser Family Foundation, "Food for Thought," p. 57.
8. Deirdre Barrett, *Supernormal Stimuli: How Primal Urges Overran Their Evolutionary Purpose* (New York: W. W. Norton, 2010).
9. There were three main forms of regulation. First, the FCC insisted on some programming not supported by advertising. Second, the FCC maintained a "Fairness Doctrine" to ensure that alternative points of view would be heard. Third, the FCC imposed ownership limits on the media, to prevent the monopolization of the local airwaves or the joint control of print, radio, and TV in a local market. These three mechanisms tamed the worst excesses of privately owned television as late as the 1970s. Then came the deregulation of the 1980s, which continues today.
10. Wilhelm Röpke, *A Humane Economy: The Social Framework of the Free Market* (Wilmington: ISI Books, 1960), p. 137.
11. Max Weber, *The Protestant Ethic and the Spirit of Capitalism* (Mineola, N.Y.: Dover, 2003), p. 53.
12. John Maynard Keynes, *The Economic Consequences of the Peace* (Toronto: University of Toronto Libraries, 2011), Chapter 2, Paragraph 20.
13. Andrew Carnegie, "The Gospel of Wealth and Other Timely Essays."
14. Google: "Google Search Advertising Revenue Grows 20.2% in 2010," January 20, 2011. Facebook: "Facebook's Ad Revenue Hit $1.86b for 2010," January 17, 2011.
15. Emily Steel, "A Web Pioneer Profiles Users by Name," *Wall Street Journal*, October 25, 2010.
16. The following data are from Roger Bohn and James Short, "How Much Information? 2009 Report on American Consumers," Global Information Industry Center, December 2009.
17. National Endowment for the Arts, "To Read or Not to Read: A Question of National Consequence," Research Report No. 47, November 2007, Sections 1 and 2.
18. Mark Bauerlein, *The Dumbest Generation* (New York: Penguin, 2008), p. 16.

19. Pew Research Center for the People & the Press, "Public Knows Basic Facts About Politics, Economics, but Struggles with Specifics," November 2010.

Part II: The Path to Prosperity

Chapter 9: The Mindful Society

1. Attributed to Aristotle in Stobaeus, *Florilegium*, transl. J.E.C. Welldon.
2. For GDP data, see World Bank Data and Statistics, http://siteresources.world bank.org/DATASTATISTICS/Resources/GNIPC.pdf. For life expectancy data, see World Health Organization Global Health Observatory Data Repository.
3. Geoffrey Miller, *Spent* (New York: Penguin, 2009), p. 65.
4. Elizabeth Dunn, Daniel T. Gilbert, and Timothy Wilson, "If Money Doesn't Make You Happy Then You Probably Aren't Spending It Right," *Journal of Consumer Psychology* 21, no. 2, pp. 115–25.
5. Ibid., p. 123.
6. U.S. Bureau of Labor Statistics, "Economic News Release: Table A-4— Employment Status of the Civilian Population 25 Years and Over by Educational Attainment."

   The education gradient is stark. Among those twenty-five years and older, the unemployment rate in December 2010 was 15.7 percent for those with less than a high school education, 9.8 percent for those whose highest education attainment was a high school diploma, 7.9 percent for those with some post– high school education, but without a degree; and 4.6 percent for those with a bachelor's degree or higher.
7. The fact that the carbon dioxide in the atmosphere warms the planet was first accurately elaborated in 1824 by French scientist Joseph Fourier and in numerical detail by Swedish chemist Svante Arrhenius in 1896.
8. Pew Research Center for the People & the Press, "Public Praises Science; Scientists Fault Public, Media," July 2009.
9. Bob Altemeyer, "Why Do Religious Fundamentalists Tend to Be Prejudiced?," *International Journal for the Psychology of Religion* 13, no. 1 (2003): 17. Altemeyer concludes that "strong, early emphasis of the family religion may . . . produce a template for 'us-them' discrimination that facilitates acquiring later prejudices." Similarly, Hall, Matz, and Wood find that religiosity and racism are correlated. They too surmise that "a strong in-group identity was associated with derogation of racial out-groups. Other races might be treated as out-groups because religion is practiced largely within race, because training in a religious in-group identity promotes general ethnocentrism, and because different others appear to be in competition for resources." (Deborah Hall et al., "Why Don't We Practice What We Preach? A Meta-Analytic Review of Religious Racism," *Personal Social Psychology Review* 14, no. 1 [December 2009], p. 126.)
10. Robert Putnam, "E Pluribus Unum: Diversity and Community in the Twenty-first Century: The 2006 Johan Skytte Prize Lecture," *Scandinavian Political Studies* 30, no. 2 (June 2007).

11. Senate floor statement by Senator James Inhofe, July 28, 2003.
12. Hans Jonas, *The Imperative of Responsibility: In Search of an Ethics for a Technological Age* (Chicago: University of Chicago Press, 1985).
13. National Intelligence Council, "Global Trends 2025: A Transformed World," November 2008.
14. Hans Küng, "Manifesto for a Global Economic Ethic," Tübingen: Global Ethic Foundation, 2009, p. 5.
15. John F. Kennedy, Address before the Irish Parliament, June 1963, http://ua_tuathal.tripod.com/kennedy.html.
16. John F. Kennedy, Remarks at American University Commencement, June 1963.

Chapter 10: Prosperity Regained

1. U.S. Department of Education, National Center for Educational Statistics, "The Condition of Education 2010," June 2010, p. 214.
2. In the early years, the government should subsidize the purchases of electric vehicles, to help the industry "move down the learning curve." Later on, electric vehicles will compete on their own vis-à-vis the traditional alternatives, assuming of course that gasoline use is properly taxed to account for its adverse environmental externalities.
3. U.S. Department of Education, "Mortgaging Our Future: How Financial Barriers to College Undercut America's Global Competitiveness," A Report of the Advisory Committee on Student Financial Assistance, September 2006, p. iii.
4. See U.S. Bureau of Labor Statistics, "Economic News Release: Table A-15—Alternative Measures of Labor Underutilization."
5. Organisation for Economic Co-operation and Development, "Public Expenditure and Participant Stocks on LMP," Statistical Database.
6. U.S. Department of Education, "Mortgaging Our Future: How Financial Barriers to College Undercut America's Global Competitiveness."
7. U.S. Department of Education, "Revenues and Expenditures for Public Elementary and Secondary School Districts: School Year 2007–2008 (Fiscal Year 2008)," NCES 2010-323, August 2010, p. 6.
8. U.S. Department of Education, "The Condition of Education 2010," p. 277.
9. McKinsey & Company, "Winning by Degrees: The Strategies of Highly Productive Higher-Education Institutions," November 2010, p. 8.
10. America's Promise Alliance, "Building a Grad Nation: Progress and Challenge in Ending the High School Dropout Epidemic," November 2010, p. 16.
11. Ibid.
12. Ibid., p. 50. This study concluded: "Although 17 percent of these [charter] schools provide a superior education to traditional public schools, half of them offer an education that is comparable, and more than a third of them provide an education that is significantly worse than the local public school."
13. For more information on James Heckman's research on early childhood investment, see http://www.heckmanequation.org/.

14. U.S. Census Bureau, "Table 3: Poverty Status of People, by Age, Race, and Hispanic Origin: 1958–2009," Current Population Survey, Annual and Social Economic Supplements.
15. Gösta Esping-Andersen et al., *Why We Need a New Welfare State* (Oxford: Oxford University Press, 2002); particularly see Chapter 3, "A Child-Centered Social Investment Strategy," pp. 26–67); and Gösta Esping-Andersen, "Unequal Opportunities and the Mechanisms of Social Inheritance," in *Generational Income Mobility in North America and Europe*, ed. Miles Corak (Cambridge: Cambridge University Press, 2004).
16. For U.S. data, see U.S. Census Bureau, *Income, Poverty and Health Insurance Coverage in the US: 2009*, p. 15. For Sweden data, see Gösta Esping-Andersen, "Unequal Opportunities and the Mechanisms of Social Inheritance," p. 308.
17. Organization for Economic Co-operation and Development, "OECD Family Database."
18. George Halvorson, *Health Care Will Not Reform Itself* (New York: CRC Press, 2009). His point is this: health care providers are making a bundle of money, and have no incentive to give it up:

> Many health care providers have set up shop in America. From a pure business perspective, those businesses are almost all economic successes—winners—not economic losers. . . . Expecting our current massive, very well-financed, high-revenue, high-margin, high-growth, high-cost health care infrastructure to voluntarily take steps to reduce costs and prices, and expecting our care infrastructure to also voluntarily and spontaneously improve either care outcomes or care quality is unfortunately naïve. . . . Health care in America is a robust and growing nonsystem of immense size, scope, and scale. It is very well fed. (p. 2)

Halvorson explains that the huge costs in America come from treating patients with multiple chronic conditions requiring a large number of doctors: "[O]ver 75 percent of care costs in America currently result from patients with chronic conditions, and 80 percent of those costs come from patients with both chronic care conditions and 'co-morbities'" (p. xix).

When many doctors are involved, there are often major duplications of testing, examinations, billing services, record keeping, administration, and with poor medical coordination as well. There is also far too little help for individuals to avoid or reduce their chronic conditions in the first place, through healthier lifestyles, diet, exercise, or other choices that might be within their means and reach. The reimbursement system creates incentives to maximize costs. Employer-provided health care coverage is heavily subsidized because it is tax-deductible and doctors are reimbursed for the procedures and services they offer, not for the health outcomes that result. As Halvorson grimly notes: "Hospitals in America do not get paid more money if they do great work and are completely infection free. They do get paid a lot more money for patients with infections" (p. 11). He recounts cases where reengineering of services led to lower costs—and a revolt by the doctors, who felt that their incomes and jobs were jeopardized.

19. McKinsey & Company, "Accounting for the Cost of Health Care in the United States," January 2007, p. 10.
20. For classification details, see Organisation for Economic Co-operation and Development, "OECD Health Data, Part II: International Classification for Health Accounts (ICHA)."
21. U.S. Energy Information Administration, "Net Generation by Energy Source: Total," January 2011.
22. Lawrence Burns, Vijay Modi, and Jeffrey Sachs, "Transition to a Sustainable Energy System for the United States," December 16, 2010, unpublished paper.
23. U.S. Department of Defense, "DoD Request: FY 2011," http://comptroller .defense.gov/Budget2011.html.
24. Robert F. Kennedy, Remarks at the University of Kansas, March 18, 1968.
25. American Human Development Project, "The Measure of America 2010–2011: Mapping Risks and Resilience."
26. Karma Ura, "Gross National Happiness," Centre for Bhutan Studies.
27. For a recent useful survey, see David Blanchflower and Andrew Oswald, "International Happiness," NBER Working Paper No. 16668, January 2011.
28. For more information on these studies, see Organization for Economic Co-operation and Development, "Global Project on Measuring the Progress of Societies"; William Nordhaus and James Tobin, "Is Growth Obsolete?," in *The Measurement of Economic and Social Performance*, NBER Book Series Studies in Income and Wealth, 1973; *Economist* Intelligence Unit, "The *Economist* Intelligence Unit's Quality-of-Life Index," *The World in 2005*; Joseph Stiglitz and Amartya Sen, "Commission on the Measurement of Economic Performance and Social Progress"; Paul Dolan et al., "Measuring Subjective Well-Being for Public Policy," Office for National Statistics—Government of the United Kingdom, February 2011.

Chapter 11: Paying for Civilization

1. Congressional Budget Office, "An Analysis of the President's Budgetary Proposals for Fiscal Year 2012," Table 1.5.
2. See Table 7.1 of the Office of Management and Budget Historical Tables.
3. Congressional Budget Office, "An Analysis of the President's Budgetary Proposals for Fiscal Year 2012," Table 1.5.
4. See Table 8.4 of the Office of Management and Budget Historical Tables.
5. Justice Oliver Wendell Holmes, Jr., attributed in Felix Frankfurter, *Mr. Justice Holmes and the Supreme Court* (Cambridge: Harvard University Press, 1961), p. 71.
6. Center for Responsive Politics, "Congressional Members' Personal Wealth Expands Despite Sour Economy," November 2010.
7. All the calculations that follow are based on the Congressional Budget Office report "The Budget and Economic Outlook: Fiscal Years 2011 to 2021," January 2011. I do not report the CBO estimates exactly, but rather adjust them according to specific alternative assumptions that I believe form a more

accurate baseline. For example, the CBO baseline for 2015 assumes a budget deficit of 3 percent of GDP (Tables 1–4). The CBO baseline assumes that the Bush tax cuts, currently in effect until 2012, are allowed to lapse after 2012. I instead assume for purposes of my baseline that they are continued after 2012. This adds around 2 percentage points of GDP to the CBO baseline deficit. The CBO baseline also assumes that civilian discretionary spending keeps up with inflation but not with GDP growth, causing discretionary civilian spending in 2015 to fall to 3.5 percent of GDP. I instead start with a baseline of discretionary civilian spending of 4 percent of GDP. I also assume that debt servicing in 2015 is 3 percent of GDP, while the CBO assumes 2.5 percent of GDP. The overall effect is a baseline of 6 percent of GDP, rather than the CBO's 3 percent of GDP.

8. See Tables 1.2 and 8.4 of the Office of Management and Budget Historical Tables.

9. "In FY 2010, Congress approved more than 9,000 earmarks costing taxpayers close to $16 billion." See U.S. Government Executive Office, "The National Commission on Fiscal Responsibility and Reform: The Moment of Truth," December 2010, p. 27.

10. See Table 3.2 of the Office of Management and Budget Historical Tables.

11. There is a pervasive belief that foreign aid eats up an enormous share of the budget, so that if we would simply stop our foreign assistance to foreign tyrants, we'd close much of the gap. The confusion about foreign aid is breathtaking. In a November 2010 opinion survey, Americans were asked their "hunch" about the percentage of the federal budget that goes to foreign aid. The median answer was 25 percent. The respondents were then asked what would be an "appropriate" percentage. The median response was 10 percent. The correct answer in fact is that foreign aid accounts for 0.8 percent of the budget (and 0.2 percent of GDP). The public is off by a factor of thirty times. While it demands a "cut" in foreign aid, its target of 10 percent of the budget would actually require an increase in aid of twelve times! (World Public Opinion, "American Public Opinion on Foreign Aid," November 30, 2010.)

12. The "Medicaid and Related" category comprises the following: Medicaid, Refundable Premium Assistance Tax Credit, Reinsurance and Risk Adjustment Program Payments, and Payments to Reduce Cost Sharing in Qualified Health Plans. The "Other" category comprises the following: Other Health, Children's Health Insurance, Family and Other Support Assistance, Earned Income Tax Credit, Child Tax Credit, Making Work Pay Tax Credit, Payment to States for Foster Care, Housing Assistance, and Other. (Office of Management and Budget Historical Table 8.5.)

13. Neil King, Jr., and Scott Greenberg, "Poll Shows Budget-Cuts Dilemma," *Wall Street Journal*, March 3, 2011.

14. Means-tested spending is aid that is provided to individuals who meet certain low income qualifications.

15. The FY 2011 budget estimate for TANF programs was approximately $17.4 billion. The total outlays for Means Tested programs in FY 2011 was approximately $498 billion (OMB Budget Table 8.2), and the U.S. GDP is projected to be $15.1 trillion. (U.S. Department of Health and Human Services, "Temporary Assistance for Needy Families: FY 2012 Budget," p. 305.)

16. See Office of Management and Budget Historical Budget Table 11.3 for the category "Family Support Payments to States and TANF," divided by GDP in Historical Table 1.2.

17. See Office of Management and Budget Historical Table 8.7.

18. U.S. Government Executive Office, "The National Commission on Fiscal Responsibility and Reform: The Moment of Truth," December 2010.

19. Angus Maddison, *The World Economy: A Millennial Perspective/Historic Statistics* (Paris: Development Centre of the Organization for Economic Co-operation and Development, 2006), p. 264.

20. Calculated using total federal receipts from Office of Management and Budget Historical Table 1.2 and total tax collection per OECD statistical database.

21. New Hampshire collects taxes on dividends and interest income only.

22. Charles M. Tiebout, "A Pure Theory of Local Expenditures," *Journal of Political Economy* 64, no. 5 (October 1956), pp. 416–24.

23. Pew Research Center for the People & the Press, "Trends in Political Values and Core Attitudes: 1987–2009," May 21, 2009, p. 131.

24. See Office of Management and Budget Historical Table 12.1.

25. Data for calculations from Thomas Piketty and Emmanuel Saez, "How Progressive Is the US Federal Tax System? A Historical and International Perspective," *Journal of Economic Perspectives* 21, no. 1 (Winter 2007), pp. 3–24; Congressional Budget Office, "Average Federal Taxes by Income Group," June 2010.

26. See Office of Management and Budget, "A New Era of Responsibility," February 2009, p. 9, and Edward N. Wolff, "Recent Trends in Household Wealth in the United States: Rising Debt and the Middle-Class Squeeze—an Update to 2007," Levy Economics Institute of Bard College, March 2010.

27. Federal Reserve Statistical Release, "Flow of Funds Account of the United States: Flows and Outstandings Fourth Quarter 2010," March 10, 2011.

28. Internal Revenue Service, "Reducing the Federal Tax Gap: A Report on Improving Voluntary Compliance," August 2007.

29. American Petroleum Institute, "Motor Fuel Taxes."

30. The New York State Department of Taxation and Finance, "Stock Transfer Tax."

31. Gerald Prante and Mark Robyn, "Fiscal Fact: Summary of Latest Federal Income Tax Data," Tax Foundation, October 6, 2010.

Chapter 12: The Seven Habits of Highly Effective Government

1. John Paul Stevens, *Opinion of Stevens, J. Supreme Court of the United States. Citizens United Appellant vs. Federal Election Commission*, January 2010.

2. John F. Kennedy, Remarks of President John F. Kennedy at American University Commencement, June 1963.

3. John F. Kennedy, Address at Rice University on the Nation's Space Effort, September 12, 1962.

4. Jennifer Manning, "Membership of the 111th Congress: A Profile," Congressional Research Service, November 2010.
5. Partnership for Public Service, "Ready to Govern: Improving the Presidential Transition," January 2010, p. iii.
6. National Park Service Organic Act.
7. At previous junctures of American history, third-party movements were able to intrude upon established parties to shift national politics in a fundamental way. The Republican Party arose in the 1850s to defeat the Whigs and lead the nation through the Civil War and the end of slavery. The Populist Party arose in the 1880s to demand significant reforms to public administration, the direct election of senators, women's suffrage, and the control of giant industrial trusts. The Populist platform, though never dominant electorally, led the way to the Progressive Era, including the reformist presidencies of Theodore Roosevelt and Woodrow Wilson.

Chapter 13: The Millennial Renewal

1. Alexis de Tocqueville, *The Old Regime and the French Revolution*, trans. John Bonner (New York: Harper & Brothers, 1856), p. 124.
2. Henry Ashby Turner, Jr., *Hitler's Thirty Days to Power: January 1933* (London: Bloomsbury, 1996).
3. Pew Research Center for the People & the Press, "Millennials: Confident, Connected, Open to Change," February 24, 2010.
4. U.S. Census Bureau, "Population by Age and Race 2009."
5. Johan Rockström, "A Safe Operating Space for Humanity," *Nature* 461 (September 2009), pp. 472–75.
6. See Jeffrey D. Sachs, *Common Wealth: Economics for a Crowded Planet* (New York: Penguin, 2008), Chapter 5.
7. For 2011 Gross World Product data, see International Monetary Fund, "World Economic Outlook Database: April 2011."
8. Donald Pfaff, *The Neuroscience of Fair Play: Why We (Usually) Follow the Golden Rule* (New York: Dana Press, 2007). In one of the most fascinating areas of recent scientific advance, neurobiologists have begun to unravel the basic neural and chemical pathways of conflict and cooperation. The Golden Rule and nurturing behavior more generally, speculates neuroscientist Donald Pfaff, emerged from a mother's behavior toward her offspring, involving the hormones estrogen, cortisol, prolactin, and oxytocin. On the other hand, aggression seems to be related mostly to male behavior rooted in protecting the offspring and defending territory. These behaviors are mediated by hormonal and brain systems that involve testosterone, vasopressin, and serotonin, among other regulators.
9. See Foreword, Jeffrey D. Sachs, *Common Wealth: Economics for a Crowded Planet*, p. xii.
10. John F. Kennedy, Remarks of President John F. Kennedy at American University Commencement, June 1963.
11. Ibid.

WORKS CITED

ABC News, "Summary of Polling on a 'Public Option,'" http://abcnews.go.com/images/PollingUnit/PublicOptionPolls.pdf.

Altemeyer, Bob. "Why Do Religious Fundamentalists Tend to Be Prejudiced?" *International Journal for the Psychology of Religion* 13, no. 1 (2003).

American Human Development Project. "The Measure of America 2010–2011: Mapping Risks and Resilience," http://www.measureofamerica.org/.

American Petroleum Institute. "Motor Fuel Taxes," http://www.api.org/statistics/fueltaxes/.

American Society of Civil Engineers. "2009 Report Card for America's Infrastructure," March 2009, http://apps.asce.org/reportcard/2009/grades.cfm.

America's Promise Alliance. "Building a Grad Nation: Progress and Challenge in Ending the High School Dropout Epidemic," November 2010, http://www.americaspromise.org/Our-Work/Grad-Nation/Building-a-Grad-Nation.aspx.

Angelova, Kamelia. "Worst CEOs Ever: Angelo Mozilo," June 8, 2009, http://www.businessinsider.com/worstceosever/angelo-mozilo.

Aristotle. In Stobaeus, *Florilegium*, transl. J.E.C. Welldon.

Bacevich, Andrew J. *Washington Rules: America's Path to Permanent War.* New York: Henry Holt, 2010.

Barrett, Deirdre. *Supernormal Stimuli: How Primal Urges Overran Their Evolutionary Purpose.* New York: W. W. Norton, 2010.

Bartels, Larry. "Homer Gets a Tax Cut: Inequality and Public Policy in the American Mind." *Perspectives on Politics* 3, no.1 (March 2005).

Bauerlein, Mark. *The Dumbest Generation.* New York: Penguin, 2008.

Bernays, Edward. *Propaganda.* 1928, http://sandiego.indymedia.org/media/2006/10/119695.pdf.

Bishop, Bill. *The Big Sort: Why the Clustering of Like-Minded America Is Tearing Us Apart.* New York: Houghton Mifflin, 2008.

Blanchflower, David, and Andrew Oswald. "International Happiness." NBER Working Paper No. 16668, January 2011.

Bohn, Roger, and James Short. "How Much Information? 2009 Report on American Consumers." Global Information Industry Center, December 2009, http://hmi.ucsd.edu/pdf/HMI_2009_ConsumerReport_Dec9_2009.pdf.

Brickman, Philip, and Donald Campbell. "Hedonic Relativism and Planning the

Good Society." In M. H. Apley, ed., *Adaptation Level Theory: A Symposium*. New York: Academic Press, 1971.

Burns, Lawrence, Vijay Modi, and Jeffrey Sachs. "Transition to a Sustainable Energy System for the United States," December 16, 2010, unpublished paper.

Business Wire. "Business and Financial Leaders Lord Rothschild and Rupert Murdoch Invest in Genie Oil & Gas," November 15, 2010, http://www .businesswire.com/news/home/20101115007704/en/Business-Financial -Leaders-Lord-Rothschild-Rupert-Murdoch.

Campaign Finance Institute. "New Figures Show That Obama Raised About One-Third of His General Funds from Donors Who Gave $200 or Less," January 8, 2010, http://www.cfinst.org/Press/Releases_tags/10-01-08/ Revised_and_Updated_2008_Presidential_Statistics.aspx.

Carnegie, Andrew. "The Gospel of Wealth and Other Timely Essays," http:// us.history.wisc.edu/hist102/pdocs/carnegie_wealth.pdf.

Center for Responsive Politics. "Banking on Connections," June 3, 2010, p. 1, http://www.opensecrets.org/news/FinancialRevolvingDoors.pdf.

———. "Congressional Members' Personal Wealth Expands Despite Sour Economy," November 2010, http://www.opensecrets.org/news/2010/11/ congressional-members-personal-weal.html.

Clinton, Bill. Radio Address, January 27, 1996, http://www.presidency.ucsb .edu/medialist.php?presid=42.

CNN Election Center 2008, http://www.cnn.com/ELECTION/2010/results/ main.results/.

Coen Advertising Expenditure Dataset, quoted in Douglas Galbi, "U.S. Advertising Expenditure, 1998–2007," Purple Motes blog, February 16, 2009, http:// purplemotes.net/2009/02/16/us-advertising-expenditure-1998-2007/.

Cohen, Jon. "Most Americans Say Regulate Greenhouse Gases." *Washington Post*, June 10, 2010, http://voices.washingtonpost.com/behind-the-numbers/ 2010/06/most_americans_say_regulate_gr.html.

Congressional Budget Office. "An Analysis of the President's Budgetary Proposals for Fiscal Year 2012," http://www.cbo.gov/doc.cfm?index=12130.

———. "Average Federal Taxes by Income Group," June 2010, http://www.cbo .gov/publications/collections/collections.cfm?collect=13.

———. "Estimate of Direct Spending and Revenue Effects of H.R. 2," February 18, 2011, http://www.cbo.gov/ftpdocs/120xx/doc12069/hr2.pdf.

———. "The Impact of Unauthorized Immigrants on the Budgets of State and Local Governments," December 2007, http://www.cbo.gov/ftpdocs/87xx/ doc8711/12-6-Immigration.pdf.

Dewitt, Larry. "The Decision to Exclude Agricultural and Domestic Workers from the 1935 Social Security Act." U.S. Social Security Administration, 2010, http://www.ssa.gov/policy/docs/ssb/v70n4/v70n4p49.html.

Di Leo, Luca, and Jeffrey Sparshott. "Corporate Profits Rise to Record Annual Rate." *Wall Street Journal*, November 24, 2010.

Dobuzinskis, Alex. "Mozilo Settles Countrywide Fraud Case at $67.5 million." Reuters News, October 15, 2010, http://www.reuters.com/article/2010/10/ 15/us-sec-mozilo-idUSTRE69E4KN20101015.

Dolan, Paul, et al. "Measuring Subjective Well-Being for Public Policy." Office for National Statistics—Government of the United Kingdom, February 2011, http://www.statistics.gov.uk/articles/social_trends/measuring-subjective-wellbeing-for-public-policy.pdf.

Drucker, Jesse. "Google 2.4% Rate Shows How $60 Billion Lost to Tax Loopholes," Bloomberg News, October 21, 2010, http://www.bloomberg.com/news/2010-10-21/google-2-4-rate-shows-how-60-billion-u-s-revenue-lost-to-tax-loopholes.html.

Dunn, Elizabeth, Daniel T. Gilbert, and Timothy Wilson. "If Money Doesn't Make You Happy Then You Probably Aren't Spending It Right." *Journal of Consumer Psychology* 21, no. 2, pp. 115–25.

Duverger, Maurice. "Factors in a Two Party and Multiparty System." In *Party Politics and Pressure Groups.* New York: Thomas Y. Crowell, 1972.

Easterlin, Richard. "Does Economic Growth Improve the Human Lot? Some Empirical Evidence." In Paul A. David and Melvin W. Reder, eds., *Nations and Households in Economic Growth: Essays in Honor of Moses Abramovitz.* New York: Academic Press, 1974.

Economist Intelligence Unit. "The *Economist* Intelligence Unit's Quality-of-Life Index," *The World in 2005,* http://www.economist.com/media/pdf/QUALITY_OF_LIFE.pdf.

Edsall, Thomas Byrne, and Mary D. Edsall. *Chain Reaction: The Impact of Race, Rights, and Taxes on American Politics.* New York: W. W. Norton, 1991.

Eisenhower, Dwight D. "Farewell Address," January 17, 1961, http://www.americanrhetoric.com/speeches/dwightdeisenhowerfarewell.html.

Esping-Andersen, Gösta. "Unequal Opportunities and the Mechanisms of Social Inheritance." In *Generational Income Mobility in North America and Europe,* ed. Miles Corak. Cambridge: Cambridge University Press, 2004.

Esping-Andersen, Gösta, et al. *Why We Need a New Welfare State.* Oxford: Oxford University Press, 2002.

"Facebook's Ad Revenue Hit $1.86b for 2010," January 17, 2011, http://mashable.com/2011/01/17/facebooks-ad-revenue-hit-1-86b-for-2010/.

Federal Reserve Statistical Release. "Flow of Funds Account of the United States: Flows and Outstandings Fourth Quarter 2010," March 10, 2011, http://www.federalreserve.gov/releases/z1/current/z1.pdf.

Ferguson, Thomas. *Golden Rule: The Investment Theory of Party Competition and the Logic of Money-Driven Political Systems.* Chicago: University of Chicago Press, 1995

Forbes. "The World's Billionaires," 2011, http://www.forbes.com/wealth/billionaires.

Gallup Poll. "Automobile, Banking Industry Images Slide Further," August 17, 2009, http://www.gallup.com/poll/122342/Automobile-Banking-Industry-Images-Slide-Further.aspx.

———. "In general, are you satisfied or dissatisfied with the way things are going in the United States at this time?," May 5–8, 2011, http://www.pollingreport.com/right.htm.

———. "Republicans, Democrats Still Fiercely Divided on Role of Government," June 2010, http://www.gallup.com/poll/141056/republicans-democrats-fiercely-divided-role-gov.aspx.

———. "Views of Income Taxes Among Most Positive Since 1956," April 13, 2009,

http://www.gallup.com/poll/117433/views-income-taxes-among-positive
-1956.aspx.

Garretsen, H., and Jolanda Peeters. "Capital Mobility, Agglomeration and Corporate Tax Rates: Is the Race to the Bottom for Real?" *CESifo Economic Studies* 53, no. 2 (2007): 263–93.

General Electric annual 10-K filing, http://ir.10kwizard.com/filing.php?ipage=7438579&DSEQ=1&SEQ=14&SQDESC=SECTION_PAGE&exp=&source=329&welc_next=1&fg=24.

Gibbons, John. "I Can't Get No . . . Job Satisfaction." The Conference Board, January 2010, http://www.conference-board.org/publications/publication detail.cfm?publicationid=1727.

Goldman Sachs website, http://www2.goldmansachs.com/our-firm/investors/financials/current/10k/2009-10-k-doc.pdf.

"Google Search Advertising Revenue Grows 20.2% in 2010," January 20, 2011, http://www.telecompaper.com/news/google-search-advertising-revenue-grows-202-in-2010.

Gravelle, Jane G. "Tax Havens: International Tax Avoidance and Evasion." Congressional Research Service Report for Congress, July 2009.

Hajnal, Zoltan, et al. "Immigration and the Political Transformation of White America: How Local Immigrant Context Shapes White Policy Views and Partnership." University of California, San Diego Center for Comparative Immigration Studies, International Migration Conference, March 12, 2010, http://weber.ucsd.edu/~zhajnal/page5/files/immigration-implications-and-the-political-transformation-of-white-america.pdf.

Hall, Deborah, et al. "Why Don't We Practice What We Preach? A Meta-Analytic Review of Religious Racism." *Personal Social Psychology Review* 14, no. 1 (December 2009).

Halvorson, George. *Health Care Will Not Reform Itself.* New York: CRC Press, 2009.

Hayek, Friedrich. *The Road to Serfdom.* Chicago: University of Chicago Press, 1944.

Henry J. Kaiser Family Foundation. "Food for Thought: Television Food Advertising to Children in the United States," March 2007, http://www.kff.org/entmedia/upload/7618.pdf.

Holmes, Justice Oliver Wendell, Jr., attributed. In Frankfurter, Felix, *Mr. Justice Holmes and the Supreme Court.* Cambridge: Harvard University Press, 1961.

Hurtado, Patricia, and Christine Harper. "SEC Settlement with Goldman Sachs for $550 Million Approved by US Judge." Bloomberg News, July 21, 2010.

Inhofe, James, Senate floor statement, July 28, 2003, http://inhofe.senate.gov/pressreleases/climate.htm.

Innes, Robert, and Arnab Mitra, "Is Dishonesty Contagious?," June 2009, http://www.agecon.purdue.edu/news/seminarfiles/Innis_abstract.pdf, and the references therein.

Institute for Democracy and Electoral Assistance, "Voter Turnout by Country," http://www.idea.int/vt/country_view.cfm?country.

Internal Revenue Service. Internal Revenue Code, http://www.law.cornell.edu/uscode/html/uscode26/usc_sup_01_26_10_A_20_1.html.

———. "Reducing the Federal Tax Gap: A Report on Improving Voluntary

Compliance," August 2007, http://www.irs.gov/pub/irs-news/tax_gap _report_final_080207_linked.pdf.

International Energy Agency, Data Services, http://wds.iea.org/WDS/ TableViewer/dimView.aspx.

International Monetary Fund, "World Economic Outlook Database: October 2010," http://www.imf.org/external/pubs/ft/weo/2010/02/weodata/index.aspx.

————. "World Economic Outlook Database: April 2011," http://www.imf.org/ external/pubs/ft/weo/2011/01/weodata/index.aspx.

Jargowsky, Paul, and Todd Swanstrom. "Economic Integration: Why It Matters and How Cities Can Get More of It." Chicago: CEOs for Cities, City Vitals Series, http://www.ceosforcities.org/pagefiles/EconomicIntegration.pdf.

Jingjing, Shan. "Blue Book of Cities in China." Chinese Academy of Social Science, http://www.chinadaily.com.cn/china/2009-06/16/content_8288412 .htm.

Jonas, Hans. *The Imperative of Responsibility: In Search of an Ethics for the Technological Age.* Chicago: University of Chicago Press, 1985.

Kaiser, Robert. *So Damn Much Money: The Triumph of Lobbying and the Corrosion of American Government.* New York: Alfred A. Knopf, 2009.

Kennedy, John F. Address at Rice University on the Nation's Space Effort. September 12, 1962, http://www.jfklibrary.org/Research/Ready-Reference/ JFK-Speeches/Address-at-Rice-University-on-the-Nations Space Effort -September-12-1962.aspx.

————. Address before the Irish Parliament, June 1963, http://ua_tuathal .tripod.com/kennedy.html.

————. Remarks of President John F. Kennedy at American University Commencement, June 1963, http://www.jfklibrary.org/Research/ Ready-Reference/JFK-Speeches/Commencement-Address-at-American -University-June-10-1963.aspx.

Kennedy, Robert F. Remarks at the University of Kansas, March 18, 1968, http:// www.jfklibrary.org/Research/Ready-Reference/RFK-Speeches/Remarks -of-Robert-F-Kennedy-at-the-University-of-Kansas-March-18-1968.aspx.

Keynes, John Maynard. *The Economic Consequences of the Peace.* Toronto: University of Toronto Libraries, 2011.

King, Neil, Jr., and Scott Greenberg. "Poll Shows Budget-Cuts Dilemma." *Wall Street Journal*, March 3, 2011, http://online.wsj.com/article/SB1000142405 2748704728004576176741120691736.html.

Küng, Hans. "Manifesto for a Global Economic Ethic." Tübingen: Global Ethic Foundation, 2009, http://www.globaleconomicethic.org/main/pdf/ENG/ we-manifest-ENG.pdf.

Lee, John Michael, and Anita Rawls. "The College Completion Agenda: 2010 Progress Report." The College Board, 2010, http://completionagenda .collegeboard.org/sites/default/files/reports_pdf/Progress_Report_2010 .pdf.

Lucchetti, Aaron, and Stephen Grocer. "On Street, Pay Vaults to Record Altitude." *Wall Street Journal*, February 2, 2011.

Maddison, Angus. *The World Economy: A Millennial Perspective/Historic Statistics*. Paris: Development Centre of the Organisation for Economic Cooperation and Development, 2006.

Manning, Jennifer. "Membership of the 111th Congress: A Profile." Congressional Research Service, November 2010, http://www.fas.org/sgp/crs/misc/R40086.pdf.

McCarty, Nolan, et al. *Polarized America: The Dance of Ideology and Unequal Riches*. Cambridge: MIT Press, 2006.

McGinniss, Joe. *The Selling of the President 1968*. New York: Trident, 1969.

McKinsey & Company. "Accounting for the Cost of Health Care in the United States," January 2007, http://www.mckinsey.com/mgi/reports/pdfs/health-care/MGI_US_HC_fullreport.pdf.

———. "Winning by Degrees: The Strategies of Highly Productive Higher-Education Institutions," November 2010.

Miller, Geoffrey. *Spent*. New York: Penguin, 2009.

Munnell, Alicia M., Anthony Webb, and Francesca Golub-Soss. "The National Retirement Risk Index: After the Crash." Center for Retirement Research, October 2009, No. 9-22.

Mysak, Joe. "Use Stock Transfer Tax Rebate to Rebuild New York." Bloomberg News, http://www.gothamcenter.org/newdeal/bloomberg_review.pdf.

National Endowment for the Arts. "To Read or Not to Read: A Question of National Consequence," Research Report No. 47, November 2007, http://www.nea.gov/news/news07/TRNR.html.

National Intelligence Council. "Global Trends 2025: A Transformed World," November 2008, http://www.dni.gov/nic/PDF_2025/2025_Global_Trends_Final_Report.pdf.

National Park Service Organic Act, http://www.nps.gov/legacy/organic-act.htm.

New York State Department of Taxation and Finance. "Stock Transfer Tax," http://www.tax.ny.gov/bus/stock/stktridx.htm.

Nordhaus, William, and James Tobin. "Is Growth Obsolete?" In *The Measurement of Economic and Social Performance*, NBER Book Series Studies in Income and Wealth, 1973.

Office of Management and Budget, Historical Tables, http://www.whitehouse.gov/omb/budget/Historicals.

———. "A New Era of Responsibility," February 2009, p. 9, http://www.gpoaccess.gov/usbudget/fy10/pdf/fy10-newera.pdf.

Organisation for Economic Co-operation and Development. "Doing Better for Children: OECD 2010," http://www.oecd.org/dataoecd/19/4/43570328.pdf.

———. "Economic Policy Reforms, Going for Growth: OECD 2010," http://www.oecd.org/dataoecd/3/62/44582910.pdf.

———. "Education at a Glance: 2009," http://www.oecd.org/document/24/0,3746,en_2649_39263238_43586328_1_1_1_1,00.html.

———. "Global Project on Measuring the Progress of Societies," www.oecd.org/progress.

———. "Growing Unequal? Income Distribution and Poverty in OECD Countries."

———. "Health Data 2010," http://www.oecd.org/document/16/0,3343,en_2649_34631_2085200_1_1_1_1,00.html.

———. "Obesity and the Economics of Prevention: Fit Not Fat," http://www.oecd

.org/document/45/0,3746,en_2649_37407_46064099_1_1_1_37407,00
.html.

———. "OECD Economic Outlook Database 88," www.oecd.org/dataoecd/
5/51/2483816.xls.

———. "OECD Factbook 2010: Economic, Environmental and Social Statistics," http://www.oecd-ilibrary.org/sites/factbook-2010-en/11/03/02/
index.html?contentType=&itemId=/content/chapter/factbook-2010-91-
en&containerItemId=/content/serial/18147364&accessItemIds=&mime
Type=ext/html.

———. "OECD Family Database," http://www.oecd.org/document/4/0,3746,
en_2649_34819_37836996_1_1_1_1,00.html.

———. "OECD Health Data. Part II: International Classification for Health Accounts (ICIIA)," http://www.oecd.org/dataoecd/3/42/1896876.pdf.

———. "OECD STAT," http://stats.oecd.org/Index.aspx?DatasetCode=
DECOMP.

———. Programme for International Student Assessment, "PISA 2009
Results," http://www.pisa.oecd.org/document/61/0,3746,en_32252351_
32235731_46567613_1_1_1_1,00.html.

———. "Public Expenditure and Participant Stocks on LMP," Statistical Database, http://stats.oecd.org/Index_aspx?DatasetCode=LMPEXP.

———. "Social Expenditure Database," http://www.oecd.org/document/9/0,
3343,en_2649_34637_38141385_1_1_1_1,00.html.

Orszag, Peter. "One Nation, Two Deficits." *New York Times,* September 6, 2010.

Page, Benjamin, and Lawrence Jacobs. *Class War? What Americans Really
Think About Economic Inequality.* Chicago: University of Chicago Press,
2009.

Partnership for Public Service. "Ready to Govern: Improving the Presidential
Transition," January 2010, www.ourpublicservice.org/OPS/publications/
download.php?id=138.

Pew Forum on Religion & Public Life. "US Religious Landscape Survey: Religious Affiliation, Diverse and Dynamic," February 2008, http://religions
.pewforum.org/pdf/report-religious-landscape-study-full.pdf.

Pew Hispanic Center. "Statistic Portraits of Hispanics in the US, 2009," http://
pewhispanic.org/factsheets/factsheet.php?FactsheetID=70.

Pew Research Center for the People & the Press. "Millennials: Confident,
Connected, Open to Change," February 24, 2010, http://pewresearch.org/
millennials/.

———. "Mixed Views on Tax Cuts, Support for START and Allowing Gays to
Serve Openly," December 2010, http://pewresearch.org/pubs/1822/poll
-bush-tax-cuts-start-treaty-boehner-pelosi-afghanistan-korea.

———. "Public Knows Basic Facts About Politics, Economics, but Struggles
with Specifics," November 2010, http://pewresearch.org/pubs/1804/
political-news-quiz-iq-deficit-defense-spending-tarp-inflation-boehner.

———. "Public Praises Science; Scientists Fault Public, Media," July 2009,
http://people-press.org/report/?pageid=1549.

———. "Taxed Enough Already?," September 20, 2010, http://pewresearch
.org/pubs/1734/taxed-enough-already-tea-party-pay right amount-taxes.

——. "Trends in Political Values and Core Attitudes: 1987–2009," May 21, 2009, http://people-press.org/files/legacy-pdf/517.pdf.

Pfaff, Donald. *The Neuroscience of Fair Play: Why We (Usually) Follow the Golden Rule*. New York: Dana Press, 2007.

Piketty, Thomas, and Emmanuel Saez. "How Progressive Is the US Federal Tax System? A Historical and International Perspective." *Journal of Economic Perspectives* 21, no. 1 (Winter 2007): 3–24, http://www.taxfoundation.org/news/show/250.html#Data.

Plato. "Apology." In *Five Dialogues,* transl. G.M.A. Grube. Indianapolis: Hackett Publishing, 2002.

Prante, Gerald, and Mark Robyn. "Fiscal Fact: Summary of Latest Federal Income Tax Data." Tax Foundation, October 6, 2010, http://www.taxfoundation.org/news/show/250.html.

Putnam, Robert D. *Bowling Alone: The Collapse and Revival of American Community*. New York: Simon & Schuster, 2002.

——. "E Pluribus Unum: Diversity and Community in the Twenty-first Century: The 2006 Johan Skytte Prize Lecture." *Scandinavian Political Studies* 30, no. 2 (June 2007).

Rasmussen Reports. "Energy Update," April 2011, http://www.rasmussenreports.com/public_content/politics/current_events/environment_energy/energy_update.

——. "Right Direction or Wrong Track," March 2011, http://www.rasmussenreports.com/public_content/politics/mood_of_america/right_direction_or_wrong_track.

——. "65% Now Hold Populist, or Mainstream, Views," January 2010, http://www.rasmussenreports.com/public_content/politics/general_politics/january_2010/65_now_hold_populist_or_mainstream_views.

——. "Support for Renewable Energy Resources Reaches Highest Level Yet," January 2011, http://www.rasmussenreports.com/public_content/politics/current_events/environment_energy/support_for_renewable_energy_resources_reaches_highest_level_yet.

Rath, Tom, and Jim Harter. *Wellbeing: The Five Essential Elements*. New York: Gallup Press, 2010.

Reagan, Ronald. First Inaugural Address, January 20, 1981, http://www.presidency.ucsb.edu/ws/index.php?pid=43130#axzz1MeL0knUW.

Rockström, Johan. "A Safe Operating Space for Humanity." *Nature* 461 (September 2009).

Romer, Christina D., "What Obama Should Say About the Deficit." *New York Times,* January 16, 2011.

Roosevelt, Franklin D. Second Inaugural Address, January 20, 1937, http://www.bartleby.com/124/pres50.html.

Röpke, Wilhelm. *A Humane Economy: The Social Framework of the Free Market*. Wilmington: ISI Books, 1960.

RTL Group IP Network. "Television 2010 International Key Facts," www.ip-network.com/tvkeyfacts.

Sachs, Jeffrey D. *Common Wealth: Economics for a Crowded Planet*. New York: Penguin, 2008.

Sachs, Jeffrey, and Michael Bruno. *Economics of Worldwide Stagflation*. Cambridge: Harvard University Press, 1985.

Saez, Emmanuel, and Thomas Piketty. Data set for "Income Inequality in the United States, 1913–1998," updated July 2010, http://elsa.berkeley.edu/~saez/.

Smith, Adam. *An Inquiry into the Nature and Causes of the Wealth of Nations*. Oxford: Oxford University Press, 1993.

Steel, Emily. "A Web Pioneer Profiles Users by Name." *Wall Street Journal*, October 25, 2010, http://online.wsj.com/article/SB1000142405270230441050457556024325941607.html.

Stein, Judith. *Pivotal Decade: How the United States Traded Factories for Finance in the Seventies*. New Haven: Yale University Press, 2010.

Stevens, John Paul. *Opinion of Stevens, J. Supreme Court of the United States. Citizens United Appellant vs. Federal Election Commission*, January 2010, http://www.law.cornell.edu/supct/html/08-205.ZX.html.

Stevenson, Betsey, and Justin Wolfers. "The Paradox of Declining Female Happiness." NBER Working Paper Series No. 14969, May 2009.

Stiglitz, Joseph, and Amartya Sen. "Commission on the Measurement of Economic Performance and Social Progress," http://www.stiglitz-sen-fitoussi.fr/en/index.htm.

Tax Foundation. "Federal Spending Received per Dollar of Taxes Paid by State, 2005," October 9, 2007, http://www.taxfoundation.org/research/show/266.html.

Tiebout, Charles M. "A Pure Theory of Local Expenditures," *Journal of Political Economy* 64, no. 5 (October 1956): 416–24.

Tocqueville, Alexis de. *The Old Regime and the French Revolution*, trans. John Bonner. New York: Harper & Brothers, 1856.

Transparency International. "2010 Corruption Perceptions Index," http://www.transparency.org/policy_research/surveys_indices/cpi/2010.

Turner, Henry Ashby, Jr., *Hitler's Thirty Days to Power: January 1933*. London: Bloomsbury Press, 1996.

UN Population Division Home Page, http://www.un.org/esa/population/.

UNCTAD. "Largest Transnational Corporations," Document 5, http://www.unctad.org/templates/page.asp?intItemID=2443&lang=1.

Ura, Karma. "Gross National Happiness." Centre for Bhutan Studies, http://www.grossnationalhappiness.com/gnhIndex/intruductionGNH.aspx.

USA Today/Gallup Poll, June 11–13, 2010, http://www.gallup.com/poll/File/140792/Government_Priorities_June_17_2010.pdf.

U.S. Bureau of Labor Statistics. "Current Employment Statistics: National," http://www.bls.gov/ces/tables.htm#ee.

———. "Economic News Release: Table A-4—Employment Status of the Civilian Population 25 Years and over by Educational Attainment," http://www.bls.gov/news.release/empsit.t04.htm.

———. "Economic News Release: Table A-15—Alternative Measures of Labor Underutilization," http://www.bls.gov/news.release/empsit.t15.htm.

———. "Employment Situation Summary," http://www.bls.gov/news.release/empsit.nr0.htm.

―――. "Establishment Data: Historical Employment," ftp://ftp.bls.gov/pub/suppl/empsit.ceseeb1.txt.

―――. "Overview of BLS Statistics on Employment," http://www.bls.gov/bls/employment.htm.

U.S. Census Bureau. "Current Population Survey: Annual Social and Economic (ASEC) Supplement," http://www.census.gov/hhes/www/cpstables/032010/pov/new01_200_01.htm.

―――. "Foreign Trade: Trade in Goods with China," http://www.census.gov/foreign-trade/balance/c5700.html#2009.

―――. "Hispanics in the US," http://www.census.gov/population/www/socdemo/hispanic/files/Internet_Hispanic_in_US_2006.pdf.

―――. *Income, Poverty and Health Insurance Coverage in the US: 2009,* http://www.census.gov/prod/2010pubs/p60-238.pdf.

―――. "No. HS-42: Selected Communications Media: 1920 to 2001," http://www.census.gov/statab/hist/HS-42.pdf.

―――. "Population by Age and Race 2009," http://www.census.gov/compendia/statab/cats/population.html.

―――. "Population Division: Historical Census Statistics on the Foreign-Born Population of the United States: 1850–2000," http://www.census.gov/population/www/documentation/twps0081/twps0081.pdf.

―――. "Table 3: Poverty Status of People, by Age, Race, and Hispanic Origin: 1958–2009." Current Population Survey, Annual and Social Economic Supplements, http://www.census.gov/hhes/www/poverty/data/historical/people.html.

U.S. Department of Agriculture. Supplemental Nutrition Assistance Program website, http://www.fns.usda.gov/snap/.

U.S. Department of Commerce, Bureau of Economic Analysis. "Comparison of Personal Saving in the NIPAs with Personal Saving in the FFAs, http://www.bea.gov/national/nipaweb/Nipa-Frb.asp.

―――. "Gross Domestic Product by State," http://www.bea.gov/regional/gsp/.

―――. "Industry Economic Accounts," http://www.bea.gov/industry/gdpbyind_data.htm.

―――. "National Economic Accounts," http://www.bea.gov/national/.

―――. "State Annual Personal Income," http://www.bea.gov/regional/spi/default.cfm?selTable=SA05N&selSeries=NAICS.

U.S. Department of Defense. "DoD Request: FY 2011," http://comptroller.defense.gov/Budget2011.html.

U.S. Department of Education. "Mortgaging Our Future: How Financial Barriers to College Undercut America's Global Competitiveness," A Report of the Advisory Committee on Student Financial Assistance, September 2006.

―――. "Revenues and Expenditures for Public Elementary and Secondary School Districts: School Year 2007–2008 (Fiscal Year 2008)," NCES 2010-323, August 2010, http://nces.ed.gov/pubs2010/2010323.pdf.

U.S. Department of Education, National Center for Educational Statistics, "The Condition of Education 2010," June 2010, http://nces.ed.gov/pubs2010/2010028.pdf.

U.S. Department of Health and Human Services. "Temporary Assistance for Needy Families: FY 2012 Budget," p. 305, http://www.acf.hhs.gov/programs/olab/budget/2012/cj/TANF.pdf.

U.S. Energy Information Administration. "Net Generation by Energy Source: Total," January 2011, http://www.eia.doe.gov/cneaf/electricity/epm/table1_1.html.

U.S. Government Accountability Office. "International Taxation: Large US Corporations and Federal Contractors with Subsidiaries in Jurisdictions Listed as Tax Havens or Financial Privacy Jurisdictions," GAO-09-157. December 2008.

U.S. Government Executive Office. "The National Commission on Fiscal Responsibility and Reform: The Moment of Truth," December 2010, http://www.fiscalcommission.gov/sites/fiscalcommission.gov/files/documents/TheMomentofTruth12_1_2010.pdf.

Veblen, Thorstein. *The Theory of the Leisure Class: An Economic Study of Institutions*. New York: Macmillan, 1902.

Weber, Max. *The Protestant Ethic and the Spirit of Capitalism*. Mineola, N.Y.: Dover, 2003.

Wolff, Edward N. "Recent Trends in Household Wealth in the United States: Rising Debt and the Middle-Class Squeeze—an Update to 2007," Levy Economics Institute of Bard College, March 2010, http://www.levyinstitute.org/pubs/wp_589.pdf.

World Bank Data and Statistics, http://siteresources.worldbank.org/DATASTATISTICS/Resources/GNIPC.pdf.

World Health Organization Global Health Observatory Data Repository, http://apps.who.int/ghodata/?vid=720.

World Public Opinion."American Public Opinion on Foreign Aid," November 30, 2010, http://www.worldpublicopinion.org/pipa/pdf/nov10/ForeignAid_Nov10_quaire.pdf.

INDEX

Page numbers in *italics* refer to figures and tables.

ABOUT THE AUTHOR

In an illustrious career stretching over three decades, JEFFREY D. SACHS has been at the forefront of globalization and international economic problem solving. His brand of "clinical economics" is unique, combining the scholarly excellence of cutting-edge economic science and the frontline problem solving of an emergency-room money doctor. His successful treatments of economic ills include the end of hyperinflations in Latin America and Eastern Europe, breakthrough strategies to resolve the debt crises of poor countries, the economic transition from communism to capitalism in Poland and other post-communist countries, the introduction of new national currencies in several crisis-ridden economies, the financing and scale-up of disease control in Africa, and the escape from extreme poverty in some of the world's most difficult settings. He has been a high-level adviser to dozens of governments around the world, including Bolivia, Brazil, China, India, Kenya, Nigeria, Poland, Russia, Slovenia, and countless other emerging economies. He currently directs the Earth Institute at Columbia University and serves as special adviser to United Nations Secretary-General Ban Ki-moon on the Millennium Development Goals.

Sachs now turns his powerful methods of clinical economics to America's economic crisis. He brings unprecedented knowledge, experience, and firsthand engagement to the challenge. Throughout his career, Sachs has consulted with presidents, Treasury secretaries, senior White House officials, senators and House members, Federal Reserve Board members, and lead economists throughout the U.S.

government and state governments. Many top officials are his former students or academic colleagues.

Sachs's message is clear: there are solutions for America's economic ills, but implementing them will require America to recommit to our core civic virtues and to the deep reform of America's political and economic institutions.

ABOUT THE TYPE

This book was set in a digital version of Bodoni
Book, a typeface named after Giambattista
Bodoni, an Italian printer and type designer
of the late eighteenth and early nineteenth century. It is not actually one of Bodoni's fonts but
a modern version based on his style and manner
and is distinguished by a marked contrast between the thick and thin elements of the letters.